EFFECTIVE SECURITY MANAGEMENT
Second Edition

AMERICAN SOCIETY FOR INDUSTRIAL SECURITY
1625 PRINCE STREET
ALEXANDRIA, VA 22314
(703) 519-6200

EFFECTIVE SECURITY MANAGEMENT
Second Edition

Charles A. Sennewald, CPP

BUTTERWORTH PUBLISHERS
Boston · London
Sydney · Wellington · Durban · Toronto

Library of Congress Cataloging in Publication Data

Sennewald, Charles A., 1931–
    Effective security management.

    Includes index.
    1. Industry—Security measures. 2. Retail trade—
Security measures. 3. Management. I. Title.
HV8290.S46   1985   658.4′7   84–23282
ISBN 0–409–90006–0

Butterworth Publishers
80 Montvale Avenue
Stoneham, MA   02180

10 9 8 7 6 5 4 3

Printed in the United States of America

CONTENTS

Preface   xv

Introduction: Managing the Organization   1
by John Sanger

    Managerial Acts   1
    Managerial Functions   2
       Planning   2
       Organizing   2
       Directing   3
       Coordinating   3
       Controlling   3
    Summary of Management Functions   4
    The Successful Manager   4
       Characteristics   4
       Leadership   5
    Time Management   6
       Time Management Tips   6

I GENERAL SECURITY MANAGEMENT

1 **General Principles of Organization**   11
    Organizational Principles   11
       Logical Division of Work   12
       Clear Lines of Authority and Responsibility   14
       Span of Control   16
       Unity of Command   16
       Responsibility, Authority, and Accountability   17
       Coordination to Meet Organizational Goals   18
    Where Security Fits in the Organizational Structure   19
       The Changing Role of Security   19
       Security's Contribution to Profits   20
       To Whom Does Security Report?   20
       The Difference Between Corporate and Company
          Security   21
    Summary   25
    Review Questions   25

2   Organizational Structure   27
The Informal Organization   27
Sub-Unit Structures   31
Summary   33
Review Questions   33

3   Security's Role in the Organization   35
The Protective Service Role   35
Special Services   37
    Executive's Home Security Surveys   37
    Investigative Assistance   38
    Bodyguard/Escort Service   38
    Emergency Service   39
Educational Services   39
    General Security Programs   40
    Supervisory Training Sessions   40
    Employee Self-Protection Programs   41
    Unit or Departmental Presentations   41
Management Services   42
Summary   42
Review Questions   42

4   The Director's Role   45
The Security Director as a Leader   45
As a Company Executive   46
As an Executive with High Visibility   46
As an Executive with a Broad Profile   47
As an Innovator   47
As a Counselor and Adviser   49
As a Trainer   49
As a Contemporary Professional   50
As a Goal Setter   51
The New Security Director   51
Summary   52
Review Questions   53

5   The Security Supervisor's Role   55
The Supervisor as an Inspector   55
The Supervisor and the Individual Employee   56
Supervisory Authority   57
The Supervisor as the "In-Between" Man   58
The Supervisor's Span of Control   58
One Boss   59
Automatic Shifting in the Line of Command   60
Functional or Staff Supervision   61
Supervisory Training   61

	Summary	62
	Review Questions	63
6	**The Individual Security Employee**	**65**
	Standards of Conduct	66
	Courtesy	66
	Responsibility	67
	Due Process	67
	Cooperation	68
	Personal Integrity	69
	Attitude	72
	Summary	72
	Review Questions	72

II SECURITY PERSONNEL MANAGEMENT

7	**Hiring Security Personnel**	**75**
	Hiring	77
	Recruiting	77
	Interviewing Preliminaries	78
	The Interview	79
	Secondary Interviewing	81
	Selection of the Best Candidate	82
	Background Investigation of Applicant	83
	Job Offer	84
	Summary	85
	Review Questions	85
8	**Job Descriptions**	**87**
	Accuracy and Completeness in Describing the Job	87
	Undesirable	88
	Desirable	88
	Matching Applicant to the Job	88
	Undesirable	88
	Desirable	89
	Employee's Understanding of the Job	89
	Match Training to Job Description	90
	Performance Evaluations Based on Job Descriptions	90
	Job Descriptions Are Current	91
	Composition of the Job Description	92
	Sample Job Description	92
	Summary	94
	Review Questions	94
9	**Training**	**97**
	Shortcomings of Typical "Training"	97
	Training Defined	99

"POP" Formula: Policy, Objective, Procedure   99
  Detailed Expansion of Procedure   101
Training As Ongoing Responsibility   102
Types of Security Training Programs   102
Meeting Organizational Needs   104
Security Manual   104
Summary   104
Review Questions   105

10 Discipline   **107**
The Supervisor's Role in Discipline   108
Disciplinary Problems Arising from Misunderstood
  Assignments   109
Basic Rules of the Disciplinary Process   110
Self-Discipline   113
  Self-Discipline and Vanity   113
  Self-Discipline and Temper   114
  Self-Discipline and Arguments   114
  Self-Discipline and Personal Likes and Dislikes   114
  Self-Discipline and Work Habits   114
  Self-Discipline and Humility   114
Summary   115
Review Questions   115

11 Motivation and Morale   **117**
"Theory X" and "Theory Y"   117
Organizational Behavior   119
  The Autocratic Theory   119
  The Custodial Theory   119
  The Supportive Theory   119
Work Motivation Theory   120
  Responsibility As a Motivator in Security   121
  Achievement As a Motivator   122
  Recognition of Achievement As a Motivator   123
  Growth As a Motivator   123
  Advancement As a Motivator   123
Demotivators   124
Summary   127
Review Questions   127

12 Promotions   **129**
Identifying Promotional Candidates   129
  The Candidate's Track Record   130
  Anticipated Performance in the Higher Level Job   130

Selection of the Right Candidate   131
The Board Interview   132
Following the Selection   133
Promotion from "Within"   133
Vertical Promotion Outside the Department   134
Advantages of Multiple Layers   134
"Temporary" Promotions   135
"Retreating"   135
Summary   136
Review Questions   137

13 Communications   **139**
Types of Communication   139
   Verbal—Down   139
   Verbal—Up   140
   Written—Down   140
   Written—Horizontal   142
   Written—Up   143
   Verbal—Horizontal   145
   Action   145
Summary   146
Review Questions   146

14 Career vs. Non-Career Personnel   **149**
Career Personnel   149
   Advantages of Career Personnel   149
   Disadvantages of Career Personnel   150
Part-Time Non-Career Personnel   152
   Advantages of Part-Time Non-Career Personnel   152
   Disadvantages of Part-Time Non-Career
      Personnel   153
Contractual Non-Career Personnel   154
   Advantages of Contractual Non-Career Personnel 154
   Disadvantages of Contractual Non-Career
      Personnel   155
Combining Career and Non-Career Personnel   156
Summary   157
Review Questions   157

III OPERATIONAL MANAGEMENT

15 Planning and Budgeting   **161**
What Is a Budget?   161
Why Do We Have a Budget?   162
When Is the Budget Prepared?   163

Who Participates in the Budgeting Process?   164
How Is the Budget Prepared?   166
  Salary Expense Budget   166
  Sundry Expense Budget   172
Justifying the Security Budget   174
Summary   176
Review Questions   177

16 Program Management   **179**
The Inspection Process   179
  Support of Senior Management   180
  Continuous Inspections   181
  Formal or Informal Inspections   181
  Structured or Unstructured Inspections   182
  Who Conducts the Inspection?   182
Assessment of Risks and Countermeasures   184
  Risk Assessment   184
  Selection of Countermeasures   185
  Assessment of Countermeasures   188
  Inspecting for Compliance with Procedures   189
Statistics in Program Management   190
Summary   192
Review Questions   193

17 Risk Analysis   **195**
What Is Risk?   195
What Is Risk Analysis?   195
What Is a Risk Assessment Analysis?   196
What Can Risk Analysis Do for Management?   196
The Role of Management in Risk Analysis   197
Risk Exposure Assessment   198
Risk Identification   199
Examples of the Problems of Identification   202
Security Checklist   203
Review Questions   203

18 The Security Survey   **205**
Why Are Security Surveys Necessary?   205
Who Needs Security Surveys?   206
Attitude of Business Toward Security   208
What Can a Security Survey Accomplish?   209
Why the Need for a Security Professional?   210
How Do You Sell Security to Management?   211
Review Questions   213

19 Office Administration **215**
Description of Functions 216
Supervision 216
Secretarial 216
Reception 218
Clerical 219
Records 219
Record Filing Systems 220
File Control 223
Mail 223
Office Security 224
The Office Environment 224
Summary 224
Review Questions 225

20 Written Policies and Procedures **227**
The Historical Evolution 227
Policy 228
Procedure: Psychological Testing 228
Procedure: Verification of Former Employees 228
Benefits 229
Consistency in Performance 229
Reduction of Decision-Making Time 229
Enhancement of Controls 230
Provision for Objective Performance Evaluation 230
Compliance 230
Combining Policies and Procedures 231
Free-Standing Policies 233
The Importance of the Written Policy 234
Policies, Procedures, and the Security Manual 234
Format and Mechanics 235
Summary 237
Review Questions 237

IV PUBLIC RELATIONS

21 Selling Security within the Organization **241**
How to Sell Security 242
Security First 242
New Employee Inductions 242
More Audio-Visuals 243
Executive Orientations 244
Security Tours 245
Bulletins 245
Meetings 246
Involvement Programs 247

Summary   248
Review Questions   248

22 Relationship with Law Enforcement   249
Services of the Public Sector   250
   Provides Information on Individual Criminal
     Histories   250
   Provides Information on Possible Criminal Attacks   251
   Provides Traffic Control Support for Special
     Events   252
   Accepts and Processes Crime Reports   252
   Coordinates with Secretary on Special
     Enforcement Projects   253
   Coordinates with Security on Major or Important
     Investigations   253
   Provides Intelligence on Radical or Political
     Activists   254
   Provides Protection During Labor Disputes   255
Services of the Private Sector   255
   Contributes to the Local Criminal Statistical Data   255
   Provides the Community with "Tax-Free" Law
     Enforcement   256
   Provides Liaison Between Law Enforcement and
     the Business World   256
Summary   257
Review Questions   258

23 Relationship with the Industry   259
Effective Relationship Categories   260
   Cooperation   260
   Participation   262
   Contributions   263
   Education   265
Summary   266
Review Questions   266

24 Community Relations   267
Public Speaking   268
News Press Appearances or Interviews   270
Radio Interviews   270
Participation in Community-Oriented Projects   272
General Public Contact   273
Summary   273
Review Questions   273

V MIS-MANAGEMENT

25 Jackass Management Traits   **277**
  1. The Manager Who Seeks to Be "Liked" Rather Than Respected   279
  2. The Manager Who Ignores the Opinions and Advice of Subordinates   279
  3. The Manager Who Fails to Delegate Properly   280
  4. The Manager Who Ignores the Training and Developmental Needs of Subordinates   281
  5. The Manager Who Insists on Doing Everything "The Company Way"   282
  6. The Manager Who Fails to Give Credit When Credit Is Due   283
  7. The Manager Who Treats Subordinates As Subordinates   283
  8. The Manager Who Ignores Employees' Complaints   284
  9. The Manager Who Doesn't Keep His People Informed   285
 10. The Manager Who Holds His Assistant Back   287
 11. The Manager Who Views the Disciplinary Process As a Punitive Action   288
 12. The Manager Who Fails to Back Up His People   289
 13. The Manager Whose Word Cannot Be Trusted   290
 14. The Manager Who Avoids Making Decisions   291
 15. The Manager Who "Plays Favorites"   292
 16. The Manager Who Fails to Stay Current in His Field   292
 17. The Manager Who Enjoys "Pouring On" More Work Than A Subordinate Can Handle   293
 18. The Manager Who Acts or Overreacts Too Quickly   294
 19. The Newly Promoted Managers Who Believe Their Manure is Odorless   295
 20. The Manager Who's Moody   297
 21. Managers Who Fail to Plan and Put Priorities On Their Work   298
 22. The Manager Who Lacks Emotion and Empathy   299
 23. The Manager Who Hires Relatives into the Organization   300
 24. The Manager Who Views Females As Being Limited to Pleasure, Breeding, and Menial Functions, Such As Clerical and Assembly Duties   301

25. The Manager Who Faithfully Practices the Art
    of Pessimism   302
26. The Manager Who Steals Subordinates' Ideas   303
27. The Manager Whose Style and Authority Is
    Based on Absolute Power   304
28. The Manager Who Seems Oblivious to What's
    Happening   305
29. The Manager Who Loves to "Sack" Employees   306
30. The Manager Who Embarrasses Subordinates in
    the Presence of Others   307
31. The Manager Who Follows "Double Standards"
    in the Organization   308
32. The Manager Who's a Religious or Racial Bigot   310

Summary   311

Appendix A: Employee Performance Evaluation   313

Appendix B: Security Vulnerability Survey   319

**Appendix C: Security Department Loss Prevention
            Check List**   327

Index   333

PREFACE

When I first positioned myself in front of the typewriter to write this book, there were relatively few books in, and for, the industry. For the most part they were "nuts and bolts" texts, dealing with such specific protection areas as hospital security, hotel security, office building security, retail and computer security, and sources of information.

At the same time, national seminars and other training forums sponsored by such prestigious organizations as the American Society for Industrial Security, to name but one, similarly focused on the "how-to" of security, such as how to improve facility security through the integrated use of state-of-the-art technology with a smaller staff, et cetera.

Those kinds of books and training programs were professionally done and certainly most necessary. In fact, they were indispensable in the ever-growing protection industry. Yet, little attention was being paid to the administrative, managerial, and supervisorial aspects of our industry.

We were becoming highly skilled protection technicians but remained ignorant of and insensitive to the principles and practices of good management. Security executives, as a group, had fallen behind—had become less than "whole" executives in comparison to others in the corporate structure. Men and women in other organizational and career disciplines, such as finance, marketing, production, research, and human resources, were regularly being exposed to management development trends but for a number of reasons security managers were not. One reason was that we were too busy keeping up with racing security technology. Another reason was that we were too busy with important investigations and too absorbed with the so-called emergencies and crises that rightfully belong in the security department's camp. And still another reason was that security executives are of a disciplined and hard-set mentality, stemming in part from military or other public sector organizational experience, such as the police—organizations in which people performed because they were told to perform.

It was at this time and in this vacuum that I chose to focus on what was, in my judgment, the greatest need in the industry—better management. I had personally seen so many abuses that to me the need simply cried out. Some of these management abuses were truly tragic, some were idiotic, and some were hilariously funny. The common denominator: ignorance. I wrote *Effective Security Management* with the hope that through education and awareness abuses would subside, and security managers would favorably compare with other managers regarding American attitudes and practices in management.

The field of security management has certainly had its image improved since the first edition of *Effective Security Management* was published. Security management is increasingly viewed as a professional area within a company's or an institution's management framework. I would like to think that this book, in some small way, had a part in the growth and development of the security profession.

This revised edition remains a basic introduction to the principles of management applicable to the security department. In keeping with the practical, real-life approach to the subject, I have included new chapters on job descriptions and written policies and procedures. Furthermore, since the security manager has become more involved with the subject of risk analysis, I had asked my friend and colleague, Jim Broder, if I could incorporate material he has prepared on risk management and security surveys. He graciously assented, and contributed Chapters 17 and 18.

John Sanger at Cahners Publishing Company was kind enough to give permission to reprint his material on managing the organization, which serves as the introduction. This material describes succinctly the purpose of my book—so well, in fact, that I have included it with few changes.

I have also included my "Jackass Management Traits" at the end of this book material which originally appeared in Walsh and Healy's *Protection of Assets* manuals published by The Merritt Company in Santa Monica, California. These manuals, incidentally, represent the greatest single source or collection of security data. These fun, tongue-in-cheek caricatures may indeed be the most important part of the book, since it is all very well and good to understand organizational principles and management techniques, but if a manager does not know how to manage and supervise his employees, this learning will be all for naught.

I hope that the second edition of *Effective Security Management* will continue to be an effective tool in preparing students and practitioners for the exciting challenges of security management.

Charles A. "Chuck" Sennewald, CPP

EFFECTIVE SECURITY MANAGEMENT
Second Edition

Introduction: Managing the Organization

What is management? What functions do managers perform? While these are involved questions that will be explained in more detail in various parts of this book, we still must have a concept of what management is and what a manager does before much of the material will be meaningful. Let us start, therefore, with an exploration of what management is. Then we will explore the functions of management.

MANAGERIAL ACTS

If we were to follow a manager about all day and list on a sheet of paper everything that he does as a manager, the list would probably look somewhat as follows:

- Talks to employees
- Gives directions to lower level supervisors
- Dictates letter
- Establishes loss prevention goals
- Plans new loss prevention programs
- Hires new security officer
- Reads mail and reports
- Attends meeting
- Makes decision about new alarm equipment

You will note that these activities, as well as many others that you can think of, are either physical or mental in nature. The physical activities revolve around the concept of *communications*. He is either telling someone something verbally or in writing, or he is receiving a communication via the written or spoken word.

His mental activities, however, cannot be observed directly, but we know through his communication that he thinks and makes decisions—a mental activity. The ultimate objective of both physical and mental activities is to create an environment in which other individuals willingly participate in order to achieve objectives.

MANAGERIAL FUNCTIONS

Management functions are categorized differently by different managers. Basically, though, there are five general, and separately identifiable, functions.

Planning

Every manager must, to some extent, make plans. These vary from immediate tasks to long-range objectives, from simple to involved, and from departmental to company-wide impact. A manager, for example, may plan the work for tomorrow, decide when vacations will start, determine which security systems will be purchased next month, or determine the department's objectives during the next five years. Planning is nothing more than looking ahead, a vital function performed by every manager. Determining future activities necessarily involves a conceptual or mental look ahead and a recognition of needed future actions—whether they be tomorrow or next year. It involves looking forward, conceptualizing about future events and making decisions today which will affect tomorrow.

If future events could be determined with accuracy, then a plan of action could be developed to accomplish the objectives of the firm under the conditions which the future would bring. The future, however, is not certain, and, at best, forecasting future events is a game of educated guessing. Therefore, the manager estimates or forecasts that one of several possible conditions will exist at some given future time. A manager's future planning actually consists of developing a series of plans, some of which will be put into effect, depending on the conditions existing at that future time.

Planning is not a function reserved exclusively for top management. To the contrary, it is one of the functions that every manager performs, regardless of his location in an organization. The higher the level of management, the more time spent planning.

Organizing

Managers must organize—organize people, organize materials, organize time, and organize jobs. Through organizing, the manager is creating an environment which will be conducive to achieving the organization's objectives.

Organization consists of the following:

1. Determining what activities need to be done,
2. Grouping and assigning these activities to subordinates, and
3. Delegating the necessary authority to the subordinates to carry out the activities in a coordinated manner.

When you, as a manager, direct work, establish goals, and affix authority relationships, you are performing organizing functions in addition to the previously discussed planning functions. Before you can organize, you must plan. Neither planning nor organizing is clearly or separately discernible, but both are intermixed in the overall management function.

Directing

In addition to planning and organizing, a manager must succeed in directing the activities of others. This managerial function deals directly with influencing, guiding, or supervising subordinates in their jobs. Directing cannot be performed alone. It must be executed with planning and organizing.

When directing employees in their tasks, the manager's communication is a planned and organized one. An unplanned or disorganized directive is useless.

Coordinating

Few tasks can be undertaken without coordinating the efforts of several people—inside and outside the organization. A typical security program may require coordinating the efforts of the personnel department, the contract guard company, the shipping department supervisor, and the police department.

It is the manager's job to ensure that the various tasks are scheduled and implemented in an efficient and economical manner. As with the other functions of a manager, it is difficult to single out coordinating. It, too, is part of the composite that includes planning, organizing, and directing.

Controlling

Whenever people are joined together in some common undertaking, some form of control is necessary. Orders may be misunderstood, or rules may be violated, or objectives may unknowingly shift. Whatever the reason, it seems that the larger the number of individuals concerned, the greater the probabilities that inappropriate action (or *no* action) will be taken.

Controlling merely consists of forcing the tasks that have been undertaken to conform to prearranged plans. Thus planning is necessary for control. As with the other functions of management, controlling is not performed independently. That it cannot exist alone is immediately apparent when we realize that managerial control consists of preconceived and *planned* acts which must have been *organized.* Likewise, employees must be *directed* and activities *coordinated* for control to exist.

SUMMARY OF MANAGEMENT FUNCTIONS

The management process, therefore, is not a series of separate functions (planning, organizing, directing, coordinating, controlling) but a composite process.*

If you have any doubts about the composite aspect of these functions, consider this:

- A *plan* is a course of action—an *organized* scheme for doing something. Planning without organization, therefore, is impossible. A plan, to be a plan, must be known and communicated.
- To effect communication of the plan, some *directions* must be given and some *coordination* must occur.
- To *control* is to verify something by comparing it with a standard (the plan) and taking action if necessary.

THE SUCCESSFUL MANAGER

The manager's job is to create an environment conducive to the performance of acts by others in order to accomplish personal as well as company goals. Managers should be able to inspire, motivate, and direct the work of others.

Characteristics

A truly definitive list of characteristics for a successful manager would be impossible to develop. The list below includes some of the desirable characteristics, however.

1. A manager should be able to think. Specifically, he should be able to think clearly and purposefully about a problem.
2. A manager should be able to express himself clearly. A manager's

---

Note from the author (CAS)
* Many management professionals refer to this process by the acronym PODSCORB: *P*lanning, *O*rganizing, *D*irecting, *S*taffing, *CO*rdinating, *R*ecord Keeping, and *B*udgeting. Later chapters in the book will cover each of these functions in great detail.

chief physical act is communicating. The best conceived idea is worthless if it cannot be communicated.

3. A manager must possess technical competence. He does not necessarily have to be a technician. Rather, he should possess the technical ability to enable him to manage effectively.

4. A manager should possess the ability to think broadly. Broad comprehension is necessary to see the effect of each proposed action on the whole organization.

5. A manager should be a salesman. Selling an idea—convincing others of its worth—is one of management's tasks. Selling a plan of action is a vital part of communication and motivation.

6. A manager should possess moral integrity. Both his superiors and his subordinates should have implicit confidence in him and his actions.

7. A manager should be emotionally stable. He should keep his personal feelings out of business problems.

8. A manager should possess skill in human relations and have insight into human motivation and behavior. This enables him to lead, not drive, his subordinates.

9. A manager should possess organizational ability. A logical, ordered process is invaluable to achieving established goals.

10. A manager should be dynamic—a characteristic trait of leaders.

Leadership

Leadership is a quality that inspires others to perform. It is that quality in a manager's personality that enables him to influence others to accept his direction freely or willingly.

A good leader is not necessarily a good manager, but an effective manager must have many of the qualities of a good leader. A leader must be able to recognize each of his follower's needs in order to motivate him through his needs.

The following are some general qualities that good leaders exhibit:

1. The desire to excel. A leader is never content with second best. He must always be first. He must be a self-starting individual who is willing to engage in long hours and hard work to achieve success.

2. A sense of responsibility. A leader is not afraid to seek, accept, and faithfully discharge responsibility.

3. A capacity for work. Good leaders are willing to accept the demands of success—long hours and hard work.

4. A feel for good human relations. Leaders study and analyze their followers, trying always to understand them and their problems. The ability to understand their fellow workers is probably the most important single characteristic of good leadership.

5. A contagious enthusiasm. Good leaders should impart this contagious enthusiasm to their associates.

Obviously, these are not the only qualities of good leadership. Intelligence, character, integrity, and other similar traits are also important.

TIME MANAGEMENT

Everything we have discussed so far involves time. And time management may well be the most difficult of all of your management tasks.

Time management consultants often refer to the 80/20 rule, which reflects their discovery that people tend to spend about 80 percent of their time on tasks that produce 20 percent of the results. Too many people work diligently on low-value activities. These activities may make you feel good and give you a sense of accomplishment, but they are not significantly productive.

Time Management Tips

Here are some general hints on managing your time.

1. Figure out what time of the day you are most productive and make sure that you schedule important work during those hours. If, for example, you are a "morning person," schedule less productive tasks for the afternoon.
2. Keep a detailed log of how you spend your time. You will quickly see when and how you waste time and you will probably be able to spot your most productive hours if you are not already aware of them.
3. If the log shows a lack of self-discipline, create new time management habits. Write a fairly rigid schedule for yourself, and stick to it until it becomes habit.
4. Keep a calendar, preferably covering a week at a time, so you can always see what you have to do.
5. Do similar tasks at one time; for example, do all of your telephoning or all of your letters at one time.
6. Relegate the small or routine tasks to your least productive hours. (This is the time to write letters and make phone calls.)
7. Get someone else to do work you do not absolutely have to do. If your secretary or assistant can perform the task, delegate it.
8. Use downtime—when you are riding a bus or waiting for an appointment—to do certain routine or easy tasks such as reviewing a memo, figuring your expense account, reading the morning mail, or reading trade journals.

9. Resist the urge to handle the mail as soon as it arrives. Save it for the less productive time that you have scheduled.
10. Control paper. Keep your records simple and look for ways to streamline.
11. Keep things where they belong and keep them in logical places.
12. Eliminate unnecessary meetings.
13. Establish a time for planning—"quiet time"—and handle only true emergencies during that time, should they arise.
14. Try to make your first hour at work your most productive hour.
15. Attach priorities to tasks. Do not spend more time on a project than it is worth.
16. Jot down notes of things that need to be done. Do not try to do them immediately.
17. Use your note pad for notes—do not attempt to rely on your memory for important information.
18. Keep unscheduled and social visits to a minimum.
19. When someone brings you a problem, expect them to have a suggested solution in mind.
20. Do a job right the first time so you do not have to do it again.

Time management gives managers more time to manage.

John Sanger

I

GENERAL SECURITY MANAGEMENT

1

General Principles of Organization

The framework of structured organization is nothing more nor less than a vehicle for the realization of the purposes for which a company or a department is established. That skeleton, the organizational structure itself, does not think, has no initiative, cannot act or react. Yet it is absolutely essential in the work environment. A sound organizational framework facilitates the accomplishment of tasks by members of the organization, people working under the supervision of responsible managers.

A hospital, for example, is organized for the purpose of providing health care services. A sub-unit of that master organization, the Security Department, is organized for the purpose of protecting that health care environment. Organization, then, is the arrangement of people with a common objective or purpose, in a manner to make possible the performance of related tasks grouped for the purpose of assignment, and the establishment of areas of responsibility with clearly defined channels of communication and authority.

ORGANIZATIONAL PRINCIPLES

In the design of a sound organizational framework there are six widely accepted principles:

1. The work should be divided according to some logical plan.
2. Lines of authority and responsibility should be made as clear and direct as possible.
3. One supervisor can effectively control only a limited number of people, and that limit should not be exceeded. (This principle is called Span of Control.)
4. There should be "unity of command" in the organization.
5. Responsibility cannot be given without delegating commensurate authority and there must be accountability for the use of that authority.
6. All efforts of sub-units and personnel must be coordinated into the harmonious achievement of the organization's objectives.

Each of these principles has a meaningful application within a security organization.

Logical Division of Work

The necessity for the division of work becomes apparent as soon as you have more than one man on the job. *How* the work is divided can have a significant impact on the results at the end of the day. The manner and extent of the division of work influence the product or performance qualitatively as well as quantitatively. The logical division of work, therefore, deserves close attention.

There are five primary ways in which work can be divided:

- purpose
- process or method
- clientele
- time
- geography

Purpose

It is most common for work to be divided according to purpose. In fact, the Security Department could be organized into two divisions: a Loss Prevention Division (its purpose being to prevent losses) and a Detection Division (its purpose being to apprehend those who defeated the efforts of the prevention unit).

Process or method

A process unit is organized according to the method of work, all similar processes being in the same unit. An example in security might be the polygraph examiners unit or the credit card investigators unit of the general investigative section.

Clientele

Work may also be divided according to the clientele served or worked with. An example here would be the background screening personnel, who deal only with prospective and new employees; or store detectives, who concentrate on shoplifters; or general retail investigators, who become involved with dishonest employees, shoplifters, and a host of other criminal offenders.

Division of work by purpose, process, or clientele is really a division based on the *nature* of the work itself and consequently is referred to as "functional." In other words, the grouping of security personnel to perform work divided by its nature (purpose, process or clientele) is called *functional organization.*

For a great many organizations, the functional organization constitutes the full division of work. Security, however, like police and fire services in the public sector, usually has around-the-clock protective responsibilities. In addition, unlike its cousins in the public sector, it may have protective responsibilities spread over a wide geographic area.

Time

At first glance the 24-hour coverage of a given facility may appear relatively simple. The natural reaction is to have 3 eight-hour shifts, with fixed posts, patrol, and the communication and alarm center all changing at midnight, 8:00 A.M. and 4:00 P.M. In reality a number of interesting problems surface when a department begins organizing by time, such as:

- How many security people are necessary on the first shift? If a minimum security staff takes over at midnight and the facility commences its business day at 7:00 A.M., can you operate for one hour with the minimum staff, or must you increase coverage prior to 7:00 A.M. and overlap shifts? (There are hundreds of variables to just this type of problem.)
- If you have two or more functional units, such as men assigned to patrol and men assigned to the communications and alarm center (in another organizational pyramid altogether), who is in command at 3:00 A.M.? The question of staff supervision confuses many people. (See Chapter 5, "The Security Supervisor's Role," for a detailed discussion of staff supervision.)
- How much supervision is necessary during facility down-time? If the question is not *how much,* then how is *any* supervision exercised at 3:00 A.M.?
- If there are five posts, each critical and necessary, and five men are scheduled and one fails to show, how do you handle the situation? Should you schedule six men for just that contingency?

These and other problems do arise and are resolved regularly in facilities of every kind. Organizing by time, a way of life for security operations, does create special problems that deserve consideration if organizing by time is a new undertaking for a company.

Geography

Whenever a security department is obliged to serve a location removed from the headquarters facility, and one or more security personnel are assigned to the outlying location, there is one major issue that must be resolved:

to whom do the security personnel report—to security management back at headquarters, or to site management (which is non-security)?

The real issue is: Should non-security management have direct supervision over a security employee who has technical or semi-technical skills that more often than not are beyond the competence of that non-security management?

In defining the type of authority an executive or supervisor exercises, a distinction is generally made between *line* and *staff* authority. While these terms have many meanings, in its primary sense line authority implies a direct (or single line) relationship between a supervisor and his subordinate; the staff function is service or advisory in nature.

Security personnel should only be directly supervised by security management. Site management may provide staff supervision, providing suggestions and assistance, but restricted to such matters as attention to duty, promptness in reporting, and compliance with general rules. Detailed security activities fall outside the jurisdiction of such a manager.

Non-security management should not have line authority (direct supervision) over security, not only because of the issue of professional competency but also because site management should not be beyond the "reach" of security. Site management is indeed "out of reach" if the only internal control, security, is subject to its command. Site management would be free to engage in any form of mischief, malpractice or dishonesty without fear of security's reporting the activities to company headquarters.

Clear Lines of Authority and Responsibility

Once the work has been properly divided, the organization takes on the appearance of a pyramid-like structure, within which are small pyramids, as illustrated in Figure 1.1. Each part of each pyramid defines, with exactness, a function or responsibility and to whom that function is responsible. One can easily trace the solid line upwards to the Security Manager or Director who is ultimately responsible for every function within the security organization.

Not only is it important to have this organizational pyramid documented, normally in the form of an organizational chart, but it is also essential that security employees have access to that chart so they can see exactly where they fit into the organization pattern, to whom they are responsible, to whom their supervisor is responsible, and so on right up to the top. Failure to so inform employees causes unnecessary confusion, and confusion is a major contributor to ineffective job performance.

Additionally, the organizational chart is a subtle motivator. People can see themselves moving up in the boxes; in order for goal-setting to be successful, one must be able to envision oneself already in possession of one's goal.

Figure 1.1 Repeated pyramidal forms within organizational structure.

Finally, the apparent rigidity of boxes and lines in the organizational chart must not freeze communications. Employees at the lowest layer of the pyramid must feel free to communicate directly with the Security Manager, and have the right to do so without obtaining permission from all the intervening levels of supervision.

Span of Control

There is a limit to the number of subordinates who can be supervised effectively by one person, and that limit should not be exceeded. The limit ranges from a maximum of five at the highest level in the organization, to a maximum of twelve at the lowest level. The greater the degree of sophistication of the interactions between supervisors and subordinates, the narrower is the optimum span of control.

Exceeding the limits of span of control is really no different from spreading oneself too thin in some non-work environment such as school. If a student carries a full academic load of core subjects, becomes involved in student government, goes out for varsity football, is engaged to be married, belongs to the military reserve, and works twenty hours a week in a liquor store, it is likely that some of his activities will not receive the attention they deserve and few, if any, will be done with excellence.

Slipshod, undisciplined, poorly executed security work is an almost inevitable consequence of violating the organizational principle of span of control.

Unity of Command

The fourth principle, that of unity of command, means that an employee should be under the direct control of *one and only one* immediate superior (Figure 1.2). This principle also dictates that a task or function requiring

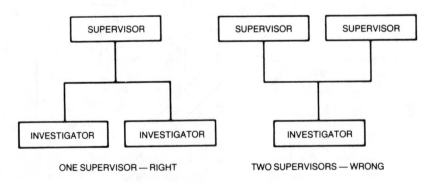

Figure 1.2 Unity of command.

the action of two or more people must also be under the direct control of but one supervisor.

Violations of the principle of unity of command are not usually found in the design of the organization, but rather occur, more by accident than design, during special events or other non-routine conditions that bring out more company executives than usual. The security officer or agent who is given conflicting orders by several superiors becomes confused, inefficient, irresponsible and, to say the least, angry.

One cannot successfully serve two masters. This will be discussed further in Chapter 5.

Responsibility, Authority, and Accountability

The fifth principle of organization is all too frequently violated by the manager or executive who gives a subordinate the responsibility to do a task but holds back the authority needed to discharge such responsibility effectively. A prime example of this is the case where a man is given the job of supervising a unit. He is told the unit is his and he will be measured by how well he performs in that assignment. The new supervisor then discovers he does not have the right (authority) to select the applicant of his choice to fill a vacancy; he discovers that disciplinary matters are decided by his superiors (and his subordinates know this); and he soon finds that his plans, suggestions and ideas are replaced with those of his boss, and thus he is totally frustrated. He has a job and yet he does not.

The true art of delegation includes giving responsibility with commensurate authority and then holding the employee fully accountable for his use of that authority. *If,* in the above example, the new supervisor had the authority to hire, discipline, and implement his own ideas, and did so without exercising good judgment, and could not be corrected or trained to use his authority properly, then he should be stripped not only of the authority but of the responsibility as well. The employee must be given *both* responsibility and authority and held accountable for both.

Perhaps the major reason why so many managers violate this principle is that they are unwilling, sometimes subconsciously, to allow subordinates to carry out the responsibilities delegated to them, because the manager knows that he is ultimately responsible. The manager knows it is true that you cannot completely delegate responsibility. This may seem confusing and sound like double-talk, so let us approach the problem from a different angle.

a.   The head of the security pyramid, the Security Manager or Security Director, is the only one accountable for his organization, the Security Department. His reputation grows brighter in the department's successes and suffers in its failures. Almost invariably, he rose to the top because of his proven ability and track record. In other words, doing things his way has proven, over the stretch of time, to be successful. That is why he is where he is.

b.   The security manager or director cannot do the entire security job alone and needs people to help him get it done. Depending on the scope of the job, he may need anywhere from two people to three hundred people. Ideally, if every person on his team thought and acted exactly as he does, he would assure himself of continued outstanding success.

c.   The manager understands, however, that no one else thinks and acts exactly as he does. He may reason that the next best thing, then, is to do the thinking for all the key people, make the decisions for them, have them run the organization his way. He holds the authority, and when things go wrong—and they will—he will probably severely criticize the party who failed. This manager has not really delegated responsibility and authority. Yet, ironically, when things go wrong he will point out to management the employee who failed, and in so doing will have someone to *share* the responsibility with, because ultimately it is his responsibility.

d.   Or, in contrast to the situation described in (3) above, the manager may open up the organization to other talented people. Within the broad guidelines he sets as a leader, he will give those key people genuine responsibility. He will make them accountable, and they will respond positively to that accountability. When things go wrong—and they will—the party who failed will judge himself critically. This manager *has* truly delegated responsibility and authority. Yet, ironically, he will take full responsibility for failure, because it *is* ultimately and rightfully his responsibility.

Coordination to Meet Organizational Goals

Theoretically, if the first five principles just discussed were adhered to, everything should function smoothly. In practice such total harmony is rare, if not impossible. Human frailties such as jealousy over assignments as well as promotions, elitism in some subunits, friction between supervisors, the historic poor reputation of certain sub-units or assignments—all these and more tend to decrease what might have been optimum efficiency.

How then does management coordinate all efforts of sub-units and personnel? Or, better, what can management do to *attempt* to coordinate all units and personnel into the harmonious achievement of the department's goals? The answer is: establish a sound security training program and good departmental communications.

Both training and communications are dealt with in separate chapters (Chapters 9 and 13, respectively). The emphasis in both cases should be on educating employees about the organization and its objectives; defining the importance of each sub-unit's contribution to the whole; developing organizational pride and individual security employee self-esteem; creating a sense of security unity and identification within the company as a whole; and, finally, developing a climate wherein the individual employee includes organizational goals within his own personal goals.

WHERE SECURITY FITS IN THE ORGANIZATIONAL STRUCTURE

The Changing Role of Security

In less than two decades the security function has climbed from the depths of organizational existence, from dank and smelly basement offices, to the heights of executive offices and a place in the sun. Gone for most organizations are the days when the Security Department reported to the superintendent of buildings, manager of buildings and grounds, head housekeeper, yardmaster, controller, plant engineer or store manager. Today security management frequently reports directly to senior management, if not the chief executive officer himself. And that vertical movement is still gaining momentum. Security is moving more and more into the ranks of senior management; more positions such as Vice President of Security, Vice President of Loss Prevention or Vice President of Assets Protection are being created yearly.

Why this sudden ascent? Simply stated, the ever-increasing contribution security makes to the organization's objectives, principally profit, has earned corresponding increased recognition from top management.

Another reason for the growing recognition of security's importance is the increasing prevalence of crime in our society. A number of socioeconomic factors, along with political and cultural conditions, have combined to create a climate in which deviant or anti-social behavior is no longer intolerable. As a result, more and more deviant behavior occurs, particularly attacks against property (theft)—until the magnitude of the problem far transcends the limited prevention ability of public law enforcement. The burden of crime prevention falls on the private sector.

In an address to the International Association of Chiefs of Police, Richard W. Velde, Administrator of the Law Enforcement Assistance Administration, stated:

> The criminal justice system, and particularly our nation's police, do perform a rather narrow function that is largely a responsive one that follows the commission of crime. There are constitutional and statutory responsibilities

in all the states that define the role of the police force and essentially they say that police are not in the crime prevention business.[1]

Without question, a large number of firms and even entire industries would fail today without their own internal security organizations. Imagine the position of a major credit card company without its security department. Who would coordinate and track the criminal abuse of that credit privilege across the country?

Security's Contribution to Profits

Security contributes to company or corporate profits by reducing or eliminating preventable losses, including those caused by criminal behavior. Consider the retail industry, for example. A major chain with sales of $1 billion might realize a 3 percent net profit as well as a 3 percent inventory shrinkage (these three figures are quite realistic). This firm, then, realizes $30 million in profits and $30 million in losses, or lost profit. If the Security Department through its efforts and programs can reduce the inventory shrinkage by just one-half of one percent, profits would rise $5 million!

Where else can management find such opportunities to increase profits? The cost of raw materials cannot be reduced; they are becoming scarcer and more expensive. The cost of labor cannot be reduced; labor's demands are only going up. The costs of so-called fixed expenses such as rent, utilities and insurance cannot be reduced; they are all rising. Because losses are so enormous, their reduction is in the hands of protection professionals who manage corporate and divisional security organizations.

To Whom Does Security Report?

With increased recognition of the need for security within the whole spectrum of company activities, all concerned directly or indirectly with the "bottom line" of business (profits), came increased responsibility; and with increased responsibility came commensurate authority. To provide the security manager with that necessary authority, he along with his organization has moved up in the organizational pyramid to report directly to senior management, usually a vice president. That vice president delegates a portion of his authority to the security chief, who can then exercise what is known as *functional* authority.

Reporting directly to a vice president places the security executive

---

[1] Velde, Richard W., quoted in *Private Security: Report of the Task Force on Private Security.* (Washington, DC: National Advisory Committee on Criminal Justice Standards and Goals, 1976), p. 19.

at the top of the middle management sector of business. The most dynamic people in the firm are now his peers. Figures 1.3 and 1.4 illustrate the place typically held in the organizational chart by a Security Director in a manufacturing and a retail organization, respectively.

The Difference Between Corporate and Company Security

Although the word *corporate* is sometimes used to describe a firm's central authority, the word more accurately refers to that small holding organization that owns a number of firms. A conglomerate is a combination of a variety of individual companies, each with its own executive team, its own goals, its own volume and its own profit performance. The financial results of each of the companies in a corporate structure (or conglomerate) are, for the sake of simplicity, forwarded to the corporate organization at the very top of the pyramid.

Many corporations have a Corporate Security Director who maintains a pure staff relationship with the individual security directors in charge of protection in the various companies within the corporate family. (Figure 1.5) The corporate director's job is as follows:

1. Establishes corporate security policies that serve as guidelines for divisional (company) security operations.
2. Serves as an advisor and counselor to divisional senior management in terms of his assessment of how effectively divisional security is functioning.
3. Serves as an advisor and counselor to Divisional Security Director, giving him support in terms of professional expertise, advice, encouragement and criticism.
4. Serves as a central clearing-house and information center for all divisions within the corporation, disseminating important information about the industry as a whole.
5. Provides for those few but important security services needed by the relatively small corporate organization comprised of, as a rule, top-ranking executives in the company.

Corporate Security Directors have other functions, such as maintaining liaison with top officials in the public sector and participating in trade association activities. But the real thrust of these corporate security jobs is one of counsel. If the corporate director has a security staff, it is usually quite small. He simply does not have direct accountability for the performance of the divisions; yet, certainly, if divisions demonstrate a consistently poor performance in security activities over a prolonged period of time, it will indeed reflect on the corporate director.

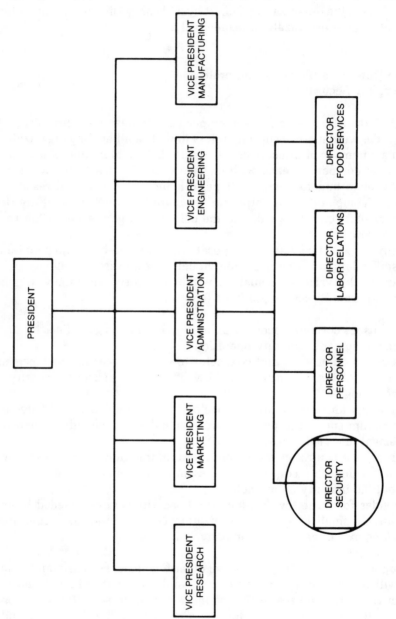

Figure 1.3 Example of manufacturing firm's organization.

22

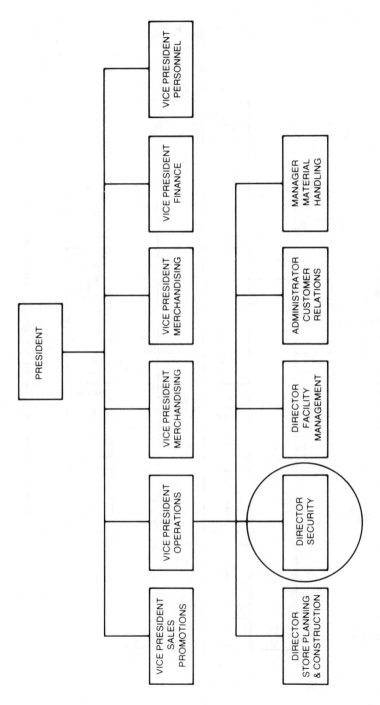

Figure 1.4 Example of retail company organization.

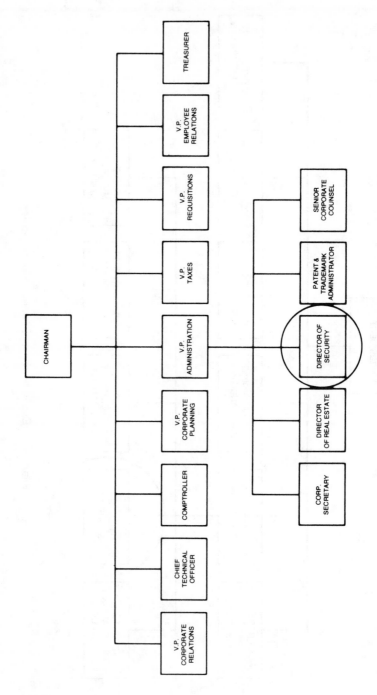

Figure 1.5 Example of corporate (conglomerate) organization.

On the other hand, the divisional or company Security Director (or Manager or whatever the head of the security department may be called) is directly accountable for the activities and results of the security organization. Throughout this text, when we refer to the Security Director, unless otherwise specified, we are talking about the divisional or company director . . . not the corporate man.

SUMMARY

Organization is the arrangement of people with a common objective in a manner that groups related tasks, establishes areas of responsibility, and defines lines of communication and authority.

There are six basic principles of organization: (1) logical division of work (according to purpose, process, clientele, time or geography); (2) clear lines of authority, visible on the organizational chart as a pyramidal structure; (3) limited span of control; (4) unity of command; (5) true delegation of responsibility and authority, with attendant accountability; and (6) coordination of efforts through training and communication.

Within the company or corporate organizational structure, security in recent years has shown a sharp vertical movement, an ascent primarily attributable to rising crime and increased recognition of security's contribution to profits. The Security Director now commonly reports to a member of senior management.

In the corporate or conglomerate structure, the Corporate Security Director serves generally in a staff relationship both to higher management and to the individual company Security Directors. In this text, discussion of the Security Director's or Manager's role refers to the security function in the individual company rather than that of the corporate organization.

REVIEW QUESTIONS

1. Explain the five methods of dividing work.

2. Discuss the problems that may arise in organizing work by time.

3. Give two reasons why non-security management should not have line authority over security employees.

4. What is meant by *Span of Control?*

5. Explain the principle of *Unity of Command.*

6. Discuss the relationship between responsibility and authority. Give an example where a manager has given a subordinate responsibility without commensurate authority.

7. How does security contribute to the company's profits?

2

Organizational Structure

The organizational structure of a department within a company will reflect the six general organizational principles discussed in Chapter 1, including:

- the logical division of tasks or responsibilities.
- clear lines of authority and responsibility—within the department specifically and within the organization generally.

The department's organizational structure is two-dimensional in its formal representation, as illustrated in Figure 2.1. On the *horizontal* plane it indicates the division of areas of responsibilities; on the *vertical* plane it defines levels of authority or rank. In the illustration shown, responsibility for security under the Security Manager has been divided into two areas, with an Assistant Manager for Loss Prevention and an Assistant Manager for Investigations. The horizontal division defines areas of responsibility for each Assistant Manager, while the vertical chart indicates that they are of equal rank, each reporting directly to the Security Manager. Similarly, Loss Prevention responsibilities are divided among the officers in charge of the Computer Room Detail, General Facility Protection, and Credit Card and Accounts Receivable. The organizational chart indicates this separation of duties, as well as showing the relationship of each officer-in-charge of these subdivisions to the officers under them and the Assistant Manager and Security Manager above them.

The organizational structure of one company's security department will differ in widely varying degrees from that of another company, *even within the same industry*. This is true for several reasons. First, organizational structures are man-made, reflecting the way in which the security director and management above him perceive departmental and company priorities. The formal pattern will also be influenced by individual personnel. Finally, the structure is and must be fluid, or highly changeable, to meet the ever-changing character of most private enterprise operations.

THE INFORMAL ORGANIZATION

It is revealing to compare the formal organizational structure outlined in Figure 2.1 with the informal organization in Figure 2.2, which illustrates how the typical organization might really work.

Figure 2.1   Formal organizational structure of a security department.

The conspicuous difference between the two organizations is that, in the informal organization—the *real* organization—five supervisors report directly to the Security Manager, not just two. In addition to the two Assistant Managers, there are the supervisors in charge of the Computer Room, Credit Card and Accounts Receivable, and Background Screening. Reasons behind such a change in structure will be many. They might include any of the following:

1. Physical protection of the computer room and of the credit card and accounts receivable areas logically belong under the Loss Prevention banner, but that Assistant Manager has limited interests and talent, favors the area of general facilities protection, and as a consequence has literally abrogated the other two functions.
2. The supervisors of those two areas of responsibility do not accept the Assistant Manager for Loss Prevention as their immediate superior and look instead to the Security Manager, who permits this condition.
3. The Security Manager has little confidence in that Assistant Manager's ability but is unable to fire him, with the result that he informally brings those sensitive units under his own wing.
4. The Security Manager has great difficulty in delegating authority in

Figure 2.2 Sample *informal* organizational structure of a security department.

sensitive areas to subordinates; consequently he tends to exercise direct authority over most activities himself.

5. The Security Manager regards such areas of activity as "toys," and he violates the organizational structure because he enjoys "playing" these games.

6. There is a personal relationship between the Security Manager and those supervisors on that second level of supervision, a friendship that interferes with the organizational integrity.

All such possible explanations—and there are many more—could also, of course, explain why the supervisor in charge of the Background Screening Unit also reports directly to the Security Manager instead of to his logical immediate superior.

Another major factor in the changeability of organizational structure is company (and therefore departmental) growth. As an example, one major retail chain had eleven stores in 1961, all located in Southern California. Sixteen years later there were 45 major department stores and two clearance centers in five states, with other stores scheduled to open. Obviously, the structure of the security department was far removed from what it had been sixteen years earlier. During that period the department experienced at least a dozen reorganizations. Contrast this flexibility with, for instance, a municipal police department with a relatively stable city population. Few, if any, major departmental reorganizations would be expected to occur during the same period of time.

Budgetary considerations also play an important role in the organizational design. As an example, consider again the organization illustrated in Figure 2.1. The chart indicates a total of six supervisors at the third level reporting directly to the two Assistant Managers. What would happen if the department's budget would allow only four supervisors at that level? How would the organization be changed?

A number of variations are possible. The Computer Room detail might be combined with the Credit Card and Accounts Receivable area into one unit or detail called the High Risk Detail, under one supervisor; similarly, the Background Screening unit might be combined with the General Assignments unit for investigations. Such horizontal shrinkage may or may not serve the best interests of the organization; however, budgetary restrictions may make such changes inevitable.

Whatever the changes required by growth or budget, the point of organization remains the same: to serve the interest of the department in getting its job done through an intelligent division of tasks and the establishment of clear lines of authority. This applies to the small organization as well as the larger one. There will be fewer vertical levels of authority or rank, and a simpler division of responsibilities on each horizontal plane, in a small department; but the *purpose* of organization and the approach to organizational structure are identical.

As we have already indicated, the structure is two-dimensional. In the ideal situation, achieving a viable organization involves three steps: (1) identify the departmental objectives, (2) identify the various tasks and divide them into logical work units, and (3) identify the levels of leadership necessary to achieve the tasks. All that remains is to "fill in" the boxes with appropriate personnel.

This is the ideal. Unfortunately, it does not normally work that way. As a rule, people—the employees to be put into the boxes—are already aboard. Thus the two-dimensional plan of organizational design becomes complicated by the introduction of what might be called a third dimension— that being, of course, the personnel. The results are almost invariably bad because the design tends to lean toward personnel considerations. Expressed in another way, there is a tendency to build jobs, and organizations, around people, rather than identifying qualified talent and placing them in the jobs defined by a plan of organization. This is true because, for policy or personnel reasons, the security manager in charge of a department for the most part has no choice but to make the best use he can of existing, in-house personnel. It is easier to change the organization than it is to change the man.

The reality of organizational structure, then, is inevitably a compromise between a pure design, based on the best possible horizontal and vertical layout, and existing security department employees. For this reason the typical organizational chart must be suspect.

The organizational chart is suspect in another significant way: it clearly defines reporting lines, or "chain of command," when, in reality, numerous informal reporting lines may exist. This aspect of organizational life clouds the levels of authority, taking from some and adding to others. In this respect the three-dimensional aspect of the organization acquires an almost sinister air in terms of who really is whose boss and who really can tell whom what to do—and who is meddling in areas outside his scope of responsibility.

SUB-UNIT STRUCTURES

In addition to the departmental organizational structure, both formal and informal, the security administrator should be aware of the existence of interdepartmental or sub-unit structures at lower levels within his own organization. The number and size of these mini-structures will be related to the size of the department. These structures will tend to have the same characteristics as the formal organization—that is, horizontal divisions (of tasks) and vertical levels (of authority).

Singling out the General Facility Protection division of our example department, consider the security officer's level on the second shift. To begin with, the second shift itself will probably represent the top of the nearly invisible hierarchical structure of security officers assigned to that division; the officers lower on the totem pole will be assigned to the least desirable shift, the first shift. The organizational structure of that second shift is shown in Figure 2.3.

In the absence of the Shift Supervisor, or Sergeant, the officer assigned to Patrol assumes leadership (in this example only). The Main Gate Officer assumes leadership for exterior protection, and the Main Lobby Officer is responsible for all security activities of an internal nature.

On the exterior protection side of this organizational pattern is a typical example of a "pecking order," or vertical line of authority; on the interior protection side, by contrast, all officers except the relief officer are of equal rank. In the latter case, in the absence of the Main Lobby Officer a struggle could ensue for position in the line of authority.

As a rule, such mini-structures of organization exist even though they have never been agreed upon by management, never been reduced to writing or charts, and in some cases never even been understood. Obviously, then, it is important for the security manager to be sensitive to the existence of such informal "structures" at the lowest levels of his organization, in order to maintain overall organizational integrity and harmony.

Consider this: How many times does a new supervisor, especially one who is not intimately familiar with the organization and its personnel, come onto the scene and commence changing operations and personnel around—

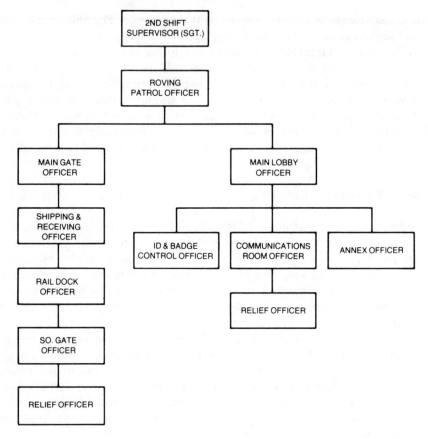

Figure 2.3 Sub-unit's structure within security department's organizational structure. Such mini-structures may exist without official departmental recognition or planning.

and meet stubborn resistance? From an administrative point of view the consequences of putting a lieutenant over a captain are clearly understood. The same is true at the bottom of the organizational ladder; these employees have their own "captains" and "lieutenants," even if they were not officially appointed as such.

Sensitivity to such organizational facts of life not only avoids disharmony—a negative advantage—but, on the positive side, such insight can be highly productive in terms of organizational performance. If a superior officer or manager wants to insure that something is done in the absence of the Shift Supervisor, he goes to the Patrol Officer. If, instead, the manager bypasses the Patrol Officer and goes to the Main Lobby Officer, the job may not get done properly.

There's no question that one key to supervisorial or managerial success is the ability to identify informal leaders and then use them for the organizational cause.

SUMMARY

Organizational structure, then, as applied to a security department, is a valuable and necessary management tool to organize tasks and people in an intelligent, meaningful and responsible structure in order to meet, and successfully discharge, the security function in any company.

In the ideal this structure is two-dimensional, defining responsibilities (horizontal) and lines of authority (vertical). In practice the structure will be affected by a third dimension: personnel. This dimension is reflected in the influence of the individual security manager, the necessity of using existing personnel, and the presence of invisible interdepartmental structures.

The organizational structure, finally, is not and should not be rigid, since it must be capable of adapting to budgetary considerations, changing goals, and company size and growth.

REVIEW QUESTIONS

1. What does the *horizontal* plane of an organizational chart represent? The *vertical* plane?

2. Why does the organizational structure of one security department differ from that of another, even within the same industry?

3. Discuss four reasons why the *informal* organization may differ from the *formal* organization.

4. What are the three steps in achieving a viable organizational structure?

5. Explain how personnel form the "third dimension" of organizational design.

3

Security's Role in the Organization

THE PROTECTIVE SERVICE ROLE

The singularly most conspicuous role of the Security Department in any organization is that of Protector or Guardian—protecting the company's property, product or merchandise, assets, equipment, reputation, and employees. And that responsibility, that duty is not limited to just the company's assets and employees. It extends to non-employees as well, be they guests, patrons, customers, or any other form of invitee on company property. Put another way, the Security Department is the guardian of all property and all people on company property.

That protective role constitutes a service to the organization; thus the security department's function is one of service.

The value of such service is better measured by what does *not* happen than by what does. For the company to operate over a given period of time without a payroll holdup, major burglary, significant disappearance of inventory, equipment or documents, or a rape, mugging, or assault in the parking lot (or parking structure—both of which are inherently dangerous areas), stairwell, or anywhere else on company property is indicative of the security function's effectiveness in its guardian role. And the posture of the guardian role is one of prevention—prevention of crime and prevention of losses by means of a strategy and philosophy of denying the criminal the opportunity to succeed. In keeping with that posture, some organizations have abandoned the name "Security Department" in favor of "Department of Loss Prevention."

Stated another way, security could easily be identified as a *protective service of prevention.*

It is beyond the scope of this text to discuss in detail all of the individual protective duties with which a security department will become involved. The specific responsibilities of any security department will be adapted to the specific organization—its buildings and curtilage, its operations, its assets, its personnel, its interaction at all levels with the public, and its general environment. Nevertheless, the role of security normally involves common elements, among which the following could be included:

- Arrests and causes prosecution of all persons committing a criminal attack on or against company property, equipment, supplies, products, goods and/or other assets.
- Designs and implements physical controls of the facility.
- Administers and conducts identification badge program.
- Conducts pre-employment and post-employment screening.
- Monitors control of DOD classified documents and information.
- Maintains liaison with local, state and federal law enforcement authorities.
- Monitors controls of company proprietary information.
- Administers employee and visitor access to facility.
- Administers vehicular access and parking controls and secures the parking environment.
- Prevents or otherwise reduces crime by maintaining a "security presence" and high visibility through such activities as patrolling company property and wearing distinctive apparel, though not necessarily military-type uniforms.
- Administers company's lock and key control program.
- Conducts security indoctrination and training.
- Investigates all criminal activity committed on company premises or against company interests, including attacks against persons.
- Administers executive protection program.
- Conducts financial stability investigations of potential vendors, merger candidates, etc.
- Coordinates special protection arrangements necessary during riots, natural disasters, strikes, etc.
- Designs and conducts security/loss prevention vulnerability surveys.
- Contracts for and administers outside security services such as professional consulting services, guard services, undercover agents, shopping services, certain investigative services, polygraph services, armored transport services, document destruction, etc.
- Provides emergency courier and escort services as needed.
- Acts as adviser to senior management on all security-related matters.

Even this extensive list by no means exhausts the possible protection services that will fall upon a given security department, responding to particular hazards. What the above catalog does suggest is the general purpose of the security function in any organization: to protect the company (people and assets) against attack or loss.

Within security's protective role, there are a host of sub-roles which are often neglected or unrecognized by security management. These sub-roles may be divided into three service categories:

- Special Services
- Educational Services
- Management Services

SPECIAL SERVICES

The Security Department's objectives are designed to contribute to the achievement of company goals. Company executives, who provide vital leadership for company goal achievement, have personal goals which are difficult to separate from company goals. More often than not, their goals *are* company goals. Service, then, to the "company" and service to management should be synonymous, for what is good for the executive team is good for the company, and vice versa. All demands for protective service, whether clearly related to the work environment or of a peripheral nature involving senior management, require attention.

The security management that understands the reasonableness and logic of providing the broadest possible range of special services moves the security function more closely to the mainstream of the business and makes a more significant contribution to the overall success of the company. A sampling of special services follows.

Executive's Home Security Surveys

The executive who wishes to "harden" his home, installing protective measures against criminal intrusion and attack, has the choice of calling the police for advice, hiring an outside security consultant, attempting to select appropriate defenses himself, or calling on the company's security staff. The latter is recommended—providing, of course, that the staff has the expertise to achieve the desired degree of security.

The homes of executives are by far more attractive targets for burglary than those of the average employees, and it only makes good sense that extraordinary precautionary measures be taken.

In one recent case, a personnel executive's rented home in the hills of Southern California was burglarized several times in a like number of weeks. The question of increasing protection or asking for company security advice never crossed the executive's mind until total frustration set in. On the occasion of each burglary, the home was entered and ransacked while the executive was away, with no evidence of forcible entry. On each occasion the police came to the home and conducted their investigation, usually a surface examination of the physical premises and a documentation of pertinent facts surrounding the loss. The police and the executive theorized that a friend of the former tenants was still in possession of the house key and was responsible for the crimes. The former tenants had moved out of state, and the identity of the friend was unknown.

Based on that theory, the executive purchased a manual burglary alarm and attached it to the door. If entry was made through the door and the alarm would sound, the subsequent examination of the device would indicate it had been activated.

The home was again burglarized and the alarm was not activated.

The executive was more than distraught over the dilemma. He finally turned to the company for assistance, and there, at his home, the security man within minutes located the point of entry used by the burglar—the louvered glass windows over the kitchen sink. The security executive temporarily secured these windows and the similar windows over the breakfast nook, and advised the executive of two alternative methods to secure those windows permanently. The executive was never victimized again. The simple technique of removing the screen and then removing the louvered window panes one at a time, and later replacing them, had escaped the police, literally as well as figuratively.

Executive home surveys will also examine the possible use of digital or central station alarming, inventorying valuable personal property (which includes recording serial numbers, photographing, video taping, and/or marking); establishing emergency procedures; and exterior lighting, to name but a few of the areas of concern, depending upon the person and properties to be protected.

Investigative Assistance

Sooner or later the whole spectrum of investigative skills can be used in peripheral service—from tracing the license plate of a hit-and-run driver who sideswiped an executive's auto, to tracking the source of an obscene letter sent to an executive's home, to locating (in cooperation with police) the runaway daughter of an executive. And such investigative service need not be limited to executive or senior management problems; someone in middle management or a key supervisor in the company could have a problem that senior management felt was deserving of company attention.

Bodyguard/Escort Service

So-called bodyguard duties constitute another dimension to the variety of special services the security organization can provide. Such a service could be any of the following:

1. Serving as an executive's chauffeur, temporarily or permanently.
2. Serving as escort for the dignitaries who are guests of the firm.
3. Serving as escorts for company executives visiting locations deemed hazardous.
4. Serving as escort for members of executives' families.
5. Intermingling with guests at special social functions.
6. Escorting couriers or messengers.
7. Serving as courier.

Emergency Service

Most security departments run a twenty-four-hour-a-day operation from either an alarm room, security operations room, or desk. Because of that twenty-four-hour telephone capability, the department can offer company management a unique emergency service, as follows: Every member of management participating in the emergency plan provides the department with a data card that lists the name, sex and date of birth of the executive and his entire family; their home address and phone number, with directions how to reach the home; the address and phone number of any summer or "second" homes, and directions how to reach those residences; the names and phone numbers of family physicians and dentists; local police department's address and phone number; local fire and rescue departments' names and numbers; local ambulance data; local hospital and emergency service data; insurance agent's identity and number; description and license numbers of family vehicles; identity of people to call (family, neighbors or friends) in the event of an emergency, etc.

That card is maintained in an alphabetical file in the twenty-four-hour operational room. When an executive is traveling, he calls in a supplement to the file, listing his itinerary, with phone numbers.

The emergency service becomes a clearing-house for processing emergency messages, dispatching emergency services, notifying appropriate people of problems, as well as expediting the flow of such information. Certainly the executive or a member of his family can call the police, fire, rescue squad, etc., directly and perhaps faster than routing the call through the Security Department. On the other hand, youngsters at home alone, or domestic servants, could be at a loss as to whom to call. Even an executive's wife might choose to call Security before calling the police if her husband is traveling—for example, if she became frightened and felt a prowler was on the property. A call from the company's Security Department reporting to the police that a prowler was on the property of an executive's home would, in all probability, receive quicker response than the semi-hysterical housewife calling the police herself.

There are a number of clear advantages to this type of service—still relatively unheard of and rare, but a growing function in the future of service-minded security departments throughout the country.

EDUCATIONAL SERVICES

An increasingly important and relatively new role for the Security Department is that of trainer and educator. As the private sector assumes more and more responsibility for law and order on private premises, there is an increasing need to educate employees and nonemployees alike on the necessity and objectives of security.

A striking example of the need for employee security education is in the retail industry. Retailers, including food, drug, department, chain, discount, specialty stores and independents, lose billions of dollars each year to dishonest employees. Part of that loss is directly attributable to the fact that the employee is ignorant of the company's security efforts and capabilities to detect dishonesty.

Every day, new or relatively new employees "discover" clever methods to misroute or deliver merchandise or funds into their personal possession, unaware of the fact that the ingenious scheme has been attempted and detected thousands of times before. Because they have not been properly educated, they contrive for unwarranted advantages in total ignorance, damaging their employer and exposing themselves to the tragic consequences of detection, termination and prosecution—all for the want of a security induction or awareness program for new employees.

Who is to conduct such training sessions? Experience tells us that the most effective presentations on the security function are made by security personnel. They know what they are talking about, and their expertise is apparent. A security presentation by a training officer or member of management lacks the same degree of conviction or credibility. Security must, therefore, assume the role of trainer/educator.

New employee induction programs are but one of a number of educational activities Security is involved in.

General Security Programs

Whereas the induction training addresses itself to the new employee and the consequences of dishonesty, the General Security Programs are aimed at creating an appreciation and understanding of the Security Department's objectives as they relate to the specific industry they serve. Thus, in retailing, the whole mix of problems—including shoplifting, credit card frauds, hide-in burglars, counterfeit passers, quick-change artists, etc.—can be an interesting, informative and *educational* experience for employees, who walk away from such sessions with a deeper insight into the problems and with ideas as to what they can do in the future to prevent them.

Supervisory Training Sessions

New supervisors, while undergoing a new set of directions aimed at assisting them in their new responsibilities as supervisors, should be exposed to security problems that are peculiar to supervisors. What can and what should supervisors do under certain circumstances? What are their limitations? What are the company's expectations of supervisors under a variety of security conditions, such as the discovery of a break-in or major loss?

Again, as in the programs listed above, the best trainer is a security professional.

Employee Self-Protection Programs

Perhaps the most dramatic and best-attended employee self-protection programs are rape prevention sessions, using one of the fine quality 16 mm motion picture commercial films or video cassettes available today. Employees are impressed that the Security Department is concerned about the protection of female employees as well as more business-related security activities.

Other employee self-protection programs, such as kidnaping prevention for executives, protection of personal property and home for regular (nonexecutive) employees, and basic self-defense are all possible programs the Security Department could offer, even on an optional basis, to employees of the company.

Again, this type of educational service is demonstrative of a security organization that cares about the company's employees. Consequently, the service tends to build a foundation of respect and support for the department's main objectives of protecting the company.

Unit or Departmental Presentations

Another important educational service role Security plays is in giving security presentations to various company units or departments. If a particular company unit—regardless of its organizational function or composition—wishes to hear from the Security Department, then the department should respond with a message aimed at that particular group. Housekeeping, Engineering, Purchasing, the Faculty Club, Merchandising Managers, the Youth Council—any group within the work environment is worthy of the Security Department's time and attention. (Sometimes it is necessary to cultivate an interest in security among the company's departments.)

The objective of each presentation, regardless of who the audience is, is twofold: first, to educate the group on the role and importance of the security function in the whole organization. This should be done in an entertaining and exciting way; the description of the security organization and its assignments can be liberally sprinkled with actual "war stories" which fascinate those not connected with the world of security. The second part of the objective is to point out to whatever group is being addressed how its role, contribution, or responsibility ties in with the security and protective efforts of the company or institution. In that way, they can identify with and relate to the security organization.

The educational efforts all strive to bridge the gap between the Security

Department and the rest of the organization. For too long the gap has been an accepted fact; indeed, it has served as an insulation for Security. Unfortunately, that insulation has bred distrust and fear of the security function— a function that must, if it is to be truly effective, have the understanding, trust, and support of all employees of the organization.

MANAGEMENT SERVICES

For the Security Department to make the maximum contribution to the organizational goals, security personnel (particularly at the managerial level) should achieve visibility as company management representatives as well as security management representatives. Specialists, as important as they may be, make limited contributions. Those who demonstrate interest in company problems and affairs, and who serve on various committees not specifically formed for pure protection purposes, play an additional, new role in the organization. They provide the company with a managerial support or service always in demand in organizational life.

This new dimension in Security's role must be sought out and cultivated, because Security has traditionally been content to limit its activities to the protective function. Organizational management, as a consequence, is accustomed to looking beyond the Security Department for general problem-solving counsel and assistance.

SUMMARY

Security is primarily a protective service of prevention, most conspicuously engaged in such general protective activities as access control, cargo protection, building security, investigation of criminal activities, inspections, and enforcement of company rules.

Security can and should also provide many related services. *Special services* might include executive protection, bodyguard service, special investigations and emergency services. Security should be actively engaged in *educational services,* bringing security awareness to new and established employees, and to supervisors whose responsibility must include loss prevention. And, wherever possible, the effective security department will seek out ways to expand its role, making its presence felt as a general problem-solving arm of management.

REVIEW QUESTIONS

1. Explain the statement, "The value of the Security Department's service is better measured by what does *not* happen than by what does."

2. Briefly stated, what is the general purpose of the security function in any organization?

3. Give four examples of special services which the Security Department might provide company management.

4. Describe how the Security Department might set up and operate an emergency service for the benefit of company management.

5. What are two objectives of the Security Department in making presentations to other company units or departments?

4

The Director's Role

Definitions of titles in the world of security in the private sector are not as clear as those in the public sector. There is little confusion over the position of the Chief of Police within the Police Department or his status within the municipal government. On the other hand, the private sector tends to be rather indiscriminate in the use of the title "Security Director." Too frequently the "Security Director" is, in fact, a Security Manager. There is a difference between the two. The easiest way to differentiate between them is to consider to whom they report. A "Director" is ranked at the highest level of middle management and should report to a member of senior management such as the President or a Vice President. If the head of security reports to a lower level of management in the company's organizational structure, he is a manager.

The effective Security Director should have a track record of success in handling people and problems. He will be a dynamic, results-oriented individual with a high level of personal integrity. He should have the ability to develop organizational plans, to evaluate personnel and their assignments, and to supply direction (including new approaches where necessary) of the security function.

While all of the Director's activities come under the single umbrella of "management," it is possible to examine each of his important roles individually. He is:

- a leader
- a company executive
- an executive with high visibility
- an executive with a broad profile
- an innovator
- a counselor and adviser
- a trainer
- a contemporary professional
- a goal setter

THE SECURITY DIRECTOR AS A LEADER

The Security Director's role as a leader means that he provides leadership to the management of the security organization. Note that he *does not directly manage* the department; he *provides leadership* for the manager and management team. Providing leadership means setting the right climate, pointing out directions, suggesting alternatives. The Security Director might be likened to the motion picture director. A fine film is a reflection of the director's talent, but he is rarely, if ever, in the film. So it is with the Security Director. He brings out the best of his people's talent and *they* perform.

The most difficult aspect of the leadership role is to refrain from making operating decisions. This is where the delicate art of good management skills comes to the fore. If the Security Director has selected and developed personnel properly, if he has given them *real* responsibility (and they understand this), if he has established a climate of confidence and professionalism, if he has motivated them—then his direction and suggested alternatives will allow his subordinates the courage, wisdom and strength to make decisions. And the Director must have the courage, wisdom and strength to let subordinates make mistakes.

AS A COMPANY EXECUTIVE

The Security Director's role as a company executive means that he identifies with and is accepted by senior and middle management as part of the company's management team. He should not be viewed narrowly as a security man, but rather as a skilled executive (first) in the security field (second). He should not have the reputation or image of simply being the company policeman.

The Director's demeanor, deportment, grooming, and attire should be equivalent to that of his peers (executives in other departments throughout the corporation).

AS AN EXECUTIVE WITH HIGH VISIBILITY

High visibility means just that: a Security Director who is well known in and out of the company and who is seen frequently. Ideally the Director should be an interesting and effective speaker who is sought after to make presentations. The advantages of a popular Security Director over an unpopular Director should be obvious in terms of creating good will toward the security organization and its objectives.

Additionally, the Director should be visible—and available—to all the security ranks. He should make every effort to meet new security personnel, irrespective of their assignments, and seize every opportunity to chat with security people. That kind of visibility pays off in terms of employee motivation.

AS AN EXECUTIVE WITH A BROAD PROFILE

A broad profile means that the Security Director has interests in and contributes to other areas of the business beyond the security function. Such exposure and activity not only enhance his executive image but have other rewards as well. One benefit is that the Security Director has the opportunity to meet, talk to and work with people in the company whom he might never meet otherwise. Conversely, these people have the opportunity to meet and exchange ideas with the Security Director. The experience can be very rewarding and positive—good for them and good for the company (let alone the Security Department).

As an example of the Security Director's involvement in other areas of the business beyond security, in one large company the Security Director takes part in two different activities: College Campus Recruiting for company management trainees, and the company's Supervisory Training School for first and second level supervisors.

The Security Director's responsibilities have nothing to do with campus recruiting, and vice versa. However, the company's approach to recruiting is to utilize interested and qualified middle management personnel as campus recruiters. This brings to the recruiting effort a diversified range of experience and talents, functioning within the selection guidelines designed by the personnel executive who is an expert in campus recruiting.

As a result of this approach to recruiting, there are young men and women moving up throughout the company today who were initially selected by the Security Director. What do you imagine their respective attitudes are about security people in general and the Security Director in particular? As time goes by these people will move into ever more important levels of responsibility—and security needs friends, the more the better.

At an in-house Supervisory Training School, the Security Director lectures on the subject of discipline and the disciplinary process. Attendance at the Supervisory Training School, a three-day program which must rank among the top in-house supervisory training programs in the industry, is highly coveted throughout the company. The program is meaningful and inspiring. Attitudes are changed. Skills are learned. Concepts open minds and eyes. In most cases the students are grateful for the experience and grateful to the lecturers who gave them that experience.

What is the beneficial consequence? The company had forty-nine separate facilities located in five states, and the Security Director could not go to a facility without former "students" waving or coming up to greet him. Those relationships fostered greater acceptance and recognition of the Security Department.

AS AN INNOVATOR

The Security Director is constantly charged with the responsibility of finding new ways to do the job—better, less expensive ways—and thus he must be an innovative, flexible administrator. The term "creative security" is apt because the very phrase sparks one's imagination. "Is there a better way?" should be the Director's continual question. Innovation means experimentation and risk. Security tasks do tend to become entrenched, routine and *safe,* tried and true. There is a tendency to discover a successful formula for solving a problem and then stick with it. The trap lies in clinging to what succeeded for a period of time and resisting change, refusing to try a new formula because it is unknown.

An excellent example of an innovative approach to a communications problem in a widely dispersed security organization was the adoption of a telephone pre-recorded message system. Each day every agent dialed the appropriate number at his appointed time to receive the Security Message of the Day; for example, the Salt Lake City agent called each day at 11:15 A.M. Rocky Mountain Time. The messages might be *instructional* (explaining a company procedure and how security could inspect for compliance), *informative* (reporting results of the department's activities, such as a major forger arrested), *warning* ("Be alert for counterfeit money orders bearing numbers L21344566 through 5699, with greasy feel around the indicia"), or *motivational* ("Keep up the outstanding work; all inspections were received prior to report deadline").

The idea of this daily communication tool solved a long-standing problem of disseminating information to the entire organization in a timely manner. Formerly, especially if the information was urgent, headquarters personnel would undertake the long and tedious task of trying to reach all members of the department by telephone. When agents were not in, messages left for them tended to become garbled and misunderstood. The innovative program not only transmitted the message to everyone each day, but also insured that all received the *same* message.

Another creative approach to a security problem in one retail organization was the shift away from total emphasis on theft detection to a rigorous loss prevention program. This shift was in answer to the staggering problem of an unacceptable inventory shrinkage figure. More arrests simply were not the answer to reducing losses. There had to be a better way than the traditional store detective and investigator approach.

Thus, because of innovative leadership at the Director's level, this company's "Red Coat" security program was born—a retail security program aimed at preventing shoplifting and other thefts instead of detecting them after the fact. Highly visible security personnel, dressed conspicuously in bright red blazers with gold emblems, have the job of discouraging, deterring, and preventing theft. If an act of theft is in progress or just completed, they attempt to "burn" it out—to discourage the thief by making him aware his conduct has been observed and he is under surveillance. If "burning" does not work, *then, and only then,* is an arrest made.

This program has finally balanced out to a remarkably successful ratio of 25:10 Prevention:Apprehension. It took courage to launch such a radically different approach to retail security in the face of long-standing tradition. But there *was* a better way!

AS A COUNSELOR AND ADVISER

Because of his wisdom and years of security experience, the Director's role as counselor and adviser is an invaluable one to the department as well as to the company.

It is interesting to point out how frequently security management seeks the Director's advice on routine operational problems. More often than not, they ask advice in order to "test" or compare their solutions against the Director's. This is good, as long as the Director does not succumb to the temptation of grabbing the reins and *requiring* management to come to him or to include him in the problem-solving and decision-making.

His role is to give advice, suggest alternatives, *help* solve problems— not to solve them. He gives the benefit of his experience and judgment to the Security Manager and his staff. Occasionally, when a particularly difficult problem is under discussion and no answer has been developed for comparison with the Director's, the Director may hit on a solution which is immediately recognized by the Manager and his staff as *the* solution and consequently is adopted. In this kind of situation, the Director did not force his will on the subordinates; the climate was one of mutual and open exchange. The Director's involvement was participatory in nature.

Of course, the Director *can* make the decisions and solve all the problems. Some do, or at least approve each and every decision. But once the Director does this, he steps down into the role of his subordinate (the Manager under the Director in a large department). He is no longer *directing;* he is now actively involved in operations.

On the other hand, the Director sometimes will be called upon to solve a problem. In these circumstances he will interject himself into the decision-making process and force his will if necessary. But these situations, especially the latter, should be rare.

The Director is also an adviser to company management in terms of policy, construction planning, special events, emergency and disaster planning, executive protection suggestions, executive problems (such as an executive's daughter running away from home), and a host of other areas wherein the Director's good counsel is sought.

AS A TRAINER

The Director's attitude about the importance of the training and development of *every* security employee sets the climate for the department. If he is supportive of an aggressive, structured training program within his organization, that is what he will get. If he is lukewarm about training and feels that it takes away time that is necessary to get the job done, he will end up with a fragmented, ineffective program, if any. The Director's role as a trainer deserves as much stature as his other roles. It is certainly the one role that has an impact down through every level of his department, with the obvious end result of improved performance.

With respect to the organization generally, the Security Director's role as trainer is primarily one of a climate-setter. With respect to the staff, particularly the Security Manager or Assistant Director, however, his role is very functional. The Director must personally train, guide and develop his immediate subordinate, with the objective of preparing that manager to take over the Directorship at the earliest possible date. One reason is that there is no one else who can do it. Second, there is a moral responsibility to the subordinate to help him grow vertically. Third, there is a moral responsibility to the company to develop talent that can function in the Director's absence. Finally, effective management dictates that a replacement be ready so that the Director can move vertically to assume more responsibility— e.g., Corporate Security Director, Vice President of Loss Prevention, same rank but with a larger division within the corporation, or a more advanced position with another company.

The training of the manager does not terminate at some fixed point in time. It is ongoing in nature and more frequently than not it lasts for several years. Every day the manager is prepared to take over. The next day he is better prepared, and so it goes.

As he must develop and train his own people, so must the Director contribute to the training and education of all company employees as it relates to security and loss prevention. His input with the Training Department on induction programs for new employees, general security or loss prevention awareness programs, and special campaigns or promotions can make the difference between a very credible production and a program that is flat and ineffective.

AS A CONTEMPORARY PROFESSIONAL

Being a contemporary professional means that the Director keeps abreast of the security industry—familiar with current case law affecting the industry, new and improved technology and systems, current trends, and the general state of the art. To accomplish this the Director must subscribe to and read trade journals, participate in local, regional or national security associations, attend seminars to hear his peers and see new products, and freely communicate and exchange ideas with contemporaries on a regular basis.

The importance of this professional role is better understood when one recognizes that the subordinate security manager and security technician are normally absorbed in the operating demands of their jobs and may be less free than the Director to peruse the vast array of information and data pertinent to the business.

The contemporary professional is constantly involved in training and educational programs. How can one be considered professional unless he is growing in his selected profession? This growth comes from broadened experiences coupled with new concepts, strategies, and tactics made known through some form of institutionalized educational process. Education in the security industry is not limited to the novice. Many security training and educational programs are specifically designed for experienced practitioners, supervisors and managers.

AS A GOAL SETTER

Establishing objectives and setting goals for the organization is an important aspect of the Director's job. Who else could do it? If security goals are set by senior management there is no need for a Director. A subordinate cannot establish objectives to be met and tell the Director the strategy to achieve those objectives.

Goals obviously set directions, provide challenge, and should require genuine effort to be achieved. Goals which are too easily achieved are not real goals. For example, if one departmental goal for the coming year is to have one hundred percent of the department's supervisors graduate from the company's Supervisory Training School, and only ten percent (representing two or three people) have yet to go when that goal is set, then this is not a real goal. It is simply one of many things to be done on an ongoing basis. A goal must be an objective, an accomplishment that requires stretch, that you must work at constantly to achieve.

Goals, which must be quantitative or qualitative in nature, could include replacing personnel with hardware to reduce payroll dollars; converting a predetermined number of units to a new access control program within a specified time frame; reducing specific losses by a set percentage; improving a certain measurable skill of security personnel such as firing range scores; or designing and implementing a new Programmed Learning program for major disasters—to name but a few.

In addition to the major roles described above, the Director should wear a number of other hats that can be significant. He may be the departmental "Court of Last Appeal," "father confessor," listener, financier, departmental defender on a white horse, taskmaster, politician, professor, and intelligence expert. He must be purer than Caesar's wife, and, finally, he must be a gentleman, or, as the case may be, a lady.

THE NEW SECURITY DIRECTOR

To be appointed the new head of security in a long-established organization, even if coming up through the ranks; or to come into an established organization from outside the company; or to be transferred from another area of the business to head up a newly created security organization; or to arrive on the company scene from outside for the purpose of setting up a program— all, to say the least, are difficult situations indeed. The new head of security is unknown and unproven (in *that* position), and most people are suspicious of the unknown.

How can this natural suspicion of "the new man" be overcome? The answer is for the new security director to come in with the lowest possible profile. He should look and listen, and speak when spoken to, except when asking necessary questions. He should have a pleasant manner and concern himself initially with the people in his pyramid. Such concern must be sincere and warm. In private chats with each of them he will learn much without going out to seek it.

The new security director should be very conservative in terms of making changes, unless such change is badly and conspicuously needed. In that case, he should allow the change to be made, but not in his own name. He should allow the credit to go to a subordinate. People will suspect that the new manager is behind the change anyhow and quietly admire his style. The new manager should not threaten to "clean house," make sweeping changes, bring in "qualified" help or in any way forecast change; to do so tenses up the organization and prolongs the period needed for his assimilation into the environment. It is never wise for the new director to criticize his predecessor, if there was one. If criticism is due, it will naturally come from below. The new man should listen to the criticism and be prudent in his responses. A neutral response is best; then he should move the conversation on to positive statements about the future.

If a problem or question arises to which the new security manager does not know the solution or answer, he should say so. Just because he is the chief does not mean he knows everything. He should ask subordinates for their advice and/or opinions.

This low-keyed, low profile, non-threatening approach—which even helps take some of the butterflies out of the new manager's stomach because he is not trying to prove anything—will buy time, and time is his ally. Changes will occur, of course, because the new man is there to insure protection for the company, and that means his style, his philosophy and his strategy will come into play with the passage of time. Loud noises and quick movements not only frighten animals and infants; they frighten adults, too.

SUMMARY

The Security Director is commonly one who reports to a member of senior management; the head of Security reporting to someone at a lower level is more properly called a Manager.

Within the Security Department the Director's role is that of *leading* rather than operational decision-making. (The Manager of a smaller department will inevitably have more direct involvement in operations.) In his leadership role, the mark of a good Director or Manager is the ability to delegate responsibility and commensurate authority.

Outside of his own department, the effective Security Director should be a highly visible company executive, a part of the management team with interests that go beyond security. And in his relationship with his staff he will be an innovator, counselor, trainer and goal setter.

The Security Director moving into a new company or position will advisedly seek a lower profile initially than the one described above. He will seek not to force events and people, but to lead with patience and example.

REVIEW QUESTIONS

1. What is the distinction between a Security Director and a Security Manager?

2. Give an example of how the Security Director may be involved in other areas of the company beyond security.

3. What are the reasons why the Security Director should prepare his subordinate to take over the responsibilities of the Security Director?

4. List three ways the Security Director can keep abreast of developments in the security industry.

5

The Security Supervisor's Role

Supervision is comprised of many facets, including but not limited to, hiring, training, discipline, motivating, promoting, and communicating. Each of these factors is a specific skill unto itself. Rather than grouping all of these skills under the single heading of "Supervision" or "The Security Supervisor's Role," each will be examined individually. This chapter will deal with the supervisor and his relationships with those higher and lower in the organizational structure, his responsibilities, and the general principles of supervision itself. Subsequent chapters will be concerned with those factors intrinsic to supervision.

In the smaller department the Security Manager may himself be directly involved in supervision, and the comments in this chapter on the supervisor's role would obviously apply to the manager.

One popular definition of supervision is the task of getting others (subordinates) to get the job done, the way management wants it done, when management wants it done—willingly. Willingness, of course, is the key aspect of this definition. We are interested in enlightened supervision, not the kind of supervision used to oversee the slaves on the plantations of years ago, or the slave labor programs of Hitler's regime, or even Soviet operations of today. Historically, such autocratic methods, by and large, do get the job done—but not always at the time or in the manner desired. In a free society the most difficult part of the supervisor's task is to get the job done willingly.

The supervisor's job, then, is to get other people to accomplish tasks, which means they must perform. *Performance* is the ultimate responsibility and goal of supervision. Everything revolves around job performance—execution at the line level. The supervisor's performance (his supervisory skills) is reflected in the performance of those who work for him.

THE SUPERVISOR AS AN INSPECTOR

There is an old adage that says, "Employees don't do what you expect, they do what you inspect." More often than not, that is true; not because they do not want to or do not care to perform their tasks, but simply because of human frailty. That same element of human failure is not limited to line employees; it can be traced to every level of every organizational structure, right to the top. From the top down, therefore, each "supervisor" must inspect the work of his subordinates. The Director inspects the Security Manager, the Manager his middle managers, the middle managers their supervisors, and the supervisors their subordinates. When that inspection process breaks down, for whatever reason, tasks break down, deadlines are missed, other tasks are temporarily neglected and eventually forgotten. It is a source of amazement to all levels of management that functions, tasks, duties, reports—all assumed to be taking place with regularity—have "slipped through the cracks" and disappeared from organizational life, all because the inspection process failed.

On the other side of the coin, inadequate inspection frequently surfaces when a change in supervision reveals tasks or reports being religiously accomplished which no longer serve their original purpose. Often, no one seems to know who started the tasks, or what they were intended to accomplish.

The inspection need not, and should not, be a negative process wherein the supervisor tries to find errors or omissions, then criticizes. That managerial style creates a climate of resentment, defensiveness, and hostility. One can *always* find fault.

The most effective managerial style in the inspection process is to find those tasks which are done properly, acknowledge and give credit for good performance in such areas, and then point out deficiencies in an objective fashion. Most employees want to do a good job. Most failures, as already indicated, are the result of human frailties and not of malicious design. Consequently, when performance deficiencies are pointed out objectively, they are usually received with some embarrassment, on one hand, and an expression of genuine desire to improve on the other hand.

To be effective, this critical process of performance inspection must be consistent, continuous, constructive, and tailored to the individual employee.

THE SUPERVISOR AND THE INDIVIDUAL EMPLOYEE

The supervisor must deal on an individual basis with each subordinate, because every employee is different. Every human being on the face of the earth is different. The differences are manifested not only in observable physical features and fingerprints, but in how each individual responds to external stimuli, how he perceives things, his beliefs, fears, aspirations and needs. Such human differences mean that different people require different handling. Some may require more supervision than others. Some respond to persuasion, some to command. Some want to set goals, some want goals set for them. Some are uncomfortable around authority figures, some are at ease. Sensitivity to employee differences is one characteristic of a good supervisor.

SUPERVISORY AUTHORITY

A supervisor must have commensurate authority to carry out his responsibilities. If a supervisor is told he has the responsibility of ten security officers to protect the facility between 4:00 P.M. and midnight, and at the same time he is told that any disciplinary action against any one of those ten will be handled by the next level of supervision, then he has been denied the necessary tools or stripped of the necessary authority to carry out his responsibility. Such conditions, which do indeed exist, make a mockery of organizational integrity and turn what should be legitimate supervisors into "straw bosses" or lackeys. The supervisor represents management and must be given the necessary authority to make that representation meaningful. If, for any reason, appropriate authority cannot be vested in a supervisor, it will still be necessary to have some form of "lead man" in charge.

The supervisor—with his officers, agents, investigators or whatever their titles—should have not only the necessary authority to discipline but should also have some input in the selection or assignments to his unit. He should be heard when his people are considered for promotion; he must have authority to require additional training; he must have the authority to communicate to his people, including sending instructions, memos, etc.; and he must have the freedom to measure his people's performance without interference.

The issue of a supervisor's need to measure his people's performance without interference is even larger than the one of disciplinary rights. Here is a typical case: The supervisor is obliged to evaluate the performance of his subordinates on an annual or semiannual basis. He follows directions in terms of completing the personnel form prepared for each employee. (A sample Employee Evaluation form is shown in Appendix A.) He marks the various boxes that represent rating factors such as "submits reports in a timely manner," and finally makes an overall evaluation as "Above Standards." He submits his evaluations.

Two weeks later he is called before his superior or the personnel office and is advised that his rating of "Above Standards" of Officer X is too high. The rating should be "Meets Standards." Despite the fact there are no flaws or inconsistencies in the various factor-ratings with the overall rating, the supervisor is instructed, for whatever reason, to reduce the rating to the next lower. Or, for that matter, he is instructed to raise the overall rating to the next higher.

The above problem is frequently a point of concern in any discussion of supervisory training and practice. Those raising the question say, "I don't want to get into trouble with anyone, so I changed the rating, even though

I felt my evaluation was correct. What should I have done, or what should I do next time?"

For the responsible supervisor, the answer is clear. If he is convinced that his evaluation is not incompatible with the firm's definition of standards, and the evaluation is not inconsistent with his other evaluations, then he should seek to support his own rating. If, after sufficient discussion, he is still asked to change that rating, he may have no alternative but to make the change as requested. In such circumstances, he should indicate on the evaluation form that the rating is not his own.

If a supervisor is not capable of disciplining, then he should not be a supervisor. By the same token, if he is incompetent to evaluate the performance of subordinates, he should not be a supervisor. If it is a question of skills in disciplining or evaluating performance, the onus rests with management to provide adequate training to develop such skills—not to take that authority away.

THE SUPERVISOR AS THE "IN-BETWEEN" MAN

The supervisor is the vital link between the employee and security management. The supervisor represents management's needs and views to those below and at the same time has the responsibility of representing the needs and views of his people up to his management. Failure to discharge this function objectively and faithfully, in a timely manner, can have disastrous results. The supervisor who, being closest to the scene, is aware of sentiments, grievances or problems, yet does not inform management, fails twofold. First, he fails his subordinates by not carrying the message to management. The condition, whatever it may be, is allowed to deteriorate, to the disservice of his subordinates in terms of morale, accidents, or turnover, depending upon the problem. Second, he fails management by withholding information that could provide them with answers, explanations, or decisions to resolve the issue.

This intermediary status is usually well understood by line personnel. It makes sense. Yet that status can easily serve as a crutch for the weak supervisor, providing an excuse to shirk responsibility so that all distasteful duties or assignments, or decisions which may be unpopular, are passed off (even if they are his own) with the disclaimer, "Management wants it this way." The weakness is apparent: this supervisor wants to be popular all the time. Fortunately, that kind of supervisory weakness cannot be concealed for too long.

THE SUPERVISOR'S SPAN OF CONTROL

Span of control, the number of employees a supervisor can manage, depends upon a number of factors. One important factor is the supervisor himself—

his skill level in handling people and his ability to delegate responsibility. Another factor is the job description of his subordinates. Field investigators with relatively sophisticated assignments require more attention from the supervisor than a uniformed staff assigned to one location on one shift. In the former case, the proper span of control might be six and in the latter, twelve. Long-standing and widely accepted span of control standards suggest the following ratios:

Supervisors	:	Employees
Ideal	1 :	3
Good	1 :	6
Acceptable	1 :	12

These numbers represent spans of control under normal operating conditions on an ongoing basis. However, under certain circumstances, for a relatively short period of time and with a homogeneous group, one leader could handle up to two dozen employees.

ONE BOSS

The Principle of Unity of Command is the classic or traditional way of saying that every employee must report to only one superior. Find a situation where a person is being directed by more than one superior, and you will find that subordinate coping with conflicting instructions and confusion, resulting in diluted performance.

Consider the frustrations experienced in one actual situation by the Chief of Campus Police for a group of adjacent private colleges in Southern California. In that position the Chief was responsible to five college presidents, each of whom had his own particular point of view. In one incident, a group of students had gathered off campus in a neighboring county for a Friday afternoon T.G.I.F. (Thank God It's Friday) party. The Sheriff's Department of that county took this large group of students into custody for possession and consumption of alcoholic beverages. One student slipped away, advised the Chief of Campus Police of the events, and stated that the Sheriff's officers were calling in buses to transport the students to the county jail.

At the scene the Campus Chief discussed the matter with the officer in charge and convinced him the best interests of justice would be served if he would release the students to the Chief, who in turn would process them through their respective college student court systems. The Sheriff's office could see the wisdom of avoiding the booking hassles and subsequent difficulties of proving in the county court just which student was doing what (there were close to 100 students).

The Chief of Campus Police escorted all the students back to his office and had them line up for identification purposes. He then submitted lists to three different college student courts. The courts, as expected, levied substantial fines and built up the coffers of the student body fund, and justice prevailed—at least the Chief thought so.

The outcome of all this was that one college president expressed warm appreciation for the Chief's intervention, which had saved the school from what would have been certain unfavorable publicity at the hands of the local press, and most of all for the avoidance of criminal booking records for his students. However, one of the other college presidents took exception to the Chief's intervention. His position was that the students sooner or later had to assume responsibility for their conduct. They had been warned about assembling at that particular location for "beer busts" before, and therefore they should have experienced the full consequences of their conduct.

The point is, this security director could have lived with either position had he worked for either president, but he worked for both. His job was to serve both, and obviously he could not please both.

The employee, then, who has more than one supervisor can find himself in an unworkable situation. The organization must follow the principle of Unity of Command to avoid such counterproductive conditions.

AUTOMATIC SHIFTING IN THE LINE OF COMMAND

There are necessary and legitimate exceptions to the principle of Unity of Command. Conditions that require another supervisor are:

1. Emergencies.
2. When the failure of a ranking employee to take command would jeopardize the department's objectives or reputation.

An example of Number 1: A uniformed guard, immediately following a natural disaster such as an earthquake, is approached by a security investigator (who is in an entirely different departmental pyramid or line of command but has rank over the guard). The investigator instructs the guard to run to the side of the building and cut off the gas supply. The guard cannot refuse this shifting in supervision.

An example of Number 2: A uniformed guard on a parking control assignment for a major event has been instructed by his supervisor to deny access to one reserved parking lot. A supervisor other than the guard's, because of his mobility and overview of the parking and traffic conditions, reaches the opinion that the congestion can only be relieved by routing traffic into the empty lot. Not to relieve the growing congestion could have serious repercussions on the event itself. The supervisor, knowing he is accountable for his decision, can command the guard to let the cars in.

Such direct orders out of the normal chain of command are invariably given under a time pressure; that is, a decision and action must be immediate. The consequences of delaying action in order to locate the proper supervisor could be serious, if not grave.

Such automatic shifting in the line of command, always of a short duration, requires full understanding on the part of all department members at all levels. It is interesting to note that such shifting *does not* violate the principle of Unity of Command; rather, it enhances and supports the principle by having a rule and understanding of the exception. Exceptions add credence to rules.

FUNCTIONAL OR STAFF SUPERVISION

Although every employee has his own supervisor, there are numerous occasions and conditions where the employee must perform at a time or location outside the immediate control of his supervisor. An example would be an alarm operator and alarm serviceman working the graveyard shift. Their supervisor works the day shift. By agreement, the graveyard watch commander, in another pyramidal structure within Security, assumes functional (or staff) supervision over these two security employees. As a functional supervisor he has responsibility for a limited degree of supervision, but not complete control.

There are two aspects to this functional supervision. The first is that the watch commander in all probability has no technical competence in alarm operations or servicing, so he cannot give commands which would interfere with performance. This means his supervision is limited to such things as promptness, following general orders applicable to all personnel, and demeanor on the job.

The second aspect of functional supervision is that it is essentially advisory in nature. The functional supervisor can discuss problems with the subordinate, make suggestions, point out mistakes, but—and this is most important—he lacks authority to take disciplinary action. Certainly he can cause disciplinary action by reporting the problem to the subordinate's supervisor; that supervisor can take the corrective action, but the staff supervisor cannot.

SUPERVISORY TRAINING

Perhaps the most common shortcoming in the security industry is the failure to properly prepare and equip new supervisors with the tools to discharge their important responsibilities. A line employee on Friday may become a new supervisor on Monday, with no distinguishable difference in the eyes of former peers.

It is better to give the new supervisor a week off with pay and have him sit in the library studying books on the fundamentals of supervision than to put him in his new assignment immediately. If he is off for a week and the employees believe he is attending some special training just for supervisors, they see him, upon his return, with entirely different eyes.

The library trip, of course, is a barely acceptable alternative in the absence of what should really happen. Ideally, the new supervisor, before he takes command, should attend a workshop, seminar or training session for new supervisors. If an in-house program is not available, he should be sent to a commercially conducted program, of which there are many to choose from in most communities.

The problem in this area is the false assumption that, because a man was an outstanding investigator or officer, he will make a good supervisor. That simply does not follow automatically. A new supervisor must master an entire new set of skills that have absolutely nothing to do with investigative ability. Such skills must be learned; they are not inherited and do not come into play automatically upon promotion. And new supervisors are quick to discover that they are ill prepared for their new responsibilities. They are sensitive to their deficiencies and lack confidence in handling problems and people. Subordinates are very quick to sense this absence of confidence, and some will not be at all sympathetic but will capitalize on the apparent weakness to their own advantage—especially those who are of the opinion *they* should have received that promotion.

If, for a variety of reasons, it is impossible to send the supervisor to a school immediately, or to the library, the next best thing is to arrange for his attendance at a later date. Subordinates, knowing the new boss will indeed be attending special training in the near future, will respond in a more supportive posture than in the complete absence of training.

SUMMARY

Supervision has been defined as the task of getting work done how and when management wants it done—willingly. *Performance* is the ultimate goal of supervision.

The effective supervisor will best assure the performance of his subordinates by constant *inspection.* He will be sensitive to individual employee differences in providing both criticism and encouragement. He must have the *authority* to carry out his responsibilities, both in discipline and in employee evaluations. And as the man-in-the-middle between management and the employee, the supervisor should play an active part in the process of communication both upward and downward.

Important principles of effective supervision are *limited span of control* and *unity of command.* The latter principle (no man can serve two bosses) is not violated by *functional supervision,* which is exercised over employees only temporarily under a supervisor's control. Functional supervision is both limited and advisory in nature.

A good employee does not necessarily make a good supervisor. Effective security management will provide adequate training for new supervisors. Training inspires confidence in both the supervisor and those who will serve under him.

REVIEW QUESTIONS

1. Define *supervision*. What is the ultimate responsibility and goal of supervision?

2. Explain how you would handle the situation if you were asked by a superior to change your rating of a subordinate's performance.

3. In what way is the supervisor "the vital link between the employee and security management"?

4. What are two factors influencing a supervisor's effective span of control?

5. Give two examples of legitimate exceptions to the principle of Unity of Command.

6

The Individual Security Employee

Relatively little instructive material is available concerning the individual security employee's role, contribution, or importance in the overall security function. The truth of the matter is, the good reputation of the Security Department and the successful achievement of the department's objectives are, ultimately, the result of the employee's execution of his job. Poor performance, poor reputation. Good performance, good reputation. Excellent performance, excellent reputation.

Regardless of how knowledgeable security management may be, the line employee's performance is the measurement of success. This performance has two dimensions: application of skills, and general conduct. Specific skill development, skill levels and execution of skills are the subject of many texts and will not be our concern here. Rather, we will examine the issue of conduct, not only because it has been touched on so lightly within the industry, but because, in its critical importance, conduct frequently transcends skills. In other words, if a security administrator had to choose between good skills but poor conduct and poor skills but good conduct, more often than not he would choose the latter.

Conduct, then, plays a significant role in the Security Department's general reputation. The company which Security serves expects exemplary conduct of its security force. Security management must demand exemplary conduct. Line employees will respond to such expectations and demands if they know and understand what the standards of conduct are. It is a truism that most employees will do what management wants, *if they know what management wants.*

In the absence of any generally circulated or official standards of conduct in the security industry,[1] the following is submitted:

---

[1] For additional discussion of this subject, see *Private Security: Report of the Task Force on Private Security* (Washington, DC: National Advisory Committee on Criminal Justice Standards and Goals, 1976), especially Standard 3.2, "Conduct of Security Personnel."

STANDARDS OF CONDUCT

1. Security employees are habitually courteous and attentive to those seeking assistance, reporting conditions, or lodging complaints.
2. Security employees are punctual and expeditious in the discharge of their duties.
3. Security employees conduct themselves in a just and objective manner, treating all with equal reasonableness.
4. Security employees consistently exhibit a spirit of cooperation with all and do not allow personal feelings to interfere with their work.
5. Security employees conduct their personal and business life in an exemplary fashion, above reproach in terms of stability, fidelity and morality.
6. Security employees have a cheerful and positive approach to their work.

Today these standards may sound idealistic if not old-fashioned, but if they are adopted and followed the end results will have a favorable impact on a department's reputation.

Courtesy

Courtesy starts at home, granted; but the development of courtesy on the job starts with mutual respect for fellow security employees. And one cannot be expected to respect his associates unless he respects himself first. Security management's responsibility in this area is to ensure that the employee has dignity—dignity in terms of pride in his uniform, his work place, his personal responsibility in his work. Standards set in these areas have a definite influence on an employee's assessment of his own worth.

Issuing or permitting the use of shabby uniforms, for example, takes away from a man's sense of pride. High standards for uniforms, on the other hand, automatically instill self-pride and, hence, self-respect. Old and inadequate office equipment and furniture in poor condition have a demoralizing effect, whereas equipment and furniture in fine condition make employees feel valuable to the organization. And, of course, the knowledge that each day's work is important and contributes to the overall success of the department is most necessary. The trouble is that many employees do not understand or see that their daily contribution is significant, usually because management has not bothered to tell them.

When an employee works within a climate which fosters feelings of self-worth, he will normally feel that his co-workers are also important and worthy of respect. Respect and courtesy will radiate beyond the Security Department—*if they are an understood standard of conduct.*

The emphasis on "if they are an understood standard of conduct" is important because of the nature of the security business, particularly those types of security organizations that are heavily engaged in the detection and apprehension of criminal offenders. Frequent, regular contact with negative or antisocial people tends to harden the security officer, just as it tends to desensitize law enforcement officers in the public sector. Unless courtesy is demanded under all circumstances, it may be practiced within the organization but may not be demonstrated consistently outside the organization.

Of the six standards suggested, the one of courtesy is the most conspicuous and visible to the beholder. Courteous behavior is not restricted to personal contacts; telephone courtesy, or the absence of same, is also very visible. A great deal of security business is conducted over the phone, and employees in the security organization, including clerical workers, must understand the importance of telephone courtesy.

Everyone, including scoundrels, needs and likes to be treated with courtesy.

Responsibility

Standard number two speaks to "punctual and expeditious" performance. The individual who is not punctual is not a responsible person. To be late for duty, to be late with reports due, to be late with assignments, all reflect a lack of responsibility. Such a person is expressing the attitude, "I don't really care about what's happening." Children lack responsibility; maturity is a factor in assuming responsibility. Children are impatient and soon weary of details. Concern for details, including time, is another measure of responsibility and maturity.

Webster's New Collegiate Dictionary defines *expeditious* as "characterized by or acting with promptness and efficiency."

For the department to have a reputation of being prompt and efficient, every member must be prompt and efficient. Much security work involves reporting facts (details). A lackadaisical approach, an absence of concern over details, and unnecessary delays are all serious reflections on an organization. Every security employee must be punctual, attentive and accurate. Company as well as security management relies on the security employee's sense of responsibility.

This may seem self-evident. It is a question of self-discipline, and the setting of standards imposes self-discipline.

Due Process

Standard three requires that security employees act "in a just and objective manner, treating all with equal reasonableness." Essentially this means respect for the rights of others. To be other than just or to be subjective, particularly in the enforcement aspects of security work, is to give more rights to some and to deny the rights of others. Such conduct is intolerable in the public sector, as evidenced by many appellate court decisions restricting law enforcement, as well as by the public outcry over the Watergate scandal. As of this writing, the courts have not yet reached down into the private sector with binding restrictions in terms of our enforcement activities, but that is not to say that they will not.

Actually, respect for the rights of others is a state of mind and should not require legislation. Security professionals can create the proper state of mind through standards of conduct expected of their employees.

The *due process* concept is very meaningful in an organization, such as a large retail store or any organization which takes scores of people into custody every month of the year. To be objective and treat each one with equal reasonableness is a challenge in view of many attempts at violence as well as verbal abuses. But it is both practical and humane to treat all suspects with respect; after all, once they have been apprehended the victory is already won. There is no need to harass or further embarrass them, to be verbally abusive or gloat over their misfortune in having been caught. Even in the face of vile verbal attacks, members of the staff should impassively and objectively go about their business of completing reports and related tasks with an air of quiet dignity which evokes nothing but respect from onlookers, from management on the scene, and from the police who arrive to assist.

A store detective with an abiding respect for the rights of others is a store detective with the smallest ratio of false arrests. Some may say the smallest false arrest ratio is purely skill-related; in truth, however, the best detective not only has masterful skills, he or she is also sharply tuned into the consequences of a questionable arrest—consequences not only to the store and the possible civil liabilities connected therewith, but also the mental trauma and anguish of the innocent person. They are sensitive to human rights. Insensitive detectives tend to be rash. They will gamble, will act on "instinct," will take the word of another rather than what they know through their own senses. Insensitive detectives, and all other classifications of security personnel, can become sensitive through adoption of standards of conduct.

Cooperation

A reputation of willingness to work with and for others, to serve and assist, materially contributes to the department's good image. Far too many departments attempt to find reasons not to do a job or reasons why they cannot. From the Security Director down to the newest employee with the most limited responsibilities, the watchword should be "Why, certainly"—assuming, of course, that the requested service is possible and not contrary to the best interests of the organization and there is no specific rule against it.

For example, the lobby desk officer may not have facilities to store briefcases. He could easily turn down a request from a visiting dignitary to watch his briefcase. But if he says, "Why, certainly," and places the case behind the desk for fifteen minutes, he creates a most favorable impression. It is the spirit of cooperation that counts. The dignitary would not ask unless he had a need, and he would not ask a particular person unless he felt that person was responsible. A response of "no" or "I can't" is difficult to accept.

The more Security can do as a service, the more important the entire operation becomes and the more company management will look to Security for such service. For example:

Executive: Could you spare a security man to pick up a visitor at the airport? The taxis are on strike, you know.

Security: Why, certainly.

Public Relations Officer: Could you have one of your men help out at the entrance to the special event? We need another pair of hands to collect the passes—we're afraid of gatecrashers.

Security: Why, certainly.

Employee (to security patrol in the parking lot):   Could you call on your radio and ask for a tow truck to come out here? My starter won't turn over.

Security: Why, certainly.

Every member of the department should be coached to look for ways to serve instead of looking for ways not to. "Why, certainly" is a magic phrase. And it is attitudinal. Develop that spirit in the security organization, and the Department's reputation will be enhanced.

Personal Integrity

Standard of conduct number five states: "Security employees conduct their personal and business life in an exemplary fashion, above reproach in terms of stability, fidelity and morality." The terms "above reproach" and "exemplary fashion" are very broad but hint of such qualities as self-respect, honesty, cleanliness, fair play—qualities of universal appeal. At the risk of becoming trapped by moralistic values and definitions and the interpretations of same, let us consider some of these standards as they relate to the security officer's job.

Self-respect

As discussed earlier in this chapter, self-respect means dignity and pride in oneself and what one does. An individual's sense of pride and self-respect is mirrored in the way he walks, dresses, holds his head, looks others in the eye, and executes his assignments. A security employee who takes pride in his reputation and his work will perform in an exemplary fashion.

Honesty

Honesty here refers to the smallest corners of our character, areas such as the tendency to exaggerate. Honesty in words as well as deeds is required of every security professional at every level.

Security people are subjected to more temptations than perhaps any other career field—an "occupational hazard" of a sort. Only a strong conviction of what is right and what is wrong can provide the necessary strength to resist the temptations. Again, more often than not it is the little things that test men. Everyone has heard others say, "If I ever steal, it's got to be worth it—say five million!" The truth is that most of these people would not really have the courage to commit a substantial theft, but might take something small and unnoticeable, like a handful of salted nuts from a candy counter display, or a glass of root beer from the soda fountain in the employees' lounge.

Cleanliness

A person's personal habits can be pleasant and rewarding to others or can be loathsome and offensive. Most security people are highly visible, and their contact with other company employees or the public must be positive. People notice other people. Dirty fingernails, ear wax, nose hairs, body odors are all correctable.

Stability

Consistency in action and reaction is most important. The luxury of being moody cannot be permitted in the security organization. A moody security officer at the front lobby desk would not last long.

Excitability is another unacceptable characteristic in a security man's personal makeup. Being moody, excitable, having a tendency to lose one's temper—these types of mental peaks and valleys detract from exemplary conduct.

Fidelity

Fidelity means the careful observance of duties as well as loyalty. A loyal security employee is steadfast and true, dedicated to the organization. To complain about departmental policies, procedures, assignments, or personnel is not disloyalty but lacks the true ring of fidelity. That is not to say, however, that a legitimately channeled and righteous complaint takes away from one's loyalty. There is a fine line between what one could call a positive complaint and a negative one. Perhaps the difference lies in the manner in which the complaint is levied. The writer can immediately call to mind a supervisor with years of faithful and loyal service whom he considered absolutely dedicated to the organization. Rarely did this man complain, but when he did, it was always very quietly stated, upward.

Dissatisfaction on the job does reflect in one's performance. This obviously suggests that poor or questionable job performance could be an indicator of unhappiness and dissatisfaction. Dissatisfaction erodes loyalty. It must be identified and dealt with as early as possible in a very up-front, open and honest manner. If the source of dissatisfaction cannot be corrected or explained satisfactorily and the employee is still not happy, he should be advised that the organization cannot change to accommodate him. He must adapt to the organization; if he cannot, he will remain dissatisfied. If he remains dissatisfied it will affect his performance and his work record. In view of that, it should be pointed out to him that under such circumstances the honest thing to do is to change organizations, for his best interests as well as the organization's.

Morality

The security officer should observe a standard of excellence in terms of right or proper conduct. Because of the high visibility of security personnel, employees in that capacity with questionable or low moral standards attract attention. Once a poor reputation is established, it is difficult, at best, to reverse.

Not only does the poor reputation of individual officers impinge on the department's reputation; the real threat or hazard, from the administrator's point of view, is compromise. Once just *one* security employee is compromised, the organizational objectives are compromised. To maneuver for compromise based on sexual behavior is a commonplace of intelligence, political and organized crime strategy today. To treat so-called sexual freedom lightly in the security context would be naive and counterproductive.

There are obvious limitations on security management's influence on employees' standards of morality. Management cannot dictate what movies they can or cannot see; what books they should or should not read; or what personal relationships would or would not be acceptable. What management can do is to discourage improper conduct by (1) setting high standards; (2) ensuring that every security employee knows those standards; (3) educating the employees as to the hazards of compromise; and (4) prohibiting fraternization with company employees. How effective those actions prove depends a great deal on the effectiveness of the organization's employee selection and screening processes.

Attitude

Of all the characteristics or virtues one brings to the job, none, including educational achievement, can exceed that of attitude. Attitude determines one's conduct and bearing toward others and their reaction to him. Good attitude produces good reaction; bad attitude, bad reaction. Attitude is contagious. It is a key ingredient in success or failure.

Take a security employee exemplifying the other five standards of conduct—one who is courteous, punctual, objective, cooperative, above reproach—imbue that employee with a cheerful and positive attitude and you will have the finest security employee. And the department's reputation is a reflection of that composite.

SUMMARY

The Security Department's performance ultimately depends on the performance of the individual security employee. And that performance is measured by conduct as well as by specific job skills.

Standards of conduct for the security employee should emphasize basic *courtesy* toward fellow employees and others, even in the handling of transgressors; *responsibility* in carrying out his duties; *fairness and objectivity*, respecting the rights of others; a spirit of *cooperation;* personal *integrity*, both on the job and in personal life; and a cheerful, positive *attitude.*

Security employees who exemplify these standards enhance both the reputation and the effectiveness of the security function.

REVIEW QUESTIONS

1.   What can management do to foster feelings of self-worth among security employees?

2.   Explain the concept of *due process.*

3.   What would you include in your own "Standard of Conduct" for security employees?

II

Security Personnel Management

7

Hiring Security Personnel

Hiring new security employees is one of, if not the most, important functions and responsibilities of security management, be the employer a proprietary security department or a security service company. The real magnitude of that responsibility is best appreciated in light of the old adage about sending a fox to guard the hen house. Hence, great care and attention is required to avoid hiring that "fox." The standards of care and attention applied in hiring security applicants must far exceed those used for other applicants. Not only must the hiring standards in terms of *effort, care, and attention* be higher for security applicants, but the very standards set for the applicant, as an individual, must be higher than for other employees.

In my judgment an applicant must meet the following minimum standards (and that minimum applies to the lowest entry level position, typically a uniformed security officer):

1. must be free from any physical or emotional disorder or handicap that would preclude meeting pre-determined performance standards,
2. must demonstrate responsibility, maturity, and honesty through a verifiable history of prior employment and/or pursuit of education, and
3. must not have a conviction of any crime involving moral turpitude.

A number of states in this country now "license" security officers and such states have set a standard, as it pertains to a criminal conviction, too low, i.e., security officers must not have suffered a *felony conviction*. What that low standard does is *to suggest* that anyone with a lesser conviction (misdemeanor or petty crime) is okay or is indeed suitable for security employment and "licensing." With all due respect to the good intentions of those states, that premise is ridiculous for a number of reasons, including:

1. Many felonious acts are intentionally reduced to misdemeanors to accommodate the judicial process.
2. Excluded evidence may result in the conviction of a lesser but included offense.
3. Many so-called misdemeanors would become felonious if not interrupted or intercepted (caught or arrested).

4.   The felony "cut-off" by licensing states is probably an arbitrary and expeditious solution to an awesome workload in a relatively high volume, high turnover industry being processed by an underfunded, short-handed state staff.

Moral turpitude must be the standard in the security industry, not the felony conviction. To better understand that phrase, *moral turpitude,* it is best defined as any act characterized by a violation of trust or an act contrary to justice, honesty, or good morals. Answer the following questions:

- Would you hire a man convicted of indecent exposure (an exhibitionist) to work as a security guard in a summer camp for girls? That offense is not a felony. It's only a misdemeanor!
- Would you hire a woman convicted of shoplifting a blouse from a department store as a store detective? That offense is not a felony. It's only a misdemeanor!
- Would you hire a man convicted of filing a false crime report as a security employee? Such falsification is not a felony!
- Would you hire a person convicted of a misdemeanor—involuntary manslaughter committed while driving intoxicated—and with two other convictions for drunk driving? Would you hire him or her as a security driver of an armored truck? No felonies here!
- Would you hire a hospital security officer who has been convicted of peeking in bedroom windows at night, a "Peeping Tom"? That's a misdemeanor!
- Would you hire a man or woman convicted of possession of and smoking marijuana, a misdemeanor, as a security officer for the university?
- Would you hire a man caught and convicted of fondling another man's private parts in a public toilet—a misdemeanor—and place him in a position of trust to safeguard highly valuable proprietary data?

The security industry has a grave responsibility to those it serves. It must set higher standards than state licensing bodies. After all, it is the employer who is ultimately accountable for its service and the employees who provide that service—not the state!

How we avoid placing the fox by the chicken coop is amplified later in this chapter in the section entitled "Background Investigation of Applicant." Not only must we be concerned about the negative aspects of hiring the unsuitable or undesirable candidate, we must also want to create a hiring process that will help find people who are intelligent, well groomed, with sense of purpose and well being, who are motivated to achieve and who, by their membership in the department, will help establish a reputation of quality service.

HIRING

Hiring is a step-by-step process that eventually leads to the applicant's acceptance of a job offer. These steps are:

- Recruiting activity
- Interviewing
- Secondary interviewing activity
- Selection of best candidate
- Background investigation of candidate
- Job offer

Recruiting

Entry or First Level Positions

A direct approach in advertising the fact that a vacancy exists is usually desirable. This openness can include information such as company name, the fact that it is an Equal Opportunity Employer, location of job, uniform benefits (or requirements), starting salary, minimum requirements, and the fact that the position is an entry level job. As a rule the Personnel Department of the company administers the recruiting activity; however, they look to the individual managers for direction. *Within the limitations of company policy,* the Personnel Department strives to meet the manager's wishes. Policy restrictions such as "No salary quotations in newspaper advertising" would obviously have an impact, although not an adverse one, on the degree of openness in advertising.

The issue of advertising salary is quite controversial. The salary question must be answered at some point, and it will indeed be a factor in the applicant's decision. Just as the company is in the market for new employees, the applicant is shopping for a new employer. Based on certain data available in the newspaper ad (or whatever the medium may be), the applicant *selects* prospective employers. How many used automobile advertisements in the newspaper go unanswered because the seller withheld the price of the car?

In addition to newspaper ads, entry level security applicants may be solicited by posting announcements on bulletin boards in the security administration or criminal justice departments of local community colleges. If a college does not have a security or criminal justice program, the opening may be posted with the school's placement office. College students constitute a great reservoir of manpower for entry level positions—sometimes with, but more frequently without, career intentions. They are quick to learn and are usually willing to work those shifts or hours considered least desirable.

The recruiting approach for skilled, technical, and managerial personnel is different from that for entry level positions. Rather than the direct, open approach, the "blind ad" technique is recommended. Such advertisements are designed to attract career or professional people. Advertisements must appeal to and solicit their specific talents; for example, the copy might read, "Major banking firm's Security Department accepting applications for position of Fraud Investigator. Applicants must have minimum five years credit fraud and/or forgery investigative experience."

Some candidates reading such an ad will say to themselves, "That's me. I qualify." If they are in the market for a change or a new job, they will respond. The "blind ad" is simply one in which the company's identity is not revealed. Instead, interested parties are directed to submit their resumes to a post office box number or to some other third party.

The unidentified advertisement permits the company to prescreen candidates and interview on a highly selective basis. It also allows some time for at least a preliminary background investigation into the candidate's qualifications prior to the initial interview. This is the key to the two opposing types of recruiting techniques. The entry level positions require rather broad, general qualifications that are possessed by a greater segment of the labor market. Such applicants select their employers. In the advanced positions in the department, on the other hand, the company is seeking specific candidates with specific skills. The organization knows exactly what it wants, and it will select the future employee.

Finally, skilled, technical or managerial candidates will be filling far more sensitive positions in the security organization than will entry level candidates. For this reason, far greater care must be exercised in the selection of advanced candidates.

Interviewing Preliminaries

An applicant's first contact with the company should be with the Personnel Department. Even though the applicant has submitted a resume of his background and experience, his application for employment with the company should be formalized and documented by the completion of the company's standard job application form.

Every applicant's first interview should be with a personnel interviewer who will review the data on the application, making any corrections and clarifications as appropriate. This initial personnel interview is not for the purpose of selection or making an employment decision. Rather, it is an official preliminary, preparing the applicant for the coming interview with the Security representative.

The applicant is then escorted or sent to the Security offices with his employment application, preferably sealed, for the real interview. (Many applicants look upon the personnel interview as a nuisance and are anxious to talk to the person they believe has the authority to make a hiring decision— the Security official.)

Following the interview, the Security representative will make notes on the reverse side of the application form concerning the decision he or she has made. The security interviewer must, however, be properly trained in those laws specifically pertaining to hiring practices, both at the federal and state level, that prohibit discrimination against applicants based on sex, age, race, creed or color. For example, the notation on a female candidate's application that "mother-in-law baby-sits" could be construed as sexually discriminatory should the applicant not get the job. (Would the interviewer ask a male applicant if he would have trouble getting to work because of baby-sitting problems?)

The question of discrimination becomes particularly important when an applicant is rejected. Any subsequent claims of discrimination in hiring practices will then be processed and administered by the Personnel Department. It is the Personnel Department that has the expertise and resources to handle such problems efficiently, not the Security Department. For this reason, it is foolhardy to bypass the Personnel Department and talk to possible candidates about employment opportunities privately.

The Interview

The purpose of the interview is for the interviewer to determine if there is a match between the interests and qualifications of the applicant and the needs of the department. This can only be achieved on a personal, one-on-one basis.

Prior to the commencement of the interview, the interviewer should study the written application in private. It is disconcerting for the applicant to sit in silence watching the interviewer pore over his application. Likewise the interviewer will find it difficult to concentrate on the application with the applicant staring at him. As he reviews the application, the interviewer should make a mental note of two or three highlights that he will want to explore in some depth during the interview. Throughout the questioning, the interviewer should feel free to refer to the application, but he should not make the too frequent error of repeating to the applicant the same data presented on the application.

For example:

Interviewer: I see that you worked for Bignam Glass Works for three years as an Investigator.
Applicant: Yes, sir.

That exchange does nothing to help determine whether the applicant offers the qualifications desired. It is better to give him a chance to provide that information in his own words.

For example:

Interviewer: Tell me a little about your experience at Bignam Glass Works.
Applicant: Okay. I joined them as a trainee when I graduated from State U., on a special projects assignment . . . mostly compiling statistics for department manpower and budget projections. Six months later an investigator position came up and I got the promotion. I was assigned to background investigations while I was there.

This exchange gives the interviewer some meaningful information to consider or explore further. For example, the next question might ask the applicant how much time it took to complete a typical background check.

- Rule #1 in interviewing, then, is: *Ask open-ended questions that cannot be answered with a yes or no.*
- Rule #2 is: *Do not signal the answers you are looking for in your question.*

For example, the question "Did you ever have to fill in for a supervisor and have people report to you?" is a signal to the applicant that the interviewer considers some supervisory experience very important. Naturally, the applicant will tell him what he wants to hear: "Oh, yes, sir, a number of times the Special Agent in Charge had to go out of town and I took over the Screening Section."

- Rule #3 is: *Ask motivator-type questions that tend to give the applicant a chance to provide revealing answers.*

For example:

Interviewer: Think of a time while at Bignam's when you really felt good . . . a time you consider a real highlight of your time there.
Applicant: I think the high point of my time there was when the section's Special Agent in Charge was obliged to return to the Midwest on a personal leave . . . death in the family and some estate problems . . . and I was appointed acting supervisor during his absence. To think the Director had that much confidence in me, well . . . I really felt good about that.

Now the interviewer can probe that answer with the question, "Why would the Director's expressing confidence in you make you feel so good?" Probably the reply would be something to the effect, "I'd worked hard and wanted more responsibility and the Director felt I could handle it."

The original motivator-type question has revealed the following: the applicant responds to recognition, he is an achiever, and he seeks increased responsibility. These are very important factors to look for in the recruiting process of the department.

- Rule #4 is: *Ask him what* he *likes to do most on the job.* Most applicants do not have a chance to even consider what they would like to do. It is often surprising how wide a variety of talents and skills can surface in response to such a question.
- Rule #5 is: *Do not waste precious time "selling" your company or department.* By the time he gets there, the applicant has convinced himself of the desirability of the job, although he may have a few questions he would like answered.
- Rule #6 is: *At the conclusion of the interview, give the applicant a date that he can go by.*

For example, "I'd like to have you talk with my boss Friday afternoon." Or, "Our interviewing concludes on Friday. After that we will make our final selection. You can expect our decision no later than next Wednesday."

Most applicants are keyed-up and nervous prior to and during the early stages of the interview. In the security profession, which includes interrogation responsibilities, these factors make applicants easy prey to the experienced supervisor or manager. As the level of professionalism in security rises, it is to be hoped that all employment interviews will be handled in a sensitive and empathetic fashion.

Secondary Interviewing

The primary or initial interviewer in the Security Department is the person who will be the new employee's supervisor. If this supervisor has meaningful responsibility in his assignment, and if he is to conduct meaningful employment interviews, then *he* should make the selection. Why, then, should there be a secondary interview?

The secondary interview should not be a NO or GO test, but rather a consultive arrangement. The supervisor should understand that he will decide whom he wants out of all the applicants. But management must provide a climate wherein the supervisor not only wants to extend the *courtesy* of having his selected applicant meet the manager, but also sincerely wants the input, opinion and concurrence of his superior. Admittedly, this is a fine balance. But if the climate is right, the manager can actually reject an applicant with the supervisor's total concurrence and support.

Ideally, the arrangement should go something like this:

Supervisor: Out of six applicants I found a guy I really like and think he'll do the job. Before I go back to Personnel, I'd like the benefit of

your thinking. I think you'll agree, but who knows, maybe you'll see
something I missed. Can you talk to him?

Manager (following the secondary interview):   Your candidate has very
impressive credentials and I think you made a good choice.

   Or

Your applicant has impressive credentials and I believe he'll be a good
man. But did you realize the guy is quite inflexible in terms of transfers
or promotions out of town due to his mother's health and her depen-
dence on him? How would his inflexibility affect you?

If the information about the dependent mother strikes the supervisor
as news, he might very well reconsider his selection. On the other hand,
he might decide to hire the applicant anyway and modify his developmental
strategy for the applicant somewhat, knowing his restrictions which probably
are of relatively short duration. The point is that the purpose of the secondary
interview is to confirm the interviewer's choice and/or to apprise the interviewer of additional data to consider. This is not to say that the secondary
interviewer should be powerless to override the other interviewer's choice,
because under some unusual circumstances such authority may very well
have to be exercised.

The secondary interviewer may also be instrumental in selecting one
of two good candidates. This happens when the interviewer has narrowed
the field down to two and cannot decide which one he prefers.

Selection of the Best Candidate

If the interviewer understands the job function for which he is recruiting,
and if he knows precisely what job qualifications are necessary (in terms
of acquired skills, experience, education, and even temperament and personality), and if the interview is conducted in an objective manner, then one
candidate should stand above the rest. The goal is one of objectivity; the
problem is *subjectivity.* Too frequently the best candidate is not selected
because of bias on the part of the interviewer. This is not the proper textbook
to delve into the problems of personal bias, but it is important to observe
that the professional manager must recognize that personal bias exists and
does tend to distort our decisions. Overcoming such bias can be an exciting
challenge.

To discipline oneself in the interviewing and selection process to look
for the candidates with the best qualifications, regardless of their color,
age, sex, hair style, complexion, weight, shoe size, etc., will materially contribute to the selection of the best candidate.

Background Investigation of Applicant

Our purpose here is to emphasize the criticalness of the screening effort in selecting security applicants. The management team that fails to turn over every reasonable stone in clearing a candidate reflects a negligent if not derelict staff. The key word in that statement is REASONABLE. Requiring one classification of security applicants to take a polygraph examination may be a reasonable way to expose a history of theft activity, but in another classification that same strategy may not be reasonable. Before we review the various screening strategies, let us first look at what we are obliged to accomplish in the background investigation/screening process. We should, if at all possible, satisfy ourselves with the answers to the following questions:

1. Is the applicant really who he says he is?
2. Does the applicant really have the work experience he claims he has had? For the length of time he claims?
3. Does he have the education he claims?
4. Does he possess the skills he claims?
5. Is he financially stable or does he have a history of credit problems?
6. Is his apparent good character genuine or does he have a criminal history? What is his reputation in his neighborhood?

How does the security department (or security service company) reasonably satisfy themselves that they have the answers? They do this by a combination of the following:

1. By careful examination of the applicant's application for employment: looking for unanswered questions, erased answers, answers that were struck out or otherwise changed, gaps in the history of employment, and answers or statements that demand explanation, e.g., Have you ever been convicted of any crime other than a minor traffic offense? Answer: *YES.* Or, Reason for leaving job: Answer: *Quit* or *Terminated.*

   What a simple, inexpensive, intelligent, and direct way to gather information: by asking questions and asking for explanations. The answers could very well disqualify an applicant, right then and there, or provide direction for a subsequent investigation that could disqualify an unacceptable (below standards) applicant.

2. Telephone calls to former employers to verify dates of employment, reason for leaving, type of work, salary, and re-hireability.

   There are those skeptics who will say former employers won't divulge information over the phone, and in some cases that's true, but the skilled and professional investigator more often than not can obtain some of the desired information.

3. Computerized or manual referencing to negative data bases in compliance with the Fair Credit Reporting Act. Example: Stores Protective Association (commonly referred to as SPA) of Los Angeles, or TRW for credit data.

4. Neighborhood checks, i.e., actually going to the immediate neighborhood and talking to local residents.

5. Checking those criminal records that are legally available, such as court records.

6. Requiring applicants to submit to so-called "lie detectors" (which more accurately might be referred to as "truth verifiers"), such as the polygraph.

7. Requiring applicants to take the so-called "paper and pencil" tests, which are essentially psychological survey instruments that have the capability of identifying attitudes that suggest that the applicant is unsuitable for employment.

8. If time permits, written communication to former employers, schools, training centers, etc., seeking verification of information claimed on the application.

9. If military service is claimed, requiring evidence of such service by way of documentation, e.g., DD Form 214 or Discharge form.

The enlightened security administrator is fully cognizant of the fact that security employees, like police officers, are expected to serve and perform in a manner above reproach. And like police officers, if the security officer is discovered in any form of misconduct or criminal behavior, that's deemed reprehensible! And it is all the more reprehensible if that propensity for misconduct was open to discovery, but due to mismanagement, was not searched for!

Job Offer

Once the applicant has been chosen and screening is completed, we have come full circle—back to the Personnel Department. The selected candidate's application and the interviewer's comments are reviewed by the personnel representative and interviewer. The salary and starting date are agreed upon and the matter is then left in Personnel's hands. They will make the job offer. If for any reason there is a problem with the starting date or salary, the personnel representative will serve as the intermediary until the matter is resolved. This is an important service that shields Security from what could be a disagreeable or unpleasant dialogue if handled directly between the applicant and the Security Department.

SUMMARY

An organization is people, and the performance of the Security Department will benefit from care and attention to personnel selection.

Recruiting activity will be adapted to the job level, with open ads recommended for entry level positions. Blind advertisements, followed by more detailed screening, will be used for higher level positions.

Interviewing is the heart of personnel selection. After the initial screening by the Personnel Department, the primary interview should be conducted by the supervisor for whom the selected candidate will work. Questions should require meaningful answers (not signaled in the form of the question), and should be designed to allow the candidate to reveal as much of himself as possible. A secondary interview by the Security Manager is advisable, not to overrule the supervisor but advisory in nature.

If the interviewing process is based on clear knowledge of the job function and the qualities necessary for its performance, the selection of the right candidate is often easy. Above all, that selection must be based on *objective*, not *subjective*, criteria.

Background screening prior to the final job offer is critical because of the responsible role played by the security officer.

REVIEW QUESTIONS

1.   What are the six steps in the hiring process?

2.   Besides newspaper advertising, what is another method of soliciting applicants for entry level positions?

3.   Discuss the differences in the approach to recruiting for a non-entry level position vs. an entry level position.

4.   Discuss the six rules of interviewing employment applicants.

5.   What does "sending a fox to guard the hen house" mean?

6.   Name three ways to "screen" or otherwise verify an applicant's background.

8

Job Descriptions

The very underpinnings of the security department's organizational structure are the job descriptions. Indeed, Newman and Warren,[1] in their discussion on clarifying job specifications, state "If an organization is *designed properly*, we have a series of job descriptions." In fact, there's a direct relationship between the strength and effectiveness of an organization and the quality of job descriptions, quality defined in terms of:

- Accuracy in and completeness of describing each job classification in the department
- the matching of applicant/candidates to the job description
- the individual employee's understanding of the department expectations, as expressed in the job description
- the department's ability to design its training efforts to support the job descriptions, or, put another way, to match the training to the job descriptions
- performance evaluations are based on the job descriptions
- job descriptions currently reflect those tasks necessary for the larger organization (i.e., the security department) to achieve its stated objectives.

That's to say, the job description has life; it is a living, viable document that dictates success, or, conversely, in its absence, allows a climate of confusion, shoddy work practices, vague and subjective performance evaluations, and organizational disharmony. Believe it or not!

Let's analyze the quality factors listed above.

ACCURACY AND COMPLETENESS IN DESCRIBING THE JOB

An accurate and complete definition should leave no questions as to the nature of the work and the expectations of management. Compare the following "job description" for a background investigator, contrasting desirable v. undesirable.

---

[1] *The Process of Management.* Fourth Edition. (Prentice-Hall, Inc. 1977).

Undesirable

"The background investigator is responsible for those activities that either disprove or validate the information submitted by an applicant for employment."

Desirable

The background investigator's responsibility is to validate the truthfulness of an applicant's statements, and to determine his or her suitability for employment would include:

1. Confirming previous positions by contacting former employers, supervisors or personnel executives. Such contact would verify dates of employment, reason for termination (if available), general evaluation of applicant, and whether or not the applicant would be considered rehireable.
2. Conducting personal interviews with neighbors, landlord, etc., of the applicant to determine the general reputation in his or her social setting.
3. Conducting a credit check to ensure the applicant is financially responsible.
4. Conducting a search of Department of Motor Vehicle Records to determine the applicant's accident or citation history, if any.
5. Conducting a search of those available court and criminal records that could reflect former criminal activities that the applicant denies.

MATCHING APPLICANT TO THE JOB

Once we have an accurate and complete description of the assignment we should be able to identify those qualifications necessary or desirable to discharge the task. Those qualifications then become the hiring criteria or standards for that job. If the department has ten such positions, then all ten employees have at least a "floor" of similar minimum qualifications. Further, the Human Resource or Personnel Administration people, who frequently do the initial recruiting and screening of applicants, have clear goals in terms of what the security department is looking for in a given position.

Undesirable

1. No qualifications listed in the job description.
2. Vague or overgeneralized qualifications, e.g.: "Applicants must possess

a degree from an accredited college or university and three years comparable experience." Degree in *what?* If the job description is for background investigation, would a degree in astronomy be suitable? What's *comparable* experience?

Desirable

1. "Applicants must have a baccalaureate degree in Security Administration, Criminal Justice, Administration of Justice, Law, Accounting or a degree in some relatively comparable discipline in which research and investigation is the primary thrust of the career for which it's designed."
2. "Applicants must have a minimum of three years investigative experience. Experience in personnel administration may be substituted on the basis of 2 to 1 for two of the three investigative years of experience for this position in background investigations. Experience in credit reporting may be substituted on a one for one basis as long as the candidate meets the educational requirements."

EMPLOYEE'S UNDERSTANDING OF THE JOB

How many times have I discovered employees who didn't even know what a job description *was* . . . Just imagine the difference in a given employee's attitude as well as his performance if presented with the description of the company's expectations for performance, as spelled out in the detailed duties of the background investigator listed in Chapter 7.

One of the great pities in organizations is the gap between line performance and management's expectations. The pity is the gap itself. That's to say, the employee's perceptions of management's expectations are different from what, in fact, management expects! And that's not confined to the lowest level of the organization. That gap can, and does in many organizations, go all the way up to middle and senior management.

Here's the test of tests. If the organization has not been keen on or sensitive to the importance of job descriptions, have employees in a given job classification write out what they believe management expects of them in their job. At the same time, have the supervisor write down what he or she expects of those subordinates—in detail. More often than not, there will be, just on paper, a wide variance of perceptions. Is there any question then that performance variances exist? And with that, recriminations, faultfinding, resentment toward management for not recognizing good performance (when management doesn't see that "good" performance as good), etc.

MATCH TRAINING TO JOB DESCRIPTION

More security organizations than ever before are engaged in their own training of staff. Earlier, much training was so-called "on-the-job" training, which was usually sketchy at best (see more on training in Chapter 9).

Even where we find in-house or proprietary security training there's a tendency to approach it generically. That's to say, all investigators are trained in the art of interviewing and interrogations, but the finite application is missing. Certainly all investigators, be they fraud specialists, forgery specialists, dishonest employee investigators, air piracy sleuths, etc., need training and re-training on interviewing. But what about applying the principles of interviewing, as an example, to the specifics of a given investigator's daily work? More specifically, there should be a special interviewing workshop for background investigators, in which they role-play gathering information from a landlord or a neighbor. That's really making the training activity productively meaningful. After all, gaining the confidence of and encouraging an applicant's neighbor to share information is quite different from interviewing an employee who witnessed another employee roll a company forklift.

The Security Training Officer, or outside training firm working with the security executive, should build their programs on and around the department's job descriptions. It only makes sense.

PERFORMANCE EVALUATIONS BASED ON JOB DESCRIPTIONS

An employee's performance and management's reaction to that performance, i.e., disciplinary action if sub-standard or rewards (including promotions) if outstanding, have their roots in the job description (or at least should have).

Example: Harry is assigned to the Background/Screening Detail as an investigator. He doesn't think that job is as exciting as others, and when not pressed with his own work he has slipped off and climbed into the parking lot tower apprehending several teenagers for stripping parts from cars and pilfering their contents. As laudable as those arrests are, Harry cannot be rewarded for that action because it wasn't his job, either by assignment or by job description. Every employee has to be held accountable for his performance per the job description. Otherwise chaos creeps in.

Another example: Harry conducted a background investigation on a prospective manager and reported there was no derogatory information that would preclude his appointment. Within weeks that new manager is identified, confidentially, as having a serious drinking problem. A general assignment investigator is charged with a re-assessment of this manager. Part of his investigation includes a personal check of the neighborhood, where he confirms that the manager is known as a local lush and where one neighbor points out the manager's trash barrel area that's littered with vodka bottles.

A re-examination of Harry's investigation reveals no reference to a neighbor-hood check. Harry is asked about the check by his supervisor. Harry replies that he didn't think a neighborhood check was important—that neighborhood checks had never really uncovered anything important in the past and that he had thought it would be a waste of time.

In this case, Harry's work is sub-standard. Now the company has an executive who's a problem and the security department failed in its responsi-bility to screen out, in advance, these kinds of potential problems. Irrespec-tive of Harry's opinion, the job description clearly spells out what the duties of the background investigator are. It's there in black and white. There's nothing vague about expectations here. No arguments here. Harry failed to perform according to management's expectations. And he's culpable.

If Harry had indeed made the neighborhood check and missed securing the information, it would be an entirely different story.

JOB DESCRIPTIONS ARE CURRENT

If job descriptions are living, viable underpinnings of organizational perfor-mance and success (and they are), then they must be tended to and cared for—watered and fed if you please—so they reflect the present and current organization.

- If a security clerical is now responsible for a new word processor and computer, is that reflected in the job description?
- If credit fraud investigators now inquire directly into credit files by use of computerized CRT's, is that included in their job descriptions?
- If the company has absorbed a smaller firm in the next state and the Loss Prevention Auditor is now required to visit that new site on a monthly basis, is that travel and out-of-state work referred to in that job description?

The only thing that is constant is change. Modern and progressive security departments are always operating on their tip-toes, i.e., alert, sensi-tive to what's happening and what needs attention, including keeping job descriptions current.

Don't be misled by my emphasis on job descriptions. The importance and emphasis here deal with understanding, agreement, and excellence in performance. One could mistake this emphasis and compare it with the absurdities of organized labor's job descriptions in which a worker in one job category, say a carpenter, can't do another man's work, e.g., a carpenter can't unscrew a burned-out light bulb and replace it with a new one, even if he's in the dark, because it's the electrician's job. We in our industry can change assignments overnight, or sooner, to meet the protection needs of our environment. The Background Investigator can and is temporarily assigned to surveillance of the parking lot, if the needs of the organization are met by that adjustment in assignments.

COMPOSITION OF THE JOB DESCRIPTION

Examination of most job descriptions reflect they're comprised of three basic elements: 1) function, 2) responsibility and authority, and 3) relationships. I feel that's too restricting, or fails to depict the greatest possible dimension of the position. Probably the best job description would include the following:

- Objective of the position
- Dimension of the position
- Nature and scope of the position
    Position in the organization
    Mission and environment
    Specific functions of the position
    Subordinates' functions
    Primary challenge of the position
    Authority vested in the position
    Relationships
    Requisites
- Principal responsibilities

SAMPLE JOB DESCRIPTION

Let's apply the above outline for a job description to an imaginary Captain of Security in an industrial complex.

JOB DESCRIPTION
Captain

Objective of the Position

To ensure the physical plant protection program of the Security Department is effective, functional, and properly managed.

Dimension of the Position

In personnel: directly supervises five (5) sergeants and indirectly supervises twenty-eight (28) security officers.

Nature & Scope of the Position

Position in the organization: Reports to Assistant Director of Security–Physical Security Division. Directly supervises five sergeants.
Mission and environment: Protection of company property, employ-

ees and their property, twenty-four (24) hours a day, 365 days a year in a structured regimen, with emergency response capabilities.

Specific functions of the position: Selects, trains, schedules, and supervises the Sergeants.

- Reviews all security officer generated- or related-control documents, forms, logs, and reports.
- Coordinates corrective and/or maintenance follow-up activities identified by the security officers and their supervisors.
- Analyzes physical protection strategies, assignments, posts to ensure work is cost-effective and necessary and recommends appropriate modifications and revisions when appropriate.
- Develops training and communication programs for security officers to ensure staff is both knowledgeable and productive.
- Guides, assists, monitors, and counsels the sergeants to ensure they're motivated, creative and effective leaders of their subordinates.

Subordinates' functions: Sergeants ensure the necessary security controls are in place and functioning at each facility through proper scheduling and inspection activity.

Primary challenge of the position: The primary challenge is ensuring that sufficient planning and training have adequately prepared the security staff to effectively respond to and deal with the unusual/emergency/crisis event at any hour at any facility, including but not limited to a major conflagration, bombing, earthquake, cyclone, or other natural disaster.

Authority vested in the position: Captain has the authority to deny access to the facility, deny removal of property and conversely, if circumstances warrant, may allow both, contrary to procedure, if in his judgment the action is appropriate. The Captain may order evacuation of a facility, make arrests, call for public protective service assistance as a remedial strategy, but may not invite or solicit law enforcement investigative assistance.

Relationships: By virtue of high visibility of the captain's role and broad range of responsibilities, he will invariably come in contact with any member of the total employee population, vendors, resources, job applicants, business visitors and other guests, and local fire and police personnel. All such contacts will necessarily evolve around security related problems, questions, or other security activities.

Requisites: Knowledge of:

- alarm hardware and operations, including its logic;
- fire prevention suppression strategies;
- patrol procedures;
- company policies and procedures;

- state-of-the-art in physical security devices and hardware;
- security training techniques and leadership skills.

Experience: A minimum of three years' experience as a sergeant in this company, or, a minimum of five years experience as an industrial security supervisor whose duties and responsibilities included scheduling, security and safety (including fire) training; evaluating performance; scheduling of subordinates; handling disciplinary problems; conducting facility surveys or inspections; and preparing written recommendations.

Education: Minimum of two years of college with at least one quarter of the credits in Security Administration/Management, Criminal Justice or Criminal Administration, or Industrial Safety, or any combination thereof.

Principal Responsibilities

1. Ensure that the company's four (4) facilities and facility occupants are adequately protected against harm or loss, 24 hours a day, 365 days a year.
2. Ensure that the entire physical plant protection program is effectively and efficiently supervised by the sergeants.
3. Ensure that the sergeants are adequately trained and exercise good leadership skills in dealing with their subordinates.
4. Ensure that each sergeant is sufficiently trained in and knowledgeable of appropriate response strategies to any emergency that could seriously threaten life on or the property of ABC, Inc.

SUMMARY

There exists an important relationship between an organization's performance and the various job descriptions that cover the assignments of that organization. Those job descriptions must accurately and completely describe the duties; provide for the matching of candidate to the job; be understood by the employee; be the source of training for each job; be a key source in measuring performance; and reflect the current activities and responsibilities of each job.

REVIEW QUESTIONS

1. Why does the author consider a broad definition of a task undersirable?

2. How does a good description fill the gap between an employee's performance and management's expectations?

3. Cite an example of a training program that could come directly from a job description.

4. Why is it important for job descriptions to be current?

5. What does "Dimension of position" mean?

9

Training

Without question the primary contributor to poor job performance is inadequate training. Although the value and absolute necessity of sound training are extolled by all, training dollars seldom materialize. Other demands on the organization seem to push training activities down the list of priorities, and training—real, formalized training—is always going to happen "tomorrow." No other single organizational function gets as much lip service as training.

SHORTCOMINGS OF TYPICAL "TRAINING"

Further complicating the dilemma of training is the fact that training means different things to different people; the function itself is misunderstood. The following story might serve as a typical example.

Harry X receives a phone call from a representative of the Personnel Department at Company B, where he was interviewed several days earlier. Harry X accepts the job offer. He is pleased and promptly calls his friends and relatives to tell them about his good fortune. He is to report to work on the following Monday.

When Monday morning comes, Harry X is up early. He has been anticipating this day, and he dresses to look his very best. He heads for work, sensing excitement. As the building comes into view he starts to feel some nervousness and anxiety. The tension increases as he enters the personnel offices and is greeted by a somewhat impassive personnel employee who coldly directs him to complete more forms.

Harry is then herded into a "Training Room" with a number of other new and equally nervous employees, where they meet a "Training Officer" who either acts bored or is so enthusiastic that he arouses skepticism in the minds of the new employees. Each new employee is given a company booklet which is recited to them page by page as if no one could read. The booklet describes benefits, whom to call or what to do if one is ill, retirement programs, the history of the company, and major important rules.

This concludes phase one of Harry's "training." Of course, it is not training, it is orientation. Harry and his peers learned little and will retain less, for three reasons: (1) they were not prepared for the presentation; (2) they were given too much information in too short a period of time; and (3) they cannot relate the material to their work.

Harry's state of mind at this point is becoming negative. What he is hearing goes in one ear and out the other. He wants to get to the job he was hired for. He wants to see the area he will be working in, and he wants to meet his supervisor and the people he will work with. But these personnel and "training" people (training historically falls within the personnel division) will not let him go.

Phase two of training is usually a tour of the facility. There is a welcoming address by the vice president and a luncheon in the company cafeteria. By now Harry has made friends with another new employee, and they secretly concur in their negative reaction to every company representative to whom they have been exposed so far.

Finally Harry is directed to his new department and introduced to his supervisor, who, because he was not involved in the selection of Harry, eyes him coolly and suspiciously. Harry is disappointed, hurt, disgusted in part, and close to anger. Typically, the supervisor is very busy. He does make time for the new man up to a point where he calls in one of Harry's peers and charges him with showing Harry around. Thus concludes the first day of "training."

The following day, Harry starts "on-the-job training" on the lobby desk with Frank. It is a good place to start Harry because Frank needs help; he is very busy because of the badge conversion. Frank is annoyed because he knows an inexperienced employee will only be a hindrance. He had asked for an experienced assistant. He makes it a point to let Harry know how he feels.

Harry stands by helplessly, not knowing what to do or how to respond to questions, and attempting to avoid criticism. Midway through the confusing and distressing day there is a lull. Frank finally decides to accept Harry and begins to confide in him. He tells Harry everything he does not like about the company, about the department, about supervisors. He also passes on everything he learned (and he learned the same way Harry is now learning). He even advises Harry what company procedures (as Frank interprets them) are to be followed and which are to be ignored. The second day of "training" ends.

On the third day, Harry is assigned to the receiving docks to work with another officer because "the lobby desk is too busy."

New employee training resembles Harry's experience in far too many cases.

There are many conspicuous problems and lessons in the foregoing. Elaboration is unnecessary, with one exception: a very important and powerful lesson to be learned is that first impressions made upon the employee on his first day in a new job have great impact. The new employee is disoriented, somewhat frightened, nervous, self-conscious, and subconsciously he is crying out for a friend. The manager who recognizes and is sensitive to this can treat the newcomer in such a way as to quickly establish respect and loyalty that otherwise may not be developed.

TRAINING DEFINED

As stated earlier, the training function means different things to different people; it is widely misunderstood. Certainly there is a question of definition, and a typical dictionary definition (*Webster's*) tells us little when it describes training in this manner:

> "training. *Noun.* Act, process, or method of one who trains; state of being trained. *Adjective.* That trains; used in or for training; as, a *training* ship for sailors."

Even aside from its obvious circularity, what does this explanation really explain? Is it any wonder there is confusion?

A more workable definition might be the following:

> *Training is an educational, informative, skill development process that brings about anticipated performance through a change in comprehension and behavior.*

Basically there are three things that management wants the employees to know. It is important for them to understand

1. *what* management wants them to do.
2. *why* management wants them to do it.
3. *how* management wants it done.

"POP" FORMULA: POLICY, OBJECTIVE, PROCEDURE

Interestingly enough, the *what, why,* and *how* are related to *policy, objectives,* and *procedures.* From this correlation the author has developed the POP Training Formula as the basic building block for job training.

The area of the Why/Objective in Figure 9.1 deserves special attention. Too frequently the training process overlooks the necessity of informing employees *why* this should be done, *why* that should not be done, etc. When employees are informed as to the why's, their performance will improve. This point cannot be overstressed.

Figure 9.1   The POP formula for training.

Incidentally, those who are familiar with the *who, what, where, how, why,* and *when* investigative formula may wonder what has happened to the *who, when* and *where.* The *who* (the employee who is being trained) is obviously implied, and the *when* and *where,* in this context, are included in the *how.*

Now let us translate the POP Formula into training for a specific job, such as Shoplifting Detective.

Re-examining the suggested definition, it will be seen that there are three aspects of training, involving education, information and skill development. The example in Figure 9.2 makes it apparent that, of the three tiers of the formula, the How or Procedure tier addresses itself to *skill development,* while the other two tiers, Policy and Objective, are *educational* and *informative* in nature. It is not enough for the detective to know that management's policy is to arrest and prosecute every shoplifter. He must also understand the objectives which make this policy reasonable and necessary, and he must thoroughly grasp the various procedures which are essential in the detective's own execution of his responsibilities. The proper combination of education, information, and skill development round out and give substance and definition to "training."

	COMPANY PROGRAM	EMPLOYEE FUNCTION
POLICY (What Management Wants Done)	Arrest and prosecute every shoplifter.	Has been hired by the company to specifically detect and apprehend shoplifters.
OBJECTIVE (Why Management Wants It done)	Reduce shoplifting losses. Deter others by example of arrests. Punish or discourage offenders.	• Helps to reduce losses caused by shoplifting. • Deters others from shoplifting. • Helps to punish offenders through the criminal justice system.
PROCEDURE (How Management Wants It Done)	Lawful gathering of the necessary evidence to justify arrest and support prosecution of shoplifters.	• Sees customer approach merchandise. • Sees customer select merchandise. • Sees secretion of merchandise. • Sees that no payment is made. • Sees removal of merchandise from store. • Approaches customer and says, "Excuse me, etc." • Carries out arrest with justification. • Makes written report of incident, etc.

Figure 9.2   The POP formula for Shoplifting Detective training.

Detailed Expansion of Procedure

Although each tier of the training formula is important and interrelates with the others, the Procedure tier will receive, by far, the most attention. Consider another job classification, that of Lobby Desk Officer (Figure 9.3). Management's policy of controlling access and unauthorized removal of equipment, materials or supplies, and its twin objectives of preventing trespassing and theft, are quickly grasped. What remains, for the new employee, is the question of how to carry out his assignment—how to do the How. Once on this track, the skill development process of training is well on its way.

Consider, for example, just one aspect of the procedural steps:

* *Confirm visitors by telephone, issue visitor badge, and await escort.*

How should this be done? The following might be one acceptable procedure:

1. Request visitor to complete Visitor Card, form s647.
2. Use company directory to call employee whom visitor states he wishes to see.
3. If employee wishes to see visitor, request employee to come to desk to escort visitor.

	COMPANY PROGRAM	EMPLOYEE FUNCTION
POLICY **(What Management Wants Done)**	Control entry and egress of all persons to the facility.	Ensures that no person shall enter the facility without an authorized badge. Ensures that no equipment, materials or supplies may leave the facility without authorization.
OBJECTIVE **(Why Management Wants It done)**	Prevent losses from theft. Prevent trespassing. Safeguard persons and company assets.	• Helps to reduce losses from theft. • Helps to prevent unauthorized access to the facility for malicious purposes (bombing, vandalism, theft of information, etc.) • Helps to make facility safer for personnel.
PROCEDURE **(How Management Wants It Done)**	Implementing access control program (employee and visitor badging, sign-in registers, package inspection, etc.).	• Permits entry after exhibition of authorized badge. • Refers lost or forgotten badge cases to personnel. • Prior to 6:30 a.m. and after 6:30 p.m. requires signature on registry before permitting access to facility. • Confirms visitors by telephone, issues visitor badge and awaits escort. • Inspects all containers not displaying "Security Parcel OK" slip, etc.

Figure 9.3 The POP formula for Lobby Desk Officer training.

4. Issue yellow Visitor Badge to visitor and record badge number on visitor's completed Visitor Card.
5. Place Visitor Card in Visitors Aboard box.
6. Invite visitor, by his name as indicated on Visitor Card (e.g., Mr. Jones), to have a seat until his escort arrives.

The detailed expansion of procedures, then, or the "How-to-Do-the-How," will be the primary thrust of the training efforts. It is, nevertheless, only a part of the whole—a large part, granted, but still a part.

TRAINING AS ONGOING RESPONSIBILITY

Up to this point we have been discussing individualized and specific job description training. As critical as this type of training is, it is only part of the entire training picture. The training function within the security organization should be continuous and ongoing. Ideally, training should be under the direction of a Training Officer whose *sole* responsibility is Security Training.

The last person who should be placed in the Security Training Officer function would be a trained security officer. To ensure total training objectivity, an experienced trainer or a bright college graduate with an academic background in personnel, communications or teaching should be hired and charged with the responsibility of coordinating and administering the training program in the Security Department. Such a person approaches the job without preconceived notions, without bias, without an "expert's" point of view. Rather, he goes about assignment after assignment with wide-eyed, unabashed curiosity and amazement (which tends to be contagious), learning as he goes and seeing many things the experienced security officer does not see. Such people make outstanding training officers.

Note that this opinion differs from our recommendation in Chapter 3 on the conduct of training sessions on security for the *general* employee. In such sessions only the security employee can speak with authority about the security function.

TYPES OF SECURITY TRAINING PROGRAMS

Following is a list of types of training programs which security management could provide the department's employees:

*   *General Seminars*
    Usually most effective if by employee classification; e.g., all patrol and uniformed personnel, or all fraud investigators. So-called "general" programs are a potpourri of subjects that are important and meaningful

to the group. One side effect of these sessions, which could be from one to three days in duration, is the motivational aspect, which should be capitalized upon in the agenda. Following is a typical agenda:

9:00– 9:30	Welcome and Introduction	Security Director
9:30–10:15	Organizational Overview (transparencies and handouts)	Security Manager
10:15–10:30	Break	
10:30–12:30	Inter-personal Communications	Manager, Public Relations (from outside the department)
12:30– 1:15	Lunch	
1:15– 2:00	Do's and Don't's in Handling Company Employees	Training Officer
2:00– 3:30	Report Writing (work sheets and handouts)	Chief Investigator
3:30– 3:45	Break	
3:45– 4:30	Training Manual Update (revised pages)	Security Manager
4:30– 5:00	Open Question-and-Answer Period	Staff
5:00– 5:45	Motivational Film	Training Officer

This outline illustrates how flexible a general seminar can be, depending upon the objective. In this agenda, for example, the real or *primary* objective of the session might have been to introduce and explain a major organizational change for the Security Department. This objective was achieved in the morning session. Because people had to come from far and near, the balance of the day was then devoted to training.

- *Interrogation Workshop*
  Half- to full-day session of principles and techniques of interrogation with role-playing and, ideally, video play-back of role-playing.
- *Testifying in Court Seminar*
  Half- to full-day program which includes preparation of evidence, dress, demeanor on the witness stand, voice, where to look, "traps," stress and attitude.
- *Report Writing Workshop*
  90-minute review up to a full day on the principles to be followed in reducing events to paper.

- *Supervisory Training*
  Two-hour "topic" sessions up to full three-day seminar. "Topic" session could be *How to Handle Disciplinary Problems*, or *Management Styles, X, Y or ?*

MEETING ORGANIZATIONAL NEEDS

The types of training programs are limited only by organizational needs. True, much material is available at local universities and community colleges, and security personnel should be encouraged to further their education at such institutions. Specific organizational needs, however, usually must be met through "in-house" education.

Organizational needs come down to people needs. The agenda of the general seminar discussed above was in response to needs. Security management had a need to communicate the reasons for and details of a major reorganization. Security management also recognized the daily operating problems connected with poor interpersonal communication skills between security people themselves and between non-security people and security. Therefore a second need was addressed in the program. The remainder of the agenda was the result of a survey (made in advance by the Training Officer) of the employees' stated needs. Thus, training objectives are identified and material designed to achieve those objectives. Too many training programs are the master works of art of training personnel or management, but they miss the mark of satisfying what employees want and need.

SECURITY MANUAL

A Security Manual or Handbook is an absolute essential, not only as an operational tool but also as a training guide, and it must be updated on a regular basis. The subject matter should include pertinent company policies, departmental policies, job descriptions, emergency phone numbers, and a great many procedural instructions for specific incidents, such as telephone bomb threat or facility black-out. In some organizations the manual is deemed sacred and consequently most employees are not allowed to touch it—a foolish attitude. The manual should be put in the hands of all regular proprietary security personnel.

SUMMARY

Typical new employee "training" is little more than general orientation. The newcomer is usually unprepared for the presentation, and he is given too much too fast, in a manner unrelated to the work he will actually be doing. The typical orientation program, in which the employee is lumped with many others from various departments for a day and then thrown immediately into an assignment for "on-the-job" training, is actually negative training. The employee learns the wrong way—or the wrong things—and develops undesirable attitudes.

Effective training is an *educational, informative, skill-development* process. The basic building block for training can be summed up in the POP Formula:

Policy   = *What* management wants.
Objective = *Why* management wants it.
Procedure = *How* management wants it accomplished.

Although the importance of why something must be done cannot be over-stressed, primary attention in training will be on the procedural, or skill-development, phase . . . learning "how to do the how."

Training should be an ongoing process, ideally in the hands of a Training Officer selected for qualities other than security experience. Types of training programs may include *general* seminars and *specific* seminars. They should be based on specifically identified organizational needs.

The Security Manual should embody the essentials of security responsibilities, and should be in the hands of every employee.

REVIEW QUESTIONS

1. What is a workable definition of *training?*

2. What are the three basic things that management wants employees to know? How does the "POP Formula" relate to these?

3. List four possible topics for security training seminars.

4. What should the contents of a Security Manual include?

10

Discipline

As a rule, the very word *discipline* evokes an emotional reaction on the part of employees at all levels of the organizational pyramid. Most supervisors and managers would rather do anything but discipline, and it is human nature to resist and resent punishment. This negativism surrounding a critically important organizational process is unnecessary and can easily be replaced with a positive approach, called Constructive Discipline.

Before discussing Constructive Discipline, it is instructive to consider a number of dictionary definitions of the word *discipline*.

1.   Training that corrects, molds, or perfects.
2.   Punishment.
3.   Control gained by obedience or training.
4.   Orderly conduct.
5.   A system of rules governing conduct or practice.
6.   To punish or penalize for the sake of discipline.
7.   To train or develop by instruction and exercise.
8.   To bring a group under control.
9.   To impose order upon.

The majority of these explanations emphasize punishment or control, both of which are aspects of discipline. Only the first and seventh in this list call attention to the key aspect of Constructive Discipline: *the training which develops disciplined conduct.*

The word *discipline* is derived from the Latin *discipulus* ("learning"). The word *disciple* also comes from the same root; the early Christian disciples were considered "students" of Christ. The origin of the word suggests this important concept: that positive and constructive discipline is *training that corrects, molds, or strengthens* an employee in the interests of achieving departmental and company goals. Punishment, that factor which is feared and disliked by all, is secondary. Any punishment connected with discipline should always be a *means to an end,* and that end should be organizational, not personal.

In other words, the effective disciplinary process condemns the act, not the employee. It says, "You're okay, but what you did is not okay."

By addressing ourselves to, and focusing on, action rather than personalities, the whole process takes on a constructive dimension that is easy to handle and acceptable to all. Comprehension and subsequent application of this positive concept have helped many managers cope with their disciplinary problems.

It is also important that discipline be swift. The long-range effect of coming to grips with a problem immediately is better than putting off what probably will have to be faced later—irrespective of the nature of the problem, be it simple tardiness or a careless oversight. What could easily be corrected now may be far more difficult to correct later, because the real essence and secret of constructive discipline is its *preventive* nature. To train, mold, and correct *now* reduces the need for more difficult training, molding, and correction later.

THE SUPERVISOR'S ROLE IN DISCIPLINE

Discipline is a responsibility which rests squarely on the supervisor's shoulders. It cannot be passed on to a higher supervisor and should not be passed on to the Personnel Division. Some weak supervisors shirk their responsibility with the idea that enforcing the regulations will hurt their relations with subordinates. Actually, most people prefer to work in a well-ordered environment. They really do not expect or necessarily want the supervisor to be too lenient all the time, because those who fail to exercise needed discipline, who will not say "no" or "don't" to those who deserve it, can make the workload more difficult for everyone else.

The supervisor who is fair and consistent in his treatment of employees will gain rather than lose respect through being firm and expecting conformity to the rules. Once the proper atmosphere is created through constructive discipline, a request from the supervisor *is* an order. There is no need to be abrupt or overly forceful to get the job done, because employees will respect the supervisor who respects them.

Some make the mistake of believing that discipline is only directed at the inefficient worker. *All* employees require constructive discipline. There are times when disciplinary action is essential with an outstanding employee, usually because he and others have come to think he is so good that he is indispensable. The supervisor should never lose respect or control of the organization by being afraid to lose a good man.

The supervisor who understands the employees' psychological needs will generate less reactive hostility, and consequently experience less resistance, than the supervisor who approaches the employee with insensitivity and harsh tactics. An important key is to recognize the individual differences of employees, handle them on that basis to win their loyalty and support, then motivate them to greater personal success. The benefit will be a significant reduction in disciplinary problems.

All disciplinary actions commence with an interview and discussion. If handled with sensitivity (which includes understanding the employee's psychological needs and treating him or her as an important individual), the interview can accomplish its basic purpose and at the same time actually serve to improve the personal relationship between the employee and supervisor. The employee frequently expects the worst. With many supervisors the employee would leave the interview feeling misunderstood, mistreated, hostile, guilty, or dejected. If the supervisor remembers that the basic purpose of discipline is correction and training, not punishment, he will take a positive approach in the interview. That approach will leave the employee with renewed confidence in himself and in the supervisor and greater faith in and respect for the boss's good judgment and fairness.

DISCIPLINARY PROBLEMS ARISING FROM MISUNDERSTOOD ASSIGNMENTS

The following sign hangs in a number of supervisors' and managers' offices:

I KNOW YOU BELIEVE YOU UNDERSTOOD WHAT YOU THINK I SAID, BUT I AM NOT SURE YOU REALIZE THAT WHAT YOU HEARD IS NOT WHAT I MEANT.

The irony here is that the statement is an absolute indictment against the supervisor. When the subordinate has failed to do a task as assigned, and his superior proudly directs him to read the sign, the supervisor obviously fails to recognize his own responsibility to make each assignment clearly understood. The failure really rests with the supervisor, not the subordinate. Many disciplinary cases are the result of assignment failures. And most assignment failures have nothing to do with the employee's level of competence but rather with a misunderstanding of what was expected.

How many times has a supervisor stopped an employee, given instructions on what he wanted done, and then asked, "Do you understand?" The employee nods knowingly, but as soon as the supervisor walks away, the employee turns to a peer and asks, "Do you know what he wants?" The supervisor's first error is in asking the employee if he understands. Most employees will say yes rather than admit they failed to grasp the instructions.

Other assignment errors include:

- Instructions may not have been given in a logical order or sequence.
- The person giving the instructions may have spoken indistinctly or failed to use clear language.
- Instructions may have been too complicated for one simple explanation.

There are occasions when an assignment is indeed understood and yet still not followed because of the manner in which the assignment was given. The ideal way to give an assignment is by a request rather than a demand. Asking an employee to do something makes him part of the picture and gives him more opportunity to make suggestions and to feel a responsibility to perform the assignment. Requests create a spirit of willingness to do the job.

Following are ten suggestions to follow in giving assignments:

1. Know the assignment yourself.
2. Do not assign work above the employee's ability.
3. Explain the purpose of the assignment so that the employee understands why he is being asked to do it.
4. Request or suggest—do not demand. For example,
   "Would it be possible?"
   "Suppose we try it this way?"
   "Will you take care of . . . ?"
5. Give brief, exact instructions with all of the necessary details, but not too much to confuse.
6. Demonstrate if possible.
7. Do not assume the employee understands. Have him reiterate the instructions.
8. Do not watch every move; let the employee feel responsible.
9. Let the employee know you are there if he needs assistance.
10. Be certain these points have been covered:
    a. Who is to do it.
    b. What is to be done.
    c. Where it is to be done.
    d. When it is to be started and finished.
    e. How it is to be done.
    f. Why it is to be done.

Most employees want to do a good job. If care is taken in giving assignments, there will be fewer failures and fewer disciplinary problems resulting from failures.

BASIC RULES OF THE DISCIPLINARY PROCESS

There are six fundamental rules in the disciplinary process that have universal applicability.

Rule #1—*Put rules in writing* and make certain employees understand them. There should be no assumed rules. If a rule is worth having, it is worth writing down. Employees are entitled to know what the rules are if compliance is expected.

Many institutional rules are peculiar to the organization and therefore not of common knowledge, particularly to someone new to the organization.

Take, for example, the situation of a security officer who forgot his badge and, being new to the business, borrows a badge from another new officer who is going off-duty. Experienced personnel would appreciate the logic behind prohibiting an officer from wearing another officer's badge, but a newcomer might not understand. If he is to be held accountable, he should know the ground rules. Many firms provide new employees with a copy of the rules and then have them sign a statement to that effect which becomes part of their personnel file. Other companies post rules in conspicuous areas such as employee locker rooms.

Not only is it morally wrong to take punitive action against an employee who was honestly ignorant of a given rule, it is an administrative or legal wrong which can be remedied by the government, especially if the punitive action is termination. The company may be legally bound to reinstate a wrongfully discharged employee, *with full wages for all time lost due to the discharge*. Many companies have paid months of back wages under such circumstances.

In short, there must be no surprises in terms of company rules.

Rule #2—*Discipline in the privacy of an office*. To the employee, being corrected for deficiencies in conduct or performance is a sensitive and frequently embarrassing experience. To be corrected in the presence of others is considered degrading, and the end result of that approach is seething resentment and angry embarrassment—emotions which are counterproductive to the true disciplinary goal. Additionally, the privacy afforded in an enclosed office permits the participants to hear each other clearly. It is extremely important for the supervisor to hear what the employee has to say and for the employee to hear what the supervisor is saying.

Rule #3—*Be objective and consistent*. As stated at the outset of this chapter, effective discipline condemns the act, not the person. That approach is obviously objective; the issues are not, or at least should not be, personalities. The supervisor who refers to an employee as "dummy," or who makes such statements as "Can't you get it through your thick skull . . . ," or who succumbs to personal likes and dislikes, loses objectivity and consequently loses credibility and respect. Thus the supervisor is no longer practicing true Constructive Discipline but returns to the negative approach of punishing people who fail to meet standards.

Inconsistency is equally deadly. If the policy of the department is to terminate officers who sleep on the job, then all officers so caught must be terminated. To fire one and not another breeds contempt for the management of the organization. Conversely, if the same rule is consistently enforced and acted upon, genuine respect, not only for the rules, but for the management, follows.

Rule #4—*Educate, do not humiliate*. The concept here is to *help, not hurt* an employee who has failed to meet standards of conduct or performance. If the disciplinary action truly corrects, trains or molds the individual to meet standards, he comes away from the experience with better insight into himself and what the company expects. He comes away educated. If he is berated and humiliated, he comes away angry and resentful and certainly destined to fail again, sometimes by design. Both he and the department suffer as a consequence.

Rule #5—*Keep a file on all employee infractions.* This is not to suggest that a negative dossier be maintained on each employee. Rather, documented incidents of past failures are a necessary and useful reference for repeated incidents. Compare, for example, the two following situations.

Supervisor: John, I've talked to you before about your uniform, and you're out of uniform again with those blue socks.
John: You've never mentioned my socks before . . . when was that?
(Supervisor recalls the incident only vaguely, and has no documentation of it.)

Supervisor: John, I've talked to you before about your uniform, and you're out of uniform again with those blue socks. In fact, last February 15th we talked about blue socks, and again on March 30th I talked to you about your shirt cuffs being turned up. This being the third time, I'm going to place a formalized written reprimand in your personnel jacket. You must understand that we insist on every officer dressing according to the uniform code. A uniform improperly worn lacks good taste and is a poor reflection on the organization as a whole.
(The facts are obviously clear and available, and John cannot challenge those facts.)

The "file" this rule refers to is an informal record, maintained by the immediate supervisor for his own personal reference. Dates of incidents may or may not end up as formal documentation in the personnel records, depending on the employee.

Not only does the employee find it difficult to argue with these supervisorial records, so does any administrative hearing board which may someday sit in judgment over the company's more drastic disciplinary action against the employee.

Rule #6—*Exercise discipline promptly.* Consider again the situation of John and his uniform violation of wearing blue socks when he is supposed to wear black. This time, the supervisor has delayed his corrective action.

Supervisor: John, I've talked to you before about your uniform, and last week you were out of uniform again by wearing blue socks.
John: I don't recall wearing blue socks last week. What day was that?
Supervisor: Well, *I* recall your wearing blue socks, and it happened to be last Friday.

John: If I was wearing blue socks they were navy blue and no one would ever know the difference.

Supervisor: They weren't navy blue, they were bright blue—obviously and conspicuously bright blue.

John: Did you see them yourself?

Supervisor: I did.

John: Well, then, why didn't you talk to me about them *then* if they were so bad?

Good question, John!

It should be apparent that with the passage of time (and distance) from the infraction, whatever magnitude it may have, the issue becomes vague and almost argumentative. If corrective action is appropriate, then it must be handled *now* or on as timely a basis as possible. It is like catching a child with his hand in the cookie jar. If prompt action follows the detection, the youngster can relate the consequences of his action to the act itself. If he must wait until his father gets home after work, it is harder for the child to make sense out of his scolding or punishment. Besides, depending upon the level of sophistication of the youngster (or adult), he will rationalize the incident to minimize its importance, and subsequent corrective action can appear unreasonable.

The same concept of the need for prompt action is most evident in dealing with such drastic behavior as theft. If you observe an employee steal and immediately take that employee into custody and commence the interrogation, the interrogator has all the advantages and will experience little in the way of resistance. If that employee is allowed to leave the site, however, and is not interrogated until the following morning, resistance and obstacles will surface. Yet the same act occurred. The difference is timing. Delays raise questions of credibility.

SELF-DISCIPLINE

No manager or supervisor can ever hope to discipline others effectively if he cannot discipline himself. Disciplining oneself can be accomplished by controlling vanity, likes and dislikes, personal thoughts, and by always being humble. Self-discipline will lay a solid groundwork for working with other people and their failures and problems, and for setting a climate where self-discipline becomes contagious.

Self-Discipline and Vanity

The supervisor who misuses authority will earn resentment instead of respect. Barking out commands may seem the quickest way to get the job done, but that technique is a vain self-indulgence that a manager of people cannot afford. Using power in this way is not leadership. Everyone knows the extent of the manager's power; it need not be displayed. Self-control over such vanity is also detected by subordinates, and in their own behavior they will respond in kind to that example of personal discipline.

Self-Discipline and Temper

Loss of temper may make a manager feel better for a while, but it will not improve his performance in handling people or assignments. People never know how much to discount instructions issued in an intemperate manner.

Self-Discipline and Arguments

Most arguments are useless. Discussions, not arguments, produce agreement and cooperation.

Self-Discipline and Personal Likes and Dislikes

Nothing creates a better atmosphere than friendly recognition of subordinates on an equal basis. And nothing creates trouble faster than failures to control personal likes and dislikes and developing personal favorites (including outstanding employees) or exhibiting personal prejudices and dislikes. Real self-discipline is required to deal with all personnel with honest objectivity.

Self-Discipline and Work Habits

Subordinates cannot be expected to discipline themselves in terms of good work habits if the example set by management is one of poor work habits. The manager must discipline himself to be punctual, timely with his assignments, thorough, orderly and accurate, knowing that subordinates notice far more than one might suspect. Supervisors live in glass houses on the job.

Self-Discipline and Humility

The effective manager will never hesitate to acknowledge his own errors. He is not going to be right every time, and the rest of the organization knows it. He should not be embarrassed to say, "I don't know." Although it requires self-discipline, the manager should not be hesitant to ask others, including subordinates, for their opinions, knowing that they may have some ideas better than his own.

SUMMARY

Discipline is training that corrects, molds and strengthens an employee, at all levels in the organization, in the interest of achieving departmental and company goals. Constructive discipline is *positive,* focusing on correct action rather than on personalities; on the act, not the employee.

In the security organization, discipline is primarily the responsibility of the supervisor. Effective discipline begins with effective communication and full understanding of what is required. Its purpose is *corrective training, not punishment.*

The basic rules of the disciplinary process are: (1) put rules in writing; (2) discipline in privacy; (3) be objective and consistent; (4) do not humiliate the employee; (5) keep a record of infractions and disciplinary action; and (6) exercise discipline promptly.

Effective discipline will find its model in the Security Manager's own self-discipline and restraint.

REVIEW QUESTIONS

1. Define *constructive discipline.*
2. Give several possible reasons for misunderstood assignments.
3. Discuss the six basic rules of the disciplinary process.
4. Why is it a good idea to keep a file of employee infractions?

11

Motivation and Morale

The question of how to motivate employees to do more and better work and how to keep them happy and interested in their work remains a constant challenge to management, a project for researchers, and a thesis subject for academicians. What motivates one person may not motivate another. Motivators that are effective in one industry may be out of the question in another. For example, you cannot motivate a security officer to write more citations in order to win a free trip to Hawaii, but that type of motivation is used in real estate and other types of sales companies.

There is even disagreement over whether that free trip to Hawaii is a motivator. Some management theorists argue that it is an inducement or a carrot on the end of a stick that keeps employees producing at levels predetermined by management. Others say, "Call it what you will, it gets the job done, and when he gets to Hawaii, his morale will be way up there." An opposing view holds that, if you take away the "carrot," fundamentally good people will produce at the same level and poor performers will still be poor performers (they never won the Hawaiian trip anyway). The latter position suggests that perhaps motivation is internalized as opposed to externalized; that is, motivation comes from within the person and not from without. If that is the case, is it really possible to motivate another?

"THEORY X" AND "THEORY Y"

Before we attempt to deal with that question and others about motivation, morale, and human behavior on the job, we should have some understanding and insight into classical studies that have gone before us. For example, Douglas McGregor's "Theory X" and "Theory Y" are remarkably pervasive assumptions about human nature and behavior. The first three, which still have far too much acceptance in our society today, McGregor calls "Theory X" assumptions:[1]

---

[1] Davis, Keith, *Human Relations at Work.* Third Edition. (McGraw-Hill, 1967).

"Theory X" Assumptions

1. The average human being has an inherent dislike of work and will avoid it if he can.
2. Because of their dislike of work, most people must be coerced, controlled, directed, and threatened with punishment to get them to put forth adequate effort toward the attainment of organizational objectives.
3. The average human being prefers to be directed, wishes to avoid responsibility, has relatively little ambition, and wants security above all.

In contrast to the autocratic approach to employees reflected in "Theory X," McGregor's "Theory Y" encourages managers to be supportive of their employees.

"Theory Y" Assumptions

1. The average human being does not inherently dislike work. The expenditure of physical and mental effort in work is as natural as play or rest.
2. External control and the threat of punishment are not the only means of bringing about effective organizational effort. Man will exercise self-direction and self-control in seeking to obtain goals to which he has committed himself.
3. Part of the rewards of achievement are found in the ego satisfaction and self-fulfilling aspects of the individual commitment.
4. The average individual, under the proper conditions, learns not only to accept but to seek responsibility.
5. The capacity to exercise a relatively high degree of imagination, ingenuity and creativity in seeking to solve an organizational problem is quite widely distributed throughout the population.
6. Under the conditions that exist in today's industrial and economic life, the intellectual potential of the average person is only partially tapped.

Again, "Theory X" is *not* an unpopular theory today. Those who put credence in these three assumptions would have very little interest, if any, in motivation.

On the other hand, the assumptions of "Theory Y," certainly a positive and enlightened approach, suggest areas that might indeed "motivate" employees. But before we examine those suggested areas, let us look at another classical work, dealing this time with organizational behavior instead of human behavior. The three theories of organizational behavior are The Autocratic Theory, The Custodial Theory, and The Supportive Theory.[2]

---

[2] *Ibid.*

ORGANIZATIONAL BEHAVIOR

The Autocratic Theory

The Autocratic Theory has its roots deep in history, dating back to the Industrial Revolution of the mid-eighteenth century. The theory is based on absolute power. It tends to be threatening, relying on *negative* motivation backed by power. The managerial posture is one of formal and official authority.

In practice this theory means that management knows best, and it is the employees' obligation to follow orders without question. ("Yours is not to question why. Yours is but to do or die.") Employees need to be persuaded and prodded into performance, not led. Management does the thinking and employees do what they are told. Management has absolute control over the employee. The Autocratic approach is a useful way to get work done and therefore has some merit. Though just a step above the slave-master work relationship, it was the dominant and prevailing theory until very recent times. The Autocratic approach did build transcontinental railroads, run giant steel mills, and in general produced the dynamic industrial economy of the early part of this century.

The Autocratic approach gets results, but only moderate results, and does so at high human costs. And the theory does nothing to develop human potential in an organization.

The Custodial Theory

The Custodial Theory depends upon company wealth to provide economic benefits for the employee. These come in the form of pensions, insurance, medical benefits, salary increases, etc. The managerial posture or orientation is towards tangible benefits. The employee relies on the company for security instead of on the boss, as in the Autocratic Theory. The aim is to make the employee happy, contented, and adjusted to the work environment.

This approach does not motivate employees to produce anywhere near their capacity, nor are they motivated to develop their full capabilities. Consequently, employees fail to feel genuinely fulfilled or challenged on the job. Thus they must look elsewhere, such as to the bowling team or any other outside activity that holds their interest.

The Supportive Theory

The Supportive Theory depends upon leadership. Through such leadership management provides a climate in which an employee may grow and achieve those things of which he is capable—to his own benefit as well as the company's. When management creates this type of supportive work climate, employees will take on responsibility, strive to contribute to the organization, and work at improving their own skills and performance. The employees in this climate tend to think in terms of "we" rather than "they," and organizational objectives become "our" objectives. Ideally, under this approach, the employee needs little supervision. The primary need is for the employee to tell his supervisor what kind of support he needs from that supervisor in order to do a better job.

WORK MOTIVATION THEORY

McGregor's "Theory Y" assumptions and the Supportive Theory of Organizational Behavior are the basis of an enlightened approach to motivation. With those as a backdrop, let us now consider Frederick Herzberg's Work Motivation Theory, a meaningful and outstanding work of recent times.[3]

Dr. Herzberg's position is essentially that motivation—genuine work motivation—comes from the work itself, not from those factors or "things" such as salary and job security that surround the work itself. He breaks down the job into two basic categories: (1) the job surroundings, or "hygiene" factors, and (2) the job itself and its motivators.

The Job Surroundings	*The Job Itself*
Hygiene or	Motivators
"Maintenance Factors"	
• Pay	• Responsibility
• Status	• Achievement
• Policy and	• Recognition
administration	
• Interpersonal	• Advancement
relationships	
• Benefits	• Growth
• Supervision	
• Working conditions	
• Job security	

According to Dr. Herzberg, hygiene factors do not lead to work satisfaction or happiness; rather, they lead to *dissatisfaction* more often than not, whereas the work motivators are the primary cause of *satisfaction*. Further,

---

[3] Herzberg, Frederick, "One More Time: How Do You Motivate Employees?" *Harvard Business Review*, January–February, 1968.

hygiene factors are *expected;* that is to say, good pay and periodic increases are expected, and so are benefits, good supervision and good working conditions. All are *expected once they have been given.* Certainly if there had been no dental plan, for example, and the company introduced a dental plan, everyone would be pleased. Included in their conversations would be remarks like "It's about time. So-and-so's had a dental plan for years now." Next year they will expect some new benefit—perhaps eye care. The point is, employees are not motivated to produce more for any extended period of time, nor do they find satisfaction in their daily work, as a result of factors which surround the work.

Real motivation, then, comes from the work itself and those motivating factors that are intrinsic to the job. Let us analyze how such factors fit into the security environment.

Responsibility As a Motivator in Security

Genuine responsibility is perhaps the most important motivator, and in the security environment, unlike many other types of work environments, real responsibility can be a significant factor in an employee's work. Responsibility in this context includes such things as problem-solving, decision-making and accountability.

Why is security "unlike many other types of work environments"? The answer is that relatively few departments or jobs within departments deal with unusual, erratic or criminal human behavior, few deal with accidents or other emergency conditions, and fewer still *plan* to deal with such conditions. It stands to reason, then, that the security employee who is indeed given the opportunity to solve problems revolving around behavior or emergency situations, *before or after the fact,* really has responsibility. Those security employees who are permitted or are obliged to make decisions as to what to do or not to do when criminal or unusual human behavior occurs or when catastrophe strikes, really have responsibility.

If such responsibility is built into the security job, then, one might assume that all security people, by virtue of their chosen vocation, are motivated. Unfortunately, this is not the case, because many security people are given a "sense" of responsibility, which is quite different from *real* responsibility. When the chips are down, the real decisions come from above; the problems are solved by someone higher up, and no real accountability exists. For example, an officer is placed on a surveillance position with binoculars and is told, "Harry, we have information that a thief is going to penetrate our facility sometime tonight. You are responsible for this fence line and this side of the facility. We've got to catch this guy tonight, and I'm counting on you."

Does Harry have real responsibility in this assignment? At this point it sounds as if he does, but let the supervisor complete his instructions to

Harry: "If you spot the guy climbing over, cutting through, or slipping under your section of the line, immediately contact Sgt. Green on your radio and he'll get there quick and take over."

Harry has no real responsibility here; Sgt. Green has. If you want to *motivate* Harry, then give him the responsibility to capture the thief. Give him a back-up man, a peer who will respond to the radio call that penetration is being made, or match him up with a partner and charge the two with the responsibility of apprehending anyone who penetrates their assigned area. That is responsibility. They will decide when and how to move in on the thief. That problem is theirs and theirs only, and if they apprehend or lose the thief, they are totally accountable.

Similarly, giving a security supervisor the responsibility to plan for a specific segment of an upcoming special event (say the traffic flow and parking connected with the visit of foreign royalty) is, in and of itself, an exciting challenge and a motivator. But if the supervisor's manager changes the plans, not because they are wrong but because the manager prefers his way over the subordinate's (and this is common), the so-called responsibility turns out to be only a facade. In fact, it becomes a *demotivator,* inspiring indifference and breeding suspicion of future assignments.

Most security personnel crave responsibility and have the capacity to assume more than most administrators are willing to believe. Give them as much responsibility as possible and let their work motivate them to peaks of achievement.

Achievement As a Motivator

Group and collective success is certainly important to the employee who is a member of the group. But the employee, from a personal work motivation point of view, must have the opportunity to be singularly successful, even if it is but a small success or achievement. The investigator who "breaks" a case, or the store detective who catches a shoplifter, experiences the full joy of achievement. *He* did it! And each achievement tends to drive the employee on to another.

More frequently than not, achievement comes through one form or another of problem-solving. Thus, the supervisor or administrator who recognizes achievement as a motivator will provide subordinates with the opportunity to solve a problem, to come up with the answer or to catch the thief, for the motivational benefits that success brings. Opportunities, as such, are almost limitless. As an example, ask an employee if he could design a better case history form for arrestees, or an improved filing and index system for security records—any assignment within the limits of the employee's capabilities that will provide a chance for him to truly accomplish something, to be able to say proudly, "I did that," or "That's mine!"

Recognition of Achievement As a Motivator

Rare is the person who is not motivated by praise, flattery, or any other complimentary form of recognition. To say "well done" goes a long way. Not to say "well done," when it is due, goes a long way, too, but the wrong way. It is a demotivator.

Growth As a Motivator

Growth is the consequence of expanding one's horizons, increasing insight brought about by an ever-widening variety of experiences, gathering in new ideas, concepts and information, coping with new situations and problems. All of these factors increase the individual's personal and professional growth.

Thus it behooves security management to provide a work climate that not only allows for growth, but encourages it. If there is a local security seminar, send as many people as possible. If there are local security associations, encourage appropriate members of the department to join and be active. As new assignments and problems surface, do not always call on the same already proven members of the staff to handle them. Assign someone who has not had that kind of experience so he will have the benefit of the new challenge and subsequent growth. Rotate your people around the organization rather than developing specialists in narrow areas. Rotation provides for growth. Encourage non-college graduates to return to school on a part-time basis.

Care for, water and feed your people as a gardener tends his garden, and you can actually see them "grow" before your eyes. And that growth motivates them to be achievers, ever seeking more responsibility.

Advancement As a Motivator

Opportunities to move up in the department (or in another department of the company) must be clearly visible and, in the eyes of the individual, personally attainable. If vertical movement (real or imaginary) is not apparent, then the persons who seek responsibility—the achievers, the ones who have grown and are growing—will be moved by their inner motivation to seek advancement elsewhere. Ideally, advancements should be occurring throughout the organization frequently, from interdepartmental promotions to advancements to supervisory posts in other departments, to managerial positions in security departments of corporate sister companies. Such movement is motivational in and of itself.

More production, more creative contributions to the organization, more loyalty, and more dedication to excellence in performance have a better chance of actually happening in that work environment which embraces McGregor's "Theory Y," the Supportive Theory of Organizational Development, and Herzberg's Work Motivation Theory. The department and the organization can only profit when they recognize the value of human dignity and the creative and productive potential of their employees, and then give them room to work and to breathe.

DEMOTIVATORS

Naturally there is a very close relationship between motivation and morale. Highly motivated people enjoy good morale, and vice versa. Dr. Mortimer R. Feinberg, Ph.D., Professor of Psychology at the Baruch School of Business and Public Administration, has identified a number of factors that can have dramatic negative impact on employees. He calls these factors the Ten Deadly Demotivators. Every security supervisor, manager and administrator should be familiar with them.[4]

1. *Never belittle a subordinate.*
    Do not subject any employee to the ultimate put-down by calling him stupid. He might apply the term to himself for some careless mistake, but the manager should not. Generally speaking, you can call an employee almost anything else—lazy, sloppy, slipshod—and he will accept the criticism well enough. But calling him stupid will not only deflate his ego but will undermine his initiative. How can a stupid man be ambitious or enthusiastic?
2. *Never criticize a subordinate in front of others.*
    A reprimand delivered in the privacy of your office will be accepted. The same criticism delivered in front of the employee's coworkers will breed quick resentment. You have mortified the employee in front of his or her friends—and that is unforgiveable. Like most of Feinberg's Ten Deadly Demotivators, this rule is or should be familiar to all managers. When it is forgotten in a moment of anger or haste, the damage can be permanent.
3. *Never fail to give your subordinates your full attention, at least occasionally.*
    On the positive side, making each employee feel that you care about him personally is a strong motivator. Have each employee in your office occasionally—and give him your undivided attention. Have your secretary hold your calls. If you allow interruptions, lose the train of thought and have to say, "Now then, Fred, what is it you were saying

---

[4] Feinberg, Mortimer R., *Effective Psychology for Managers* (Englewood Cliffs, N.J.: Prentice-Hall, Inc., 1966), pp. 127–131.

about your family?" you will be telling Fred that you do not really care.

4. *Never give your subordinates the impression that you are primarily concerned with your own interests.*

 While your personal goals may very well be your primary concern, it is a mistake to allow your employees to think that you are "using" them for your own selfish ends. For example, if you have a subordinate work late to finish a project that will make you look good to *your* superiors, make a point of sharing the credit for getting the job done. You will still look good—not only to higher management but also to your subordinate.

5. *Never play favorites.*

 This is another cardinal rule of supervision, but—human nature being what it is—it is one of the most frequently broken. The moment you start playing favorites, especially when the person in question has been playing up to you to gain favored status, you will antagonize the rest of the staff. Dr. Feinberg cites an example that illustrates this point well.

> A supervisor regarded as "autocratic" was accused of playing favorites. He would not let any of the secretaries in his office get away with anything, except for one. He never chastised or criticized this particular secretary, even though she was notorious for spending a lot of time making personal telephone calls. His reason was that she often stayed at the office late in order to get work done. (Naturally, this was because she wasted so much time during the day.) The rest of the secretarial staff knew that the supervisor was being manipulated, and they resented it. Consequently, the girls became demotivated.[5]

6. *Never fail to help your subordinates grow—when they are deserving.*

 When employees feel that a supervisor is on their side, and will even fight for them if necessary—in the matter of obtaining raises that are deserved, for example—they will be more loyal and more strongly motivated. Support your employees in their attempts to grow, even if it means that you might lose a good man to another department. If you stand in his way, you will probably lose him anyway. Once an employee believes you are not on his side, he will be demotivated.

7. *Never be insensitive to small things.*

 Avoid loose or rash statements—you may regret them later. In one company a department manager, on being told that one worker was unhappy and might quit, responded, "Let him—we won't miss a beat"— the statement being accompanied by a contemptuous snap of the fingers. The comment was repeated and became known to the other em-

---

[5] *Ibid.,* p. 129.

ployees, who began using it as a mocking refrain. The statement said quite clearly, "The employee doesn't matter." In another example given by Dr. Feinberg, a supervisor known for his terrible temper roared to an employee one day, "I don't care how long you've been with this firm. Seniority means nothing in my department." This particular company had been non-union for the 75 years of its existence, but, exploiting this rash comment, the union finally won a foothold. Its slogan was, "Seniority means nothing."

By the same token, consideration in small things, from remembering to inquire about an employee's wife's illness to congratulating him on his son's graduation, will increase his loyalty and desire to work for you.

8. *Never "show up" employees.*
    This rule is closely related to the first two "demotivators." Just as you should not humiliate an employee by calling him stupid or criticizing him in front of others, do not show off at his expense by demonstrating how you can do a particular job better and faster than he can. The manager should be able to perform many tasks better than his subordinates—that is why he is a manager. But it is important to any employee to take some pride in his work. If you take away that pride and self-respect, you will discourage and demotivate him. Training him to do a better job is one thing; embarrassing him is another.

9. *Never lower your personal standards.*
    Care and consideration of employees should not extend to the point of accepting or tolerating inept performance. This will only demotivate the real achievers in the organization. The reasons are summed up in an analysis Dr. Feinberg quotes from the Research Institute of America:

> The mediocrity of colleagues can muzzle the initiative of the dynamic doer who has high standards for his own performance . . . especially when the "mediocres" are permitted to stand on the sidelines and throw darts at new ideas. Management often tolerates a certain percentage of people whom they have given up on . . . men who will never pull their own weight. But if these people are permitted to remain in key positions, just the simple fact of their presence can cost the company the loss of an endless chain of worthwhile people who don't have to work against such odds. And, incidentally, whether they remain on the payroll or leave for greener fields, you've lost a man if he has decided it doesn't pay to knock himself out.[6]

10. *Never vacillate in making a decision.*
    Effective management is characterized by the willingness and ability to make prompt, wise decisions. Every decision involves an element

---

[6] *Ibid.*, p. 131.

of risk—the chance that you could be making a mistake. If your employees see that you lack confidence in your own decisions, because you are afraid to take the risks involved in being a manager, they will be demotivated. Employees draw strength from visible evidence of strong supervision and management. Their initiative can be undermined by evidence of weak or vacillating management.

SUMMARY

Among classical theories of human behavior in the work environment, McGregor's "Theory X" assumptions emphasize negative aspects of employee behavior; his "Theory Y" suggests that employees do not inherently dislike work and will actually seek responsibility and better performance if encouraged to do so. This latter theory provides a more enlightened, modern approach to motivation.

Similarly, the Supportive Theory of work motivation creates a more effective climate for the development of human potential.

Herzberg's Work Motivation Theory stresses the importance of motivators *in the job itself,* as opposed to such "hygiene" factors as pay, benefits, working conditions, etc.

In the security function, effective job motivators include giving the employee real responsibility; providing opportunity for individual achievement and self-satisfaction; recognition of performance; allowing for and encouraging growth; and creating the opportunity for advancement.

Belittling or "showing up" the employee, public criticism, inattention, favoritism, denial of opportunity, insensitivity, lowering standards of performance, or vacillation in decision-making are all "demotivators" which the effective Security Manager will avoid.

REVIEW QUESTIONS

1. Briefly describe the "Theory X" and "Theory Y" assumptions about human behavior.

2. Briefly describe the Autocratic Theory, the Custodial Theory and the Supportive Theory of organizational behavior.

3. According to Herzberg's Work Motivation Theory, what are the motivators that come from the work itself? Why do the job surroundings or "hygiene" factors not lead to work satisfaction?

4. What are some of the ways in which security management can encourage growth among security employees?

5. What are the "Ten Deadly Demotivators"?

12

Promotions

Surprisingly, many employees accept mediocrity in management practices as the rule instead of the exception. The selection of new people for the department, the quality of training, departmental disciplinary standards, motivation efforts, the presence or absence of a structured communication capability—all these have a limited impact on the individual security employee, and consequently meet with limited emotional reaction from him.

This is undoubtedly attributable to the fact that people attracted to the security/law enforcement career field tend to be conservative "rugged individualists" with a high degree of self-discipline. They tend to equate what happens around them with what it means to them personally. They take note of the following: an undiscriminating process for the selection of new employees enhances the existing employee's chances for advancement; an ineffective training program provides the really ambitious security employee, who is willing to train himself, an advantage over the less ambitious; strict or erratic disciplinary standards will punish those who are poorly qualified and poorly trained, not those who are well qualified. And so it goes. Rationalization? Probably. The point is that security people are exceptionally tolerant of management practices; they can and do survive the most difficult job conditions with a minimum of complaint—*except* in the area of promotions.

Employees identify very closely with promotions—"There, but for him, go I." It is a truism that the vast majority of employees have an inflated estimation of their ability and worth. Most feel they are under-used, underpaid, and could quite easily do their supervisor's job, and even do it better. Hence, the vertical movement of a peer within the organization is an emotionally charged event, scrutinized with intensity and, unfortunately, with suspicion.

Obviously, then, management's objective in the promotion process is to identify and promote the best qualified candidate, *with resultant general acceptance and approval of the promotion.* That is both a goal and a formidable challenge.

IDENTIFYING PROMOTIONAL CANDIDATES

There is as much excitement among security management personnel in their role in the promotion process as there is among the ranks. The appointment of a new supervisor or promotion of a supervisor to a position of greater responsibility in most cases has a personal effect on existing managers and supervisors. Naturally, they want the best and most effective person moved up.

In identifying candidates, there is a tendency to get mired down in qualities desired or "qualifications" that should not be at issue. Such factors as one's educational achievements, ability to articulate, popularity, the "halo effect" of some recent incident, and length of service should be considered at some later point but should not be the initial qualifying considerations.

There are two basic qualification factors to be considered in selecting candidates for supervisory or managerial responsibility: (1) the employee's track record in job performance, and (2) the anticipated or expected performance in the higher level job. Other factors are peripheral in nature.

That is not to say that college degrees in Security Administration or Criminal Justice, at the Associate, undergraduate or graduate levels, are unimportant. Just the opposite is true. Continued higher education in the field must be indicative of professional growth as well as motivation. But, as important as growth and motivation are, they follow proven performance and anticipated performance as promotional considerations . . . as long as anticipated performance is based on some known qualitative factors.

The Candidate's Track Record

Employees whose service and job performance are rated as "above average" or "above acceptable standards" would constitute the first group of candidates. A rating of "average" performance or "meets acceptable standards" should, as a rule, disqualify the remaining peers. This is because the highly desirable quality of being an "achiever" is reflected in regular performance evaluations of above average. Average workers are doers. Above average workers are achievers; they obviously go above and beyond what is expected. By most employee performance evaluation standards, they "frequently exceed requirements of the job," always through their own initiative. (Incidentally, employees rated as "outstanding" performers are defined as those who *"consistently* exceed job requirements" as opposed to "frequently.") So the achievement-oriented employee meets the first of the two criteria.

Anticipated Performance in the Higher Level Job

The tentative candidates (the achievers) must now be analyzed, one at a time, as to how they might measure up to or perform against standards of the higher position in question. If the open position requires scheduling employees, for example, those assessing a candidate must look back on his prior performance for evidence of some demonstrated behavior or action indicating that the candidate could indeed schedule subordinates (which would include schedule revisions, emergency scheduling, appropriate degree of flexibility, etc.). It could be that the candidate has actually done some scheduling at the request of his supervisor. In that case, management could properly anticipate or expect good performance in that area if the candidate is promoted.

More often than not, those attempting to qualify candidates for promotion tend to look for disqualifiers in this anticipatory phase. That is to say, they look for duties that, because of past performance, the tentative candidate could be expected *not* to perform competently in the higher assignment.

Disqualifiers may be identified by management or by the candidate himself. For example, otherwise qualified candidates may disqualify themselves because they do not want to travel or move or do not want shift changes. Some may state frankly that they cannot discipline or evaluate others. Self-disqualification makes management's decision easier.

It is important to note that disqualifiers, as such, should be valid for one time only. Any number of things can happen to change circumstances between promotional opportunities. Management should never assume that an earlier disqualifier still stands.

The most difficult task is the projection that the candidate is not able or qualified to perform the higher job. If, for any reason, that disqualification is subject to question or is not the unanimous decision of security management, then the candidate should not be disqualified. He should move on to the actual competition with the other qualified candidates.

What has not been stated, but should be evident, is that the promotional opportunity is common knowledge; it is not a secret. Thus, when the announcement does come, it is no surprise. Most people do not like surprises in the work environment and react negatively to them. In the process of identifying candidates for the promotion, a healthy and open climate about promotions is established.

SELECTION OF THE RIGHT CANDIDATE

The best selection process comes in the form of a Promotion Board. The Board, preferably three in number, should always have as members the successful candidate's immediate superior, a person who will be a peer of the successful candidate, and someone from the next higher rank above the successful candidate's superior. If the promotion is for a sergeant's position, for example, the Board would include one sergeant, the lieutenant for whom the new sergeant will work, and the lieutenant's captain. The Board's chairman, as such, would be the lieutenant because the promotion will affect him most directly.

The Board members, except the tie-breaking chairman, should be considered as equals; thus, the captain's will does not prevail because of his rank. The lieutenant, on the other hand, assumes leadership in this case. Leadership includes responsibility because, as stated above, the selectee will be his immediate subordinate, and a very important subordinate at that.

A frequent problem in promotions has been the exclusion of the promoted person's new superior from the decision. If the lieutenant was not involved in the selection of his new sergeant, he may disagree with (if not resent) the decision, with the result that he may not work at making the new sergeant successful. And it does require effort from the superior to make a newly promoted employee successful. Subordinates, especially those moving for the first time into new and unfamiliar responsibilities, must have direction and leadership from their boss, or they may fail. The truth is, some secret pleasure is taken in such failures. In our example, it is a way for the overlooked lieutenant to strike back at management for not including him in the selection of his own people; it is a way of saying, "I-told-you-so."

On the other hand, if the man who is responsible for the new promotee is involved in and responsible for the selection, he is bound to do all he can to make that selection a successful one.

From the time the appropriate supervisors are asked for possible candidates, through the screening and identifying of those to appear before the Board, to the day of the actual Board interview itself, not more than ten days should pass. Delays and silence about who has been selected to appear and who is to receive the promotion are counterproductive. They breed suspicion.

THE BOARD INTERVIEW

Nothing can be done to ease the anxiety of the candidate on the appointed day, and perhaps that small amount of stress is acceptable as long as it is not purposefully designed into the process. This interview is an important event in an employee's career and life; he will come spruced up as he has rarely appeared before—and more nervous than he has ever been before.

Because some degree of anxiety is normal, the Board should seek to enable the candidate to relax as much as possible after he has been ushered into the room used for this event. Rather than a very formal civil service type arrangement (single chair poised in front of a table behind which sits the "oral" board), the Board members should be arranged in an informal setting of chairs and/or sofa without a table or desk between them and the candidate—similar to a living room or den arrangement.

The same questions, asked the same way, should be put to each of the candidates. General questions should be asked first, such as "Why do you want this promotion?", "Do you feel you are the best candidate for this job and if so, why?", "What special qualities and qualifications do you feel you bring to this job?" Specific job-related questions should follow, along the lines of "What would you do if . . ." and "How would you handle _____ if no one was available to give you direction?"

The answers to the questions will identify the best candidate, and the decision to promote is usually relatively easy.

FOLLOWING THE SELECTION

When a promotion follows the selection process described, the attitude of those candidates interviewed who did not get the promotion is usually one of full acceptance of the decision and appreciation for the opportunity to compete. The attitude of the organization is one of full acceptance of the promotee because he is the best of the candidates and his selection was in no way political. The attitude of management is one of pleasure and confidence that the best candidate was identified in a totally objective fashion and the newest member of the management team is properly qualified.

Other promotion processes have somewhat less to offer than the board approach.

PROMOTION FROM "WITHIN"

Certainly the policy of promoting from within the Security Department should always be followed except when such policy would not serve the best interests of the organization. When would the best interests of the organization not be served under this policy? That situation would arise when an unqualified employee (using the same qualifying criteria outlined earlier in this chapter) is moved up simply to satisfy the "promote-from-within" policy. This type of promotion will destroy, or at least damage, the person promoted; it will automatically impact on departmental performance; and, also of great importance, it will challenge the credibility of the promotional process itself.

If management determines that there is no qualified applicant for a particular post, usually in the higher echelons of the department, then those employees in the rank from which the promotion should come must be advised they fail to qualify for the position and the organization is going to look outside for the necessary talent.

Some employees will initially react against that decision and will ask for specifics as to their deficiencies. They are entitled to such information, which management should know in very specific terms if the candidates were assessed honestly and the disqualifiers were identified. To share the decision openly and to sit down and talk about it with the employees overshadows the initial resentment and paves the way for the future arrival of the selected "outsider."

If the decision is made to go elsewhere for talent and the organization is *not* advised of that decision, the result will be predictable resistance to the new arrival, as well as broad resentment not only for the new man, but for top security management as well.

VERTICAL PROMOTION OUTSIDE THE DEPARTMENT

There are still many in all levels of management who view promotions as organizationally disruptive. They are secure in the status quo. But the "disruptiveness" of vertical movement breathes life, excitement and motivation into the organization. For that reason, promotions—not only upward within the Security Department, but in the company as well—should be explored and encouraged. The advantage, not only of creating promotional opportunities within the organization, but of having good security people in responsible positions throughout the company (such as in personnel administration) should be obvious.

To purposefully hold people back because it serves the immediate purpose of the security organization is morally wrong. And the company as a whole will benefit when there is opportunity for vertical movement both within the security department and outside of it to other areas of the organization.

ADVANTAGES OF MULTIPLE LAYERS

Perhaps the best example of the organizational advantages of multiple layers of rank is in the military service. Instead of just three layers of the enlisted ranks—private, corporal and sergeant—military organizations have many layers with, at last count, six graded army sergeant ranks alone. That is true, too, in the officer ranks of the military. The obvious advantage is increased opportunity for vertical movement. The more ranks, the more chances one has to move up. The fewer ranks, the less chance—not only in terms of layers to go up through, but in frequency of openings. Obviously, the greater the number of ranks, the more frequency there is in movement.

The organizational levels in one large retail department store chain are far from typical, but its use of multiple layers may still be of value as an illustration. Starting at the lower levels and proceeding upward are the following ranks: Fitting Room Checker, Fitting Room Inspector, Lead Fitting Room Inspector, Security Agent, Special Agent, Resident Special Agent, Senior Special Agent, Special Agent-in-Charge, (Divisional) Chief Special Agent, Security Manager, and Security Director.

Obviously the small security department cannot have as many levels of rank, but within the limitations of size the opportunity for progressive movement should still exist. Truncated structures limit movement and contribute to stagnation and frustration among the ranks. Rather than few layers with big pay jumps, it is best to have more layers with smaller pay differences and more frequent advances.

Today, in our fast-moving society, people need to feel they too are on the move, and multiple layers help to satisfy that need.

"TEMPORARY" PROMOTIONS

An excellent way to measure an employee's potential for higher levels of responsibility is to appoint him temporarily to such posts during natural absences of the regular supervisors or managers—vacations, sickness, leaves of absence, etc. The subordinate's performance while filling in is a measurable indicator of his or her capacity to assume greater responsibility.

Another way to test prospective leaders is to create temporary leadership assignments for special events or projects, appointing one as "team leader" or "project leader" for the duration of the event or project. Not only can they be evaluated, but they also gain the otherwise unavailable experience that comes with increased responsibility. People have been known to excel or to fail under such conditions, and that knowledge can be invaluable to management in future promotion considerations.

"RETREATING"

No matter how carefully an organization approaches the promotional process, mistakes in selection are sometimes made. The question is, what do you do when a person is promoted to a position beyond his ability? The "Peter Principle" (rising to one's level of incompetence) is a well-known management problem because of its common occurrence.

There are but three courses of action available to management upon discovery that an employee has been promoted beyond his level of competence:

1. Permit the employee to continue performing in an incompetent fashion.
2. Terminate the incompetent employee.
3. Allow and arrange for a "retreat" back to the former rank.

Option number one, although frequently exercised, is unacceptable to a progressive and enlightened management, for three reasons: it is counterproductive to the organization; it affects the morale of the incompetent's subordinates in a very negative way; and, finally (a point often overlooked), the person who has achieved the level beyond his ability knows it as well as anyone else, and that knowledge places him in a dilemma. He knows he is in trouble but does not want to admit it. He struggles. Unhappiness sets in. Some actually become physically ill because of the dilemma. It is a rare individual who can come forward and admit he is in trouble. The tragedy is that most will not admit it.

Option number two is another popular solution. The tragedy here is that management is culpable, too. The man promoted beyond his ability was certainly competent at the lower rank. In fact, his skill level and performance evaluation were above average. He was a good worker. He is not inherently an ineffective employee—he is simply ineffective in his new responsibility. To terminate this employee is in part to hide management's mistake in promoting the wrong person.

Option number three, if it can be accomplished, serves the best interests of all concerned. Policies prohibiting voluntary demotions are unrealistic and inhumane. Certainly the man who is willing to retreat to his former rank should be given that opportunity, even though his ego is going to be bruised for a time. The total honesty in "retreat" situations is apparent to all observers. Not only is the salvaging and protection of a man's tenure with the firm important to the misplaced individual, but others in the organization also respond to this humane policy. The first two options are known to the organization; employees have a collective wisdom of some dimension.

"Retreat" should never be a structured or formalized consideration in the promotion process because, by all rights, it should be the tragic exception in organizational life. To say to each candidate, "Well, if you prove incompetent, Harry, you can always go back to the old job," would discredit the selection ability of the Board (or management), would demean the importance of striving for competence by overcoming obstacles, would turn promotions into a gamble instead of a challenge, and would be an insult to the real achiever's confidence and intelligence.

"Retreating" is the emergency valve that should be available for those rare instances when the promotional process fails to hit the mark.

SUMMARY

Because vertical movement in the organization is an emotionally charged event, management's objective in promotion is always to identify and select the best qualified candidate.

Primary qualification factors in promotions are the employee's record of performance in his present job and his projected performance in the advanced position. Current job performance should be above average to be considered for promotion.

A Promotion Board provides the selection process most likely to be fair and objective. In all cases, the supervisor for whom the candidate will be working should be a member of the Promotion Board.

The opportunity for vertical movement elsewhere within the company should not be opposed by security management. Such movement serves both the company and the security organization.

The most effective promotion process is a flexible one. It will not make promotion automatic, but will promote only the qualified candidate; it will accept the necessity to go outside the department in some circumstances to find a qualified employee; and it will also allow for the possibility of "retreat" where an employee proves out of his depth in a higher level position.

REVIEW QUESTIONS

1.   What is management's objective in the promotion process?

2.   What are the two basic qualification factors to be considered in selecting candidates for supervisory responsibility?

3.   What problems can occur if the promoted person's new superior is not involved in the selection decision?

4.   Discuss the advantages of having multiple ranks of employees.

5.   Discuss the relative merits of the three possible courses of action when an employee has been promoted to a position beyond his ability.

13

Communications

Of all the qualities, talents, and skills required of a manager, the art of effective communication must rank first. In fact, all other managerial factors are crystallized by the communication process to form the "whole" administrator and leader. Stated another way, the manager who is a strong communicator is a strong manager, and the manager who is a weak communicator is a weak manager.

Consider this: the manager's task is to get others to do the job *when* he wants it done, *how* he wants it done, *where* he wants it done, and (if he is a good manager) to make them understand *why* he wants it done. Obviously, to translate his desire into the completed task, the manager must communicate the desire, and the employees must understand. If a job is done poorly, not done at all, or done incorrectly, it is usually because the employees *did not understand.* The manager failed, somehow, to communicate clearly.

The example above reflects only one type of communication: verbal—down. Other types of communication to be considered include: verbal—up; written—down; written—horizontal; written—up; verbal—horizontal; and action. These types of communication may take place in an "Open Climate of Communication" or a "Closed Climate of Communication."

TYPES OF COMMUNICATION

Verbal—Down

Traditionally, security organizations generally operate under the Closed Climate of Communication. This is probably due to the quasi-military nature of most security forces. It is easy to visualize the Captain on the bridge of a Navy vessel shouting directions into a tube that terminates deep down in the engine room, and everyone complying with the orders. This type of communication might be called "stovepipe" communication (verbal—down only). "Stovepipe" communication may also occur when the Captain of the Guards passes word down to the officer to lock Gate 36 at 2:00 A.M. As a rule the gate will in fact be locked as required. However effective this method of communication seems, there is an obvious flaw which haunts managers (or Captains): sometimes the gate will be found unlocked. The officer at the bottom end of the "stovepipe" hears the orders, but there he stands silently without the right key!

Ideally, then, management should strive for the development of an Open Climate of Communication.

Verbal—Up

Some readers may feel that the above example, where the officer at the bottom end of the "stovepipe" hears the order, knows he does not have the key, but remains silent, is unreal. All the officer has to do is tell the superior closest to him on the "stovepipe," probably the sergeant, that he does not have the key. This is not likely to happen, however, because the officer knows that if he tells the sergeant he does not have the key, he will be reprimanded for forgetting it or be embarrassed or abused in some other manner. To protect himself he remains silent, knowing the job will not be done. Rather than feeling free and undefensive and openly communicating to his supervisor (verbal—up) so as to get the job done, he voluntarily chooses to undercut the effectiveness of the organization—all because of the Closed Climate of Communication.

In most cases the organization does not set out to purposefully design a closed climate of communication. The climate is created at the top (the Security Director or Security Manager level) by insensitivity to the importance of communication, including verbal—up.

Written—Down

There is a classic exercise or game which dramatically points out the unreliability of spoken communications. A group of people are seated around a room. Instructions, or a short story, are whispered to the first person. He, in turn, repeats in a whisper what he heard to the next person, and so on. It is hilarious to hear the last person in that room speak out loud what he or she was told—but the reality which this game illustrates can be tragic as well, because, in any organization, many failures are attributable to the misunderstanding of directions.

There are many factors in the breakdown of verbal communications:

- People tend to hear what they want to hear.
- Generalizations are narrowed to specifics.
- Different words mean different things to different people.
- The spoken emphasis on a word or phrase can be interpreted differently by the listener, so that he assumes a different meaning than the speaker intended.

It stands to reason that there is less chance for error in understanding the written word. Not only is there less chance for error, there is more acceptance and credibility in the written word, especially in organizational life. How often does one hear, "I want to see it in writing?"

Logically, then, everything that can be reduced to writing should be. General orders, post orders, patrol orders, inspection instructions, rules and regulations which are to be enforced, rules and regulations governing the Security Department, investigative procedures, emergency procedures, alarm procedures and other appropriate material and data can and should be in writing and available to members of the department.

Should all such written material be distributed to all security personnel? Probably not. All written material will fall into three categories: "Nice to Know," "Should Know," and "Need to Know." Certainly every member of the department should be provided with the "Should Know" and "Need to Know" material.

Written material should always be put into a standardized format. For example, Orders of the Day should always be on the same size and color of paper, in the same print, with the same distinctive appearance. In this way it is recognizable at a distance as an Order of the Day. The same should be true of all other written material. Standardized formats reduce confusion, make for easier organization, and give a professional touch to the department.

Department Handbook or Manual

The need for a departmental "How-to" handbook should be apparent to any Security Manager or Director. Even a small security organization typically faces the problem of relatively high turnover of personnel as well as the need for changing or rotating assignments. And as the department grows and specific roles become more specialized, the need for standardized procedures becomes even more essential. One store chain's handbook, or manual, contains an assortment of detailed instructional materials, such as a standardized confession format, investigative steps to follow in tracking a "shopping violation," and the proper procedure to follow in processing restitution from an employee's terminal wages.

The manual need not be fancy or pretentious. Many organizations use a loose-leaf format, making it easy to add or change pages as needs change.

What is important is to develop a departmental handbook that will be a truly functional tool—one that will be *used,* providing quick instruction for the new employee or the guard assigned to a new post, spelling out procedures to be followed in any given situation, serving as a source of authority to settle disagreements or resolve confusion—especially valuable where there is wide geographic dispersal of personnel, such as in a large manufacturing plant or a chain of stores.

Ideally, the security handbook or manual should also be part of the company's general managers' manual. In this way not only will security people be provided with written material about their organization and job, but so will management. Everyone will be speaking the same language.

Departmental Newsletter

In an organization with a closed climate of communication, there is a reluctance to reduce policies and procedures to writing, or, if they are put down on paper, a reluctance to make such material available to the employees.

The "written—down" type of communication goes beyond policies, procedures and how-to's. A departmental newspaper or newsletter is an excellent communication medium. In one security organization, *The Rap Sheet* is an eight- to twelve-page monthly written for the general interest of Security Department employees. A typical issue will carry a general motivational or good management techniques statement from the Director; a "Security Officer of the Month" article, with picture; a listing of promotions and transfers; an "In Response to You" column (sort of a "Dear Abby" column answered by the Security Director); pending or new laws that will have an impact on the organization; interesting arrests and/or investigations; interesting security statistics such as arrests for the year to date against last year's figures; a security question of the month, with the answer to the previous month's question; a security-oriented puzzle, and perhaps a security cartoon.

The benefits of this type of communication are innumerable. Employees more closely identify with the organization and feel a part of the department. They appreciate being kept abreast of the latest happenings; they are, in fact, well-informed. They love the recognition afforded them in print. The Director has a vehicle to make known his standards and goals. In the eyes of the company and its non-security employees, the polished security publication is another indicator of the professionalism growing in the industry today.

Written—Horizontal

An example of written—horizontal communications is a company-wide security newsletter, providing the security administrator with the magnificent opportunity to communicate what is happening in the security world to the company as a whole. Too often, security departments are considered mysterious and organizationally non-contributory functions. The good security administrator can bring recognition to his department by opening up communications and sharing information with management of the company whenever possible.

As an example, one retail security organization publishes a monthly *Security Newsletter for Management*. The objective of this publication is to make management personnel aware of the security risks and security achievements in the industry. This simple, clean-looking four-page newsletter opens with a series of condensed incidents of recent occurrence in the retail community at large. One typical incident:

> In a competitor's store in the downtown area, four adults of Latin descent, two male and two female, entered the women's sportswear area. While one of the females engaged the saleswoman in a complicated transaction, her companions removed a total of ten fur-trimmed suede coats from the racks. Techniques used: the woman rolled four coats and crotched them (placed them under her dress and held them between her thighs), and each of the men wrapped three coats around his mid-section under a raincoat. All four escaped in a white Ford station wagon bearing out-of-state license plates. Total loss: $1,700.

That story is followed by others, still concentrating on attacks against competitor stores. These might include incidents of malicious mischief (juveniles setting off sprinkler heads, with resultant water damage), use of stolen credit cards, etc.

Following these are incidents within the company, chosen for dramatic impact. Again, the objective is to make management aware of security problems and the Security Department's efforts and successes in these problem areas of the business.

Among the incidents described are stories of recent employee dishonesty cases (names of employees are omitted). Each of these vignettes concludes with information on the disposition of the incident, such as termination of an employee or police department booking. Figure 13.1 illustrates a typical page from the newsletter.

Unit managers not only read each and every word of each publication, but they circulate the newsletter to their staff members and then read it aloud at departmental manager meetings. Discussions follow. The monthly impact remains constant: renewed amazement at the scope of the security problems; amazement over cleverness in tactics; shock at the constancy of internal theft problems.

The end result is greater security awareness within the organization.

Written—Up

In recognition of the need for employees to communicate upward (and the need is as much for the Director to know what is on the minds of his subordinates as it is for every employee to have the opportunity to express himself). *The Rap Sheet* already mentioned was originally designed as a two-way communication tool: written—down and written—up.

How was this accomplished? The first, opening edition of *The Rap Sheet* stated that, in an effort to further open communications, questions, suggestions and complaints were solicited from all security employees, with

```
DISHONEST        Region I
EMPLOYEE
                 A member of the Housekeeping staff was observed leaving
                 store with a bucket and mop on his way to clean the Tire
                 Center. His bucket was checked and under the mop was a
                 Craig Stereo cassette tape deck and a Sony AM/FM radio.
                 Employee was escorted back to store where he subsequently
                 admitted theft and was terminated.

DISHONEST        Region I
EMPLOYEE
HANDOUT          An employee in Jr. World had a friend come into department.
                 The friend selected a top and a pair of pants and went into
                 the fitting room. Once her friend had entered the bank of
                 fitting rooms, the employee stood at the entrance and acted
                 as a lookout. When the accomplice emerged from the fitting
                 room she had only the pair of pants. After a brief conver-
                 sation between the two, the accomplice left the store. The
                 accomplice was later arrested in one of the Mall stores
                 where she worked. The employee was terminated and both
                 were booked by the Culver City Police Department.

ATTEMPTED        West Covina
GRAB & RUN
                 Night Service Manager, Mr. Smith, prevented a "grab and
                 run." Smith observed a car parked outside the store's door
                 in an unauthorized parking space and took down the license
                 plate number. He then waited around to see what the two
                 males in the car were waiting for. He then observed a
                 male grab an armful of Dept. 50 merchandise. Smith then
                 took after the suspect, whereupon the suspect turned around
                 and threw the merchandise at Smith.

                      License Plate Number:

                      Total Recovery:  $473.00

SHOPLIFTER       Fashion Valley

                 A Roving Security Officer observed a F/C, 5'6", 115 lbs.,
                 34 yrs. old, blonde curly hair and glasses, carrying a
                 stuffed handbag clutched tightly to her side. The "custom-
                 er" exited the store and came back shortly with an empty
                 handbag. The R.S.O. followed the "customer" to the Chil-
                 dren's Department where she rolled a child's robe and gown
                 and placed them in her handbag. On her way out, she stopped
                 in Cosmetics and picked up some lotion which she also put
                 in her purse. The "customer" was apprehended as she exited
                 the store.

                 During interrogation she confessed to having made several
                 trips into the            as well as other mall stores. Over
                 $600.00 worth of merchandise was recovered...$500.00 from
                           and the remainder from      and         .  She
                 was arrested and booked by the San Diego Police Department
                 for Grand Theft.
```

Figure 13.1   Typical page from *Security Newsletter for
Management.*

the promise that *every* such question, suggestion or complaint would be
answered. The response was gratifying.

Not all suggestions are adopted. Not all problems are solved. But all
receive response. All employees have a way, without putting themselves
in jeopardy, to have their say, to be heard by the Director and to hear
what he has to say in response.

If an Open Climate of Communication is to be established, some such
two-way avenue of expression is essential.

Verbal—Horizontal

There are two types of verbal—horizontal communications within the context of our definition of an Open Climate of Communication. The first is intradepartmental (i.e., security personnel only) and the second involves communications with other departments in the company.

"Rap sessions" constitute the interdepartmental type. One such session might have given sub-units of the Security Department, such as the Fraud Unit, sit down together without regard to rank and talk about their work— the practices, techniques, problems, failures and successes—with no specific objective in mind except to communicate. As a rule, something of value will surface in these sessions. This could be anything from a clarification of a misunderstanding between two peers to a more realistic deadline on certain types of cases. The important result is that all participants leave the session with a good feeling about themselves, their unit, and the Security Department as a whole. As individuals, they had a chance to be heard, a chance to think out loud, a chance to be themselves.

The second type of horizontal verbal communication occurs when the Security Director and any number of his staff people go out into the company and meet with various units. These meetings are also "sit-down-around-the-table-and-talk" sessions. In these settings questions are encouraged and Security speaks openly and honestly to the questions.

The benefits of broader communications within the company are invaluable. Questions such as "What right does Security have in searching our briefcases and parcels when we leave the building?" give Security the opportunity to cite the authority and talk about the *why's.* Perhaps not every person will be satisfied with the reasons, but they will leave such meetings with more understanding and appreciation for security. This assignment calls for a security representative who is comfortable and at ease in this type of challenging environment. How he handles questions and complaints can leave a very favorable impression on participants in attendance—or a very negative impression.

Communication, then, is the very lubricant that makes the managerial machinery run smoothly and efficiently.

Action

It is true that action speaks louder than words. The administrator who wants to establish a climate of open communications had better be prepared both to listen and to respond.

If management is sincere in wanting suggestions from employees about the running of the Security Department, it stands to reason that some of their ideas will have merit. In fact, the Security Manager will find it a constant source of amazement to see how smart and creative so many people are.

Some managers feel that "I am the boss, and I should have all the workable ideas!" This attitude is shortsighted, but unfortunately a not too uncommon managerial disease.

So, if you ask for ideas, you must adopt some—the ones that are meaningful and contribute to the success of the organization. If you ask for complaints, then you must be prepared to take appropriate corrective action to cure those complaints.

If you reject sound ideas, you will discover over a period of time that the source of ideas within the organization has dried up; there will be no more upward communication. If you are critical of questions or are unresponsive or evasive, the questioning will taper away to nothing; no more upward communication. And if you disregard the message contained in complaints and fail to react in a positive and corrective way, you will lose the benefit of hearing what is troubling personnel. An example in this connection would be the case where the Director hears from a number of employees that a certain supervisor engages in heavy-handed supervisory techniques and intimidates his subordinates. If the Director disregards such information and takes no action, or even promotes the supervisor in question, the credibility of his Open Climate of Communication becomes a joke. If, on the other hand, the Director causes the supervisor to be exposed to a leadership training program, his credibility and his communication "program" are maintained.

SUMMARY

Communication ranks at the top of the effective manager's skills. Both the organization and its employees will be better served by an Open Climate of Communication, both upward and downward, whether verbal or written.

Better understanding is assured when communications are in writing wherever possible. Written-down communications might include the essential Department Handbook as well as departmental newsletters. Avenues should also be provided for *written-up* communications, in which the employees have the opportunity to express their ideas and feelings to management.

Horizontal communications, both within the department and between Security and other employees and units of the company, are mutually beneficial. And an Open Climate of Communication will remain viable and credible only when management listens—and responds.

REVIEW QUESTIONS

1. What is meant by "stovepipe" communication? Give an example of the shortcomings of this type of communication.

2.   Discuss several factors in the breakdown of verbal communications.

3.   Briefly describe two types of newsletters that might be effective communications tools for the Security Department.

4.   Discuss the ways in which a security manager can establish an Open Climate of Communications in his department.

5.   Describe two types of "horizontal" communications and their potential benefits.

14

Career vs. Non-Career Personnel

The question of utilizing career or non-career personnel to discharge the security function within a given organization, with the respective advantages and disadvantages of each, is worthy of examination.

"Career" personnel may be defined as full-time (usually on a forty-hour work week) in-house employe ⌐ on a "career path," with apparent intentions and aspirations to grow in the organization, in the security career field or in another career field within the company (such as personnel services). "Career path" means, in this context, a track leading to continual vertical movement within the greater organizational pyramid.

There are two major categories of "non-career" personnel: (1) in-house part-time employees with a short work week such as twenty hours; (2) employees of another company who perform duties for the organization on a contractual or service fee basis.

At the outset it must be understood that many factors have an impact on the type of personnel to be used in the security function. The most important factor is the character and nature of the function itself. What could very well be an advantage in one security operation might be a distinct disadvantage in another. Yet, the following somewhat generalized categorization should provide some insight into the differences between career and non-career personnel.

The title of this chapter may suggest that an axiomatic choice of one approach over the other will be the ultimate result of the comparison, but that is not the case. Rather, an objective consideration will reveal good points and bad points, advantages and disadvantages, to both career and non-career personnel; and in view of that, the decision to have a *blend* of both might well be the best solution to the security manpower needs of a particular organization.

CAREER PERSONNEL

Advantages of Career Personnel

1. Companies with in-house security programs tend to attract people seeking career positions and career opportunities. Competition for such

openings allows selection of the most qualified individuals. Attractions of career jobs include salary, pension or retirement plans, profit sharing programs, the entire employee "benefit package" (which usually includes medical, hospitalization, dental and life insurance, vacation, and sick leave), and employee privileges unique to the company (such as merchandise discounts in retailing and free or near-free travel for those in the transportation industry).

2. Career personnel develop a loyalty to the department as well as to the company. They identify with the organization and see its welfare as synonymous with their own.

3. Career personnel tend to have greater knowledge of the company, its "ins and outs," and with such insight they function more efficiently and smoothly.

4. Career personnel establish an *esprit de corps* or comradeship, and the resultant pride reflects in their performance.

5. Career personnel tend to be more ambitious and motivated to work due to apparent opportunities for advancement.

6. There is more stability among career personnel in terms of turnover in an organization, primarily because of seniority and vested interest.

7. There is more communication between the security function and the rest of the company when career people are in place, usually because of mutual company identity and common company interests.

8. Career personnel tend to be better trained because training costs are "hidden"; that is, the cost of training is part of salary expense and is not identifiable as an extra expenditure. In the case of contractual service, the time which the contract personnel must spend in on-the-job training with the client company is an added cost.

9. There is a higher degree of technical proficiency among career people because the company is willing to invest the necessary time and money to train them in anticipation of pay-back through long-term service.

Example of the Advantage of Career Personnel: Telephone companies are an excellent example of the many security organizations that utilize career personnel almost exclusively. Telephone company security agents identify closely with their firm, have in-depth knowledge of the telephone communication business, and take pride in their department as well as their employer. They rarely change companies. They know people throughout the company, because in most cases they came from non-security ranks. They are well trained, and, finally, have a high degree of technical proficiency.

Disadvantages of Career Personnel

1. In terms of costs, career personnel are substantially more expensive than non-career people. For example, there is an additional cost of

about thirty percent above and beyond the payroll costs that supports the employee benefit package. Other costs, either capital or sundry, including everything from equipment and office facilities to uniforms (to name but a few), are unavoidable in a career organization. Appreciable savings in this area can usually be realized in contractual agreements because these costs have already been incurred by the contractor.

2. Career personnel constitute a fixed, limited cadre or pool of manpower resources. Special events, special problems or emergencies could well sap the organization and have an adverse impact on the daily security requirements.

3. There is a certain amount of inflexibility in the deployment of career people in terms of location and time scheduling, more frequently than not due to company policy. Personnel policy might require three, five, or seven days' notice of a shift change, which obviously limits security management's flexibility in its attempt to provide protection. Career employees often enjoy "portal to portal" pay and travel time allowance for reporting to a location other than their regular place of work, whereas contract services might have personnel already in place at the distant location, with no loss of time or additional expense.

4. Because of the employee-employer relationship between the career employee and his company, certain disciplinary restrictions can be departmentally counterproductive. The inherent obligation of management to its employees, the source of which is traceable to governmental, administrative and judicial rulings, affords every employee job security—to the point that even those employees who, for one reason or another, perform at a marginal if not substandard level, must be retained for lengthy periods of time prior to their discharge. There is no such employee-employer relationship with non-career people in place.

5. Career manpower resources have limited parameters and ceilings of talent, and departmental capabilities are restricted as a result.

6. There is the ever-present problem of those career people who "top-out" at one level or position, and upon being told or otherwise realizing they will not progress any further, become disenchanted or resentful. Such employees frequently will not leave, and even though there is an attitude problem, management cannot terminate them because their job performance meets standards, however minimally.

Example of the Disadvantage of Career Personnel: Personnel policies of many organizations require a series of job performance "cautions" and warnings, alerting the employee that he is performing below standards and giving him the opportunity to improve. For example, one company requires three such warnings, spaced at least thirty days apart, *before* the employee can be given notice. Thus the department is obliged to endure approximately 120 days or one-third of a year of substandard work.

Additionally, an individual so terminated may file a legal action against the company on the grounds that the company's entire action against him was not based on work performance but on one form or another of prejudice (race, color, creed, sex or age). The company must then assume a legal defensive posture (at no small expense) and subsequently may be obliged to reinstate the former employee *with full back wages* for all time elapsed between termination and the final determination of the issue—which could constitute a full year's wages all at once.

PART-TIME NON-CAREER PERSONNEL

Advantages of Part-Time Non-Career Personnel

1. Part-time in-house employees are less costly than career personnel because they are not entitled to the full employee benefit package.
2. Part-time employees, by virtue of the agreement made at the time of hire regarding their schedule, allow for security coverage at difficult, unusual or odd hours that otherwise could require overtime or premium pay to regulars. This allows for broad and flexible coverage.
3. Deployment of part-time people permits security management the unique opportunity to analyze their performance over an extended period of time. If a part-timer proves productive he can move into an unfilled career position if he desires that opportunity.
4. The use of part-time security employees allows management to tap particularly high-caliber people for security service. Local colleges and universities are an excellent recruiting ground for part-timers. Intelligent and capable college students can make a substantial contribution to the security function in a wide variety of capacities. Part-time schedules usually fit into their school schedules as well as their financial needs, and this employment proves to be a bargain both ways.

   Also, more and more women are returning to the labor market, many of whom have raised their children and wish to be productive members of the community but do not want or cannot handle career or otherwise full-time jobs. These people bring maturity and common sense to part-time positions.

   Finally, a number of people who have retired early still need to be productive, and they, too, can be a definite asset to the Security Department.

Example of the Advantage of Part-Time Non-Career Personnel: Providing security coverage for an amusement park that is open twelve hours a day would pose a real problem to the security administrator responsible for such coverage—if, that is, all security personnel were career people. The schedule would call for X number of people to open the park and X number to close the park the same day. Thus there would be an unproductive (and wasteful) expenditure of overlapping hours and payroll dollars.

On the other hand, if part-time security personnel were deployed along with full-time regulars, full coverage could be effected with economy. For example: ten officers are required to open and ten to close. The park is open from 12 noon to 12 midnight. With full-time employees only, the first ten officers go on duty at noon and go off duty at 8:00 P.M. The second shift must go on duty at 4:00 P.M. and work to midnight to receive their full eight-hour shift. Between 4:00 and 8:00 P.M. there are 80 manhours being expended when only 40 are required. One full-time unit is wasted each day.

With effective scheduling of part-time personnel, the coverage could be as follows: five regulars and five part-timers (working a four-hour schedule) start at 12 noon. At 4:00 P.M. the part-timers go off duty and are replaced with five regulars who will work until midnight. At 8:00 P.M. the original five regulars go off duty, replaced with five part-timers who work until midnight. The schedule of coverage is economical and efficient.

Without question, utilization of part-time personnel helps alleviate scheduling problems.

Disadvantages of Part-Time Non-Career Personnel

1. Part-time employees have a decidedly limited commitment to the job and to the organization. They do not feel the same degree of responsibility as does a career employee. The limited feeling of responsibility results in more part-time employees failing to report, calling in sick, or offering other excuses for not appearing. Therefore, part-timers are less reliable.
2. The primary interest or attention of part-time personnel is somewhere other than the job—school, family or another job. Consequently, keen interest and attention are usually lacking. They do not identify with the company, and as a result their conduct on the job is affected adversely.
3. The relationship between the company and the part-timer is essentially mercenary in nature: immediate remuneration for services rendered. That means the primary work motivator of the part-timer is money, not achievement, challenge, growth or responsibility.
4. There is a limited number of people looking for part-time work. By far most people in the job market want full-time employment.
5. By virtue of their own emergency status in the public sector, off-duty police officers who work part-time in security cannot be counted on by the company when a major disturbance or calamity occurs in the area—those very times when they are needed the most.

6. Another disadvantage of the off-duty police officer as a part-time security employee is his tendency to take more chances, because of his experience and peace officer status, than would a civilian, particularly in making arrests.

Example of the Disadvantage of Part-Time Non-Career Personnel: A department store plans coverage of a given store from opening to closing, using a part-time employee in the plan for evening protection. Because of absence of a real commitment, the part-timer fails to show for any number of reasons, leaving the store short of security help. The question of dependability is the biggest disadvantage in the use of this type of employee.

CONTRACTUAL NON-CAREER PERSONNEL

Advantages of Contractual Non-Career Personnel

1. There is a considerable cost savings, in terms of the expense of the employee benefit package and other career employee privileges, when contractual personnel from outside the organization are engaged.
2. There is complete freedom to terminate the services of an individual serving the company on a contractual basis. Such termination can be immediate and without cause. That means that if his appearance, grooming, attitude, age, demeanor or performance is for any reason below the standards set by the company, the person can be removed from the job and returned to *his* employer, without repercussions.
3. There is good flexibility in manpower resources in a contractual arrangement. The security force can be increased to meet unexpected demands overnight if need be. This can be achieved by the primary contractor sending more personnel or calling on another contractor for short-term assistance.
4. Use of contracted services reduces miscellaneous non-security expenses such as recruiting and advertising costs, personnel interviewing and administration costs, timekeeping and payroll administration costs.
5. There is freedom to terminate services of a contractual firm if that firm's services fall below required standards. Contracts, whether written or agreed upon verbally, usually allow for a thirty-day termination clause, and poor performance justifies execution of this clause.
6. Flexibility of coverage and service in a geographically dispersed operation is a decided advantage of contractual help.
7. The short-term and/or infrequent needs for personnel with unique or highly specialized skills and technical know-how, such as a polygraph operator, can effectively be met on a contractual basis.

Example of the Advantage of Contractual Non-Career Personnel: Consider a case where the Security Department causes the placement of an undercover agent into a warehouse for the purpose of gathering information on possible internal theft. The undercover agent's *primary* employer is a contract service firm. He receives a salary from them as well as a regular paycheck, like every other warehouse employee, from the company that owns the warehouse. For a period of time some useful intelligence is obtained, but after a while the undercover agent becomes personally involved with other warehouse employees and his reports become valueless. Even though he wishes to remain employed in the warehouse, his services can be terminated forthwith without violating his rights to job security, because his real employer is the firm which sent him to the warehouse and is still paying his undercover salary (although it may be less than the warehouse salary).

If, on the other hand, the Security Department had hired an applicant directly into the warehouse to serve as an undercover agent, that person would be entitled to some job protection and could not be summarily removed from the job. The use of contractual services has some very definite advantages.

Disadvantages of Contractual Non-Career Personnel

1. Except for those few firms that pay excellent salaries, most contractual firms attract personnel with minimal poor qualifications. In order for the contract firm to be competitive and make a fair profit, the individual must settle for a lesser wage than would be paid for a comparable job in a non-contractual firm.
2. There is more turnover in non-career personnel because they may find what they believe is a career or a better job elsewhere, or because their talent can best be used by the contract firm to the firm's advantage. That means, of course, that the highest rate of turnover occurs among the most talented people sent to service the client.
3. There tends to be an absence of pride among contractual service people—pride in themselves, in many cases, as well as pride in their organization—and the absence of pride reflects in performance.
4. There tends to be a resentment on the part of many contract people over the fact they work for a company (client) but are not entitled to the benefits the regular employees receive. As a result, some contract employees seek to be hired by the client company as regular employees. Most client-contractor agreements now include provisions prohibiting such job changing or requiring the payment of a fee by the client if he wants that employee. (Note: These agreements only validate the

point that contract people frequently would prefer to identify with the other employees and the client's firm.)

5.   Ambition and motivation are questionable in many cases because opportunities for advancement seem limited, or the contract firms have failed to lay out meaningful and comprehensible career paths and make their people aware of such opportunities.

Example of the Disadvantage of Contractual Non-Career Personnel: A major shopping center contracted for guard services, awarding the contract to a reputable firm with excellent leadership at the top. The securing of this particular contract was an important addition to the list of clients being served, and good people were assigned to this most visible job. As time passed, the contract firm grew and turnover increased. The guards on the site became careless of appearance, inattentive, unreliable and eventually became a source of embarrassment to the shopping center. Such a condition could not have developed had the service been proprietary, with career people in place. (On the other hand, some shopping centers, to name but one of hundreds of types of clients, have had excellent results with contract services.)

COMBINING CAREER AND NON-CAREER PERSONNEL

Clearly, then, there are many factors to be considered in weighing the pros and cons of career and non-career personnel. In addition to those factors discussed above, there are others not explored, but also most important. Those are reflected best in simple good management practices and supervisory skills. Despite their disadvantages, career personnel can excel, depending upon good management. Non-career personnel, contractual or part-time, despite the disadvantages enumerated above, can excel if given proper supervision and good management.

Early in this chapter reference was made to the possible utilization of both career and non-career people—a blend of both. That is precisely the practice in many organizations. In one retail chain the core of the Security Department is comprised of well-trained professional career personnel. Complementing them is a large cadre of part-time security employees, including a large number of college students, many of whom are studying in the criminal justice curriculum. At the time of this writing, supplemental contractual services include some uniformed guards, undercover agents, temporary "agent" assignments, and integrity shoppers. To provide adequate protection with career people exclusively would be an impossibility. To protect the company with non-career personnel exclusively would likewise be an impossibility.

An appropriate balance or blend of both is recommended. There is a need for both and room for both in the security industry.

SUMMARY

There are advantages and disadvantages to employing full-time career security personnel or non-career employees drawn from part-time workers or contract security services.

Stability, loyalty, improved "local knowledge," superior pride and motivation, and the opportunity for better communications and training are advantages of career personnel. On the other side of the coin are increased costs, limited numbers and the attendant inflexibility of deployment, and potential problems of discipline and limited skill levels.

Part-timers are less costly; provide desirable flexibility in assignment; and allow management to draw from high-caliber sources such as students and women available only on a part-time basis. However, part-time personnel tend to lack the career employee's commitment to job and company.

Contract services offer the benefits of cost savings, freedom to terminate services at any time, great flexibility both in manpower resources and in coverage of widely dispersed operations, and specialized skills. Commonly cited disadvantages include low-paid personnel, subject to high turnover, with a lower level of pride and motivation.

No one type of employee is right for all situations; in fact, many companies can best be served by an appropriate blend of full- and part-time, in-house and contract security personnel.

REVIEW QUESTIONS

1.　What is the definition of "career personnel"?

2.　What are the two categories of non-career personnel?

3.　List six of the advantages of using career personnel in the Security Department. Contrast these with six disadvantages.

4.　Give an example of how utilization of part-time personnel can help solve scheduling problems.

5.　Describe the advantages, in terms of flexibility, of using contractual personnel.

6.　Discuss the statement, "An appropriate balance or blend of career and non-career personnel is recommended."

III

Operational Management

15

Planning and Budgeting

The budgeting process might best be approached in terms of

What is a budget?
Why do we have a budget?
When is a budget prepared?
Who participates in the budgeting process?
How is the budget prepared?

Such a pragmatic approach overrides the broader spectrum of concepts, philosophies and strategies, such as "zero-based budgeting," about which entire texts have been written. The emphasis here is on fundamentals— an understanding of the basics provides a groundwork for sophistication and growth.

The established security manager, moreover, is already involved in an ongoing budget program in his organization. Even the new manager, whether promoted from within or brought in from outside the company, will inherit budgeting responsibilities in an existing framework. A pragmatic approach to the budgeting process, therefore, is most useful.

WHAT IS A BUDGET?

The management process is the coordination and integration of all resources to accomplish organizational objectives. According to this definition, management is viewed in terms of the functions a manager performs—i.e., planning, decision-making, organizing, directing and controlling. Each of these functions has an impact, to one degree or another, on the budgeting process. Controlling, for example, is that process aimed at ensuring, through overt, timely action, that *events conform to plans.* Plans must be based on good judgment and good decision-making estimates about the future. *The budget is that plan stated in financial terms.* Planning and budgeting go hand-in-hand. You cannot have a budget without a plan; and every plan, if it is viable and is to be executed, must have a budget. A budget, therefore, is:

- a plan stated in financial terms.
- a realistic estimate of the resources required to implement a plan.

- an allocation of resources to achieve planned objectives.
- an instrument which records work programs in terms of appropriations needed to place them into effect.
- a management tool intended to ensure that work programs are carried out as planned.

Obviously, the definition of the budget must include plans (or programs, which in and of themselves are plans).

The elements of a budget can be illustrated in a practical security situation. The Security Department decides to provide a rape prevention program for the female employees of the company. The objective of the program is obviously aimed at educating employees on ways to protect themselves against the possibility of rape, ways to increase their safety during movement to and from home, and so on. With the objective established, next comes the planning of how to achieve this educational goal. The plans could include the rental or purchase of a commercially prepared film on rape prevention, preparation of posters announcing the program, scheduling of a security officer's time to conduct the program, rental of a projector to show the film, retaining an outside speaker who is considered an expert on the subject, and distribution of an anti-rape booklet to the participants following the program.

Once the plan spells out what must happen to achieve the stated objective, it must then be costed-out, or restated in dollars and cents.

1.	Video tape purchase	$ 385.00
2.	Posters	
	artwork	100.00
	printing	82.50
3.	Rental of V.C.R.	35.00
4.	Guest speaker fee	400.00
5.	300 booklets @ .48	144.00
	Rape Prevention Budget	$1146.50

To repeat, then, a budget is a plan stated in financial terms; it is a realistic estimate of the resources required to implement a plan; it is an allocation of resources to achieve planned objectives; it is a way in which we record programs in terms of the dollars needed to place such programs into effect; and it is a tool intended to ensure that the program comes off as planned.

WHY DO WE HAVE A BUDGET?

The budget breathes life into a plan and gives the plan direction. It requires the manager to *manage* the plan in three dimensions:

1.   The operation or project must unfold *as planned* if the budget is followed exactly. (If we planned on a video tape for the Rape Prevention Program, the tape will in fact be used if the allocated dollars are spent to purchase the tape. Without the budget as a guide, something could easily be substituted for the tape, and thus the plan would not be followed.)

2.   The operation or project will take place *when planned* because budgets are time-phased; i.e., plans must be executed in keeping with the budgeted availability of funds. In other words, if the salary budget for a six-month period amounts to $600,000, that money is not available in one lump sum at the beginning of the six-month period, but rather is rationed out through budget management over the planned period of time.

3.   The operation or project will not exceed the planned costs if the budget is managed properly. Without a doubt, the man who proceeds to build a house from the ground up without a budget will spend more money than the man who builds the house within a planned budget.

The three variables—the actual *operation* or *project,* the *schedule* or timing of that project or operation, and the *costs*—must be kept within the parameters of the budget. The budget provides those parameters: it gives direction. That is why we have budgets. The mark of good management is reflected in how closely the budgets are followed.

WHEN IS THE BUDGET PREPARED?

Annual (twelve months) budgets may be prepared and finalized in excess of a year in advance. Biannual (six months) budgets are usually prepared and finalized mid-period, or three months prior to the new budget period.

The novice in the budgeting process finds this aspect of forecasting, or projecting into the future, the most difficult to come to grips with. This difficulty is probably due to our natural inclination to think in terms of the here and now—not nine months downstream or late next year. Experienced, effective managers more often than not have a reputation of being able to "think ahead" and having certain predictive skills that enable them to anticipate events happening in the future. The average line employee tends to think of his work in terms of today, whereas the manager thinks of work in substantially larger blocks of time. Thinking ahead is not necessarily a measure of intelligence, but rather represents a conditioning and requisite of managerial responsibilities.

How does one plan for security requirements and costs next year? How does one plan for criminal attacks and emergencies, which may or may not occur, which may be large or small in proportion, at times unknown? The answer is that one does not plan or budget for the unknown or the unpredictable; one budgets for intelligently anticipated and predictable conditions, based on known conditions in the present and the past. For example: Security management in the steel-making industry is planning for the following year. In that year labor contracts will expire; already issues are surfacing which could cause serious conflict between labor and management. Under such conditions, along with a past experience of labor violence, extraordinary security measures should be planned to commence with the expiration of the contract. As stated previously, *plans must be based on good judgment and good decision-making estimates about the future.*

As a matter of fact, the predictability of security requirements for the future is relatively accurate. Truly major emergencies of the type that would have a serious impact on the budget would be incidents of catastrophic proportion, such as an earthquake or other natural disaster. Such events, fortunately, are few and far between.

The steel manufacturing security planner, then, can count on increased security needs when the contract expires; the university security planner can count on increased problems in June (when the pressure of final exams is over); the retail security planner can count on increased needs between Thanksgiving and New Year's. All can make decisions about plans and costs in the future.

This is not to say that a security department should not have emergency or contingency plans for major catastrophes. Indeed they should have. As a rule, however, such emergency plans are broad and generalized "game plans" which include such things as who will be in command, reporting responsibilities and channels, specific asset protection steps and life-saving/first-aid setups. Such a plan has broad parameters; it is considered a guide or road map and probably has no budget. If the plan must be implemented, costs receive little attention in view of the magnitude of the problems of property destruction and the loss of human lives. Dollars, in this context, do not count . . . at least during the early stages of the emergency.

WHO PARTICIPATES IN THE BUDGETING PROCESS?

There are "bottom-up and top-down" and "top-down and bottom-up" approaches to budgeting. The latter is preferable because senior management initiates the process by establishing acceptable expenditure guidelines prior to the detailed planning by the operating or middle management. For a given upcoming budget year, the general guideline could be that middle management should continue their cost-effectiveness efforts in all operations as they have for the previous two years. Following the detailed planning by the individual managers (Security Manager or Director in our case), senior management will evaluate and then set the final budget level, based on the financial outlook for the budget period.

Top-Down and Bottom-Up Process

Phase One: Senior Management—Top-Down
   1. Establishes operating guidelines for the Security Depart-
       ment.
   2. Establishes acceptable expenditure guidelines; i.e., a
       given number of dollars.
Phase Two: Security (Middle) Management—Bottom-Up
   1. Evaluates the security operation and projects. (*Operation*
       means a continuing, ongoing function; *project* means a
       short-term activity; for example, a rape prevention pro-
       gram is a project, not an operation.)
   2. Submits courses of action for achieving organizational
       goals.
   3. Costs-out such courses of action.
   4. Develops and recommends alternative courses. For exam-
       ple, the initial plan (or course of action) for the rape pre-
       vention program came to $1146.50. Alternatives include:
       (a) Do not offer the program at all. (b) Do not buy the
       tape; rent it instead and save $300.000, bringing the cost
       to $846.50. (c) Rent the tape and do not call in a guest
       speaker; simply have a rap session following the tape,
       thus reducing the program to $446.50. (d) In addition to
       (c) above, eliminate posters and announce the program
       through supervisors, thus reducing the program another
       $182.50. And so on.
Phase Three: Senior Management—Top-Down
   1. Reviews activities, costs and alternatives recommended
       by security management.
   2. Makes decision on the security manager's recommenda-
       tions.
   3. Allocates funds on those decisions, thus establishing the
       Security Department's next budget.

The entire budgeting process follows a logical or sequential pattern
that brings about the interaction between senior and middle management.
The sequence is as follows:

1. Planning
    • setting goals and objectives
2. Budget building or budget development
    • evaluating current activities
    • identifying new activities
    • developing alternatives
    • determining costs

3. Evaluation and review of recommendations
    *   comparing against original guidelines
    *   making decisions re priorities or alternatives
4. Budget establishment
    *   allocating funds

The top security executive should work closely with key staff members in the "bottom-up" phase of the process, soliciting input on what the current practices are and what they should be. The executive should be asking such questions as, "Why are we doing it? Why are we doing it *this way?* Do we have to do it? Is there an easier or better way to do it? Can we do it with four men instead of five?" To stimulate the thinking of subordinates in this manner can prove productive in efforts to reduce costs or otherwise effect savings in the function. At the same time, subordinates become involved, at least to some degree, in the budgeting function. Subordinates who participate in budget preparation tend to be more diligent in managing their respective areas of the budget later on.

HOW IS THE BUDGET PREPARED?

Budget costs are classified under one of three categories: salary expenses, sundry expenses, and capital expenses.

Capital expenses will receive little attention in this text because they are usually handled apart from salary and sundry costs. In short, capital expenditures are for physical improvements, physical additions, or major expenditures for hardware. To pay a man for a day's work is a salary expense; to pay for the forms and papers that make up that man's personnel jacket is a sundry expense; and to pay for the metal filing cabinet which houses those personnel jackets is a capital expense. Capital expenses are generally considered "one-time" expenses, whereas salary and sundry are recurring expenses.

Salary Expense Budget

Perhaps the simplest approach to computing salary costs is to count up the security employees, by classification, average out their weekly salary, again by classification, and add it up. (Figure 15.1)

Several things should be pointed out with reference to Figure 15.1. First, the computation could reflect anticipated overtime pay *if* there is a history of overtime requirements during the regular pay periods. If that is indeed the case, then the average amount of paid overtime can be included in the weekly totals or could even be averaged out to a monthly total. Thus a four- or five-week month could reflect, for example, $500 in overtime that

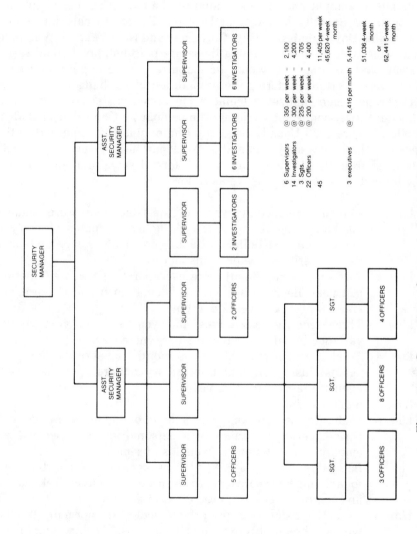

Figure 15.1 Computing salary costs for security department.

6 Supervisors @ 350 per week = 2,100
14 Investigators @ 300 per week = 4,200
3 Sgts. @ 235 per week = 705
22 Officers @ 200 per week = 4,400
45   11,405 per week
                            45,620 4-week month

3 executives @ 5,416 per month 5,416

51,036 4-week month
or
62,441 5-week month

would be part of the salary calculation for the period. Additionally, if there is any significant amount of overtime or holiday pay due employees during the budget period, that too should be included in the calculations. Otherwise, salary expenses will exceed the planned and approved budget.

A standard requirement is that all budget variances in excess of a predetermined amount must be explained by the executive responsible for the budget, the Security Manager or Director. Failure to calculate Labor Day, Veterans Day, Admission Day, Christmas and New Year's Day in holiday pay due to personnel (assuming those are paid holidays) could result in a significant "overage." It would be embarrassing to explain that such holidays were overlooked during the preparation of the budget.

First rough, then finalized calculations must be transferred to standardized budget forms, controlled by either the company's Controller or Budget Controller. (Figure 15.2) Usually one copy (the original) is submitted to the Finance Division and a copy retained in the department. Figure 15.3 reflects that transfer from the drafting stage to the formal stage. Explanations for lines 1 through 10 in Figure 15.3 are as follows:

Line 1 45 men were used last year and the same number are planned for the coming period. Although the same number of men are being used, the dollar variance represents salary increases due to merit and wage adjustments.

Line 2 Two extra units (men) were used during a two-week period last year. Because it is only a fluctuation from the norm, we know that it represents overtime.

Line 3 Three security "executives" last year and this year. Again, variance in salary is due to salary increases.

Line 4 Total use of personnel for the month of February, this year against last year, and total salary dollars spent last year against the plan for this year.

Line 5 Same as Line 1.

Line 6 Last year the department was down one man for a two-week period, perhaps because of a personal leave or because an employee quit. Salary reflects his absence.

Line 7 Budgeting on the "4–5–4" plan is most common in business today. This line represents the fifth week in a five-week month, and the odd week is so recorded in dollars.

Line 8 Executive salaries in the private sector are normally treated with confidentiality. Obviously the boss's salary would become common knowledge if recorded alone. In this instance his salary is folded in with that of his two right-hand men. This is a common practice.

Line 9 Same as Line 4.

Line 10 Actual salary dollars spent for the budget period last year, and the planned salary dollars to be spent for the same period this year.

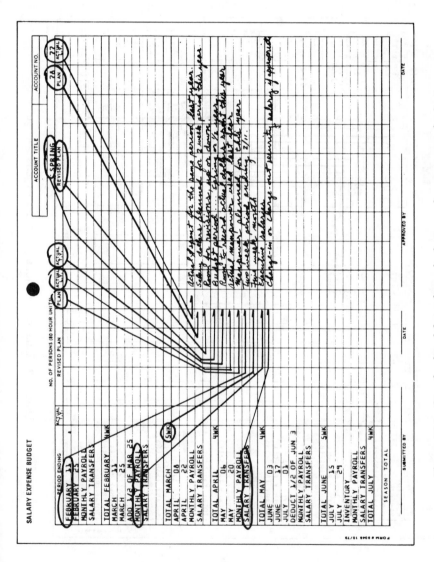

Figure 15.2 Standardized form for calculating salary expense budget.

169

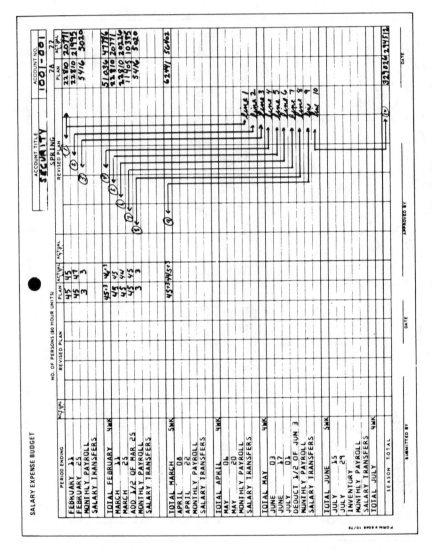

Figure 15.3 Final calculations for salary expense budget.

Company-wide pay adjustments or so-called "cost of living" increases, regardless of when they take place, force the revision of the budget at the departmental level. Random increases throughout the ranks, on the other hand, normally do not require a budget revision. Revisions, upward or downward, are recorded on a form designed for just that purpose. (Figure 15.4.)

Figure 15.4 Request form for expense budget revision.

Sundry Expense Budget

All ongoing non-salary expenses are considered sundry expenses. Figure 15.5 reflects a security "supplies" account. Those expenses charged to this particular account are somewhat arbitrary because the division of expenses into given accounts really depends on volume. In a large security organization, it is quite likely that a *separate* sundry account would be established just for uniform replacement and cleaning. In the same organization the "supplies" account would reflect only the first four items listed in Figure 15.5.

In addition to volume, another criterion for creating a sundry account would be the distinctive identity of that account; for example, a "travel expense" account, funds allocated specifically for security executives or personnel to travel between facilities and locations where their presence is required.

Sundry security accounts could include the following:

- Supplies
- Uniforms (replacement or upkeep)
- Travel
- Transportation
    lease of patrol vehicles
    maintenance of vehicles
    insurance of vehicles
- Contract services
    central station alarm contracts
    employment screening service
    polygraph examiner retainer
    undercover (intelligence) service
- Professional
    organization membership fees
    business or professional luncheons and other entertainment costs
    publication subscriptions

Again, volume and identity (or, perhaps better stated, those expenses that have a common denominator) dictate the number of sundry accounts a given department might have. If uniform-related expenses are not significant in terms of dollar volume, then those expenses can be budgeted under the next most logical account, such as Supplies (see Figure 15.5). If the only travel expense is an annual trip to a convention, then a separate Travel account would not be justified. The travel expense could be budgeted under Transportation or Professional.

Because budgets are a management tool, it is reasonable to conclude that one very large budget could be cumbersome and difficult to work with, whereas a number of smaller budget accounts are far more manageable

SUNDRY EXPENSE BUDGET

ACCOUNT TITLE: SECURITY SUPPLIES   ACCOUNT NO. 1000-50

MONTH	ACTUAL TY	DATE	DATE	REVISED PLAN DATE	DATE	PLAN	ACTUAL LY
FEB 78						1000	826
MAR 78						1000	1151
APR 78						650	997
MAY 78						950	1084
JUN 78						700	1123
JUL 78						950	1002
TOTAL						5250	6183

BUDGET AMOUNT IN MONTH IN WHICH CHARGE WILL BE MADE

DESCRIPTION OF ITEM	FEB AUG	MAR SEPT	APR OCT	MAY NOV	JUNE DEC	JULY JAN	TOTAL SEASON BUDGET	LAST YEAR
PRINTING COSTS	200	200	200	200	200	200	1200	1316
DUPLICATING MACHINE RENTAL	150	150	150	150	150	150	900	900
OFFICE SUPPLIES	50	50	50	50	50	50	300	377
TYPEWRITER MAINTENANCE POLICY - ALL MACHINES	50	50	50	50	50	50	300	300
RAILROAD SEAL RE-ORDER	350						350	700
UNIFORM REPLACEMENT		300		300		300	900	1111
UNIFORM CLEANING	200	200	200	200	200	200	1200	1391
LOCKS & KEYS		50			50		100	88
TOTAL	1000	1000	650	950	700	950	5250	6183

LIST PRINCIPAL ITEMS INCLUDED IN THIS BUDGET — GROUP SMALL AMOUNTS TOGETHER AND LIST AS MISCELLANEOUS

SUBMITTED BY   DATE   APPROVED BY   DATE

S-8040 10/73

Figure 15.5 Sundry expense budget for Security Supplies.

and easier to work with. A significant variance in a large "catchall" sundry account would require the manager to track down all sorts of expenditures to find the cause of that variance. If the same variance is in the Transportation account, the tracking time to discover the explanation is reduced. Thus, having a number of manageable sundry accounts is an efficient way to manage money.

As in the salary expense account, sundry expenses should be relatively predictable, based on good planning for the future period as well as experiences of the past. Statements or invoices should never come as a surprise to the account, except for unpredictable emergencies. In those rare cases, the budget should be revised then and there to reflect the increase.

Earlier in this chapter we discus, the three variables in the budget: the operation or project itself, the schedule or timing, and the costs. The timing of costs is most evident in Figure 15.5. So many dollars are budgeted for each month in the upper portion of the form, and then those planned expenses are broken down into specific expenditures, *by month,* in the lower half of the form. If this particular budget is properly managed, then the railroad seals will be purchased in February, not in any other month. And so it is with uniform replacements and the purchase of locks and keys.

A word of explanation is in order regarding the "Actual T.Y. (This Year)" column on the sundry as well as the salary expense budgets. As the manager works with his "tools" month by month, he records his budget management results in the "Actual T.Y." column as the figures become available. Figure 15.6 reflects actual expenses for the first two months of the budget period, as entered by the manager. This obviously serves as a red flag that he has already exceeded his budget by $210, which should force him to look for a comparable savings during the following months so as to come in within the budgeted total amount. Failure to keep a running tab on expenses, sundry or salary, can lull a manager into complacency, and the net results at the end of the budget period can be an unpleasant surprise.

JUSTIFYING THE SECURITY BUDGET

It is clear evidence of poor communications between senior management and security management if the Security Manager or Director must wrestle over the issue of "selling" company management on security. He should not be in the position of having to justify the Security Department's existence in the company, nor should he have to struggle for his fair share of the available budget dollars to be allocated among all departments. The condition where security management is attempting to justify protection to an uninformed management group is to be avoided; rather, the operating conditions should be an open communications line, an ongoing understanding of the Security Department's objectives and the methods and strategy to

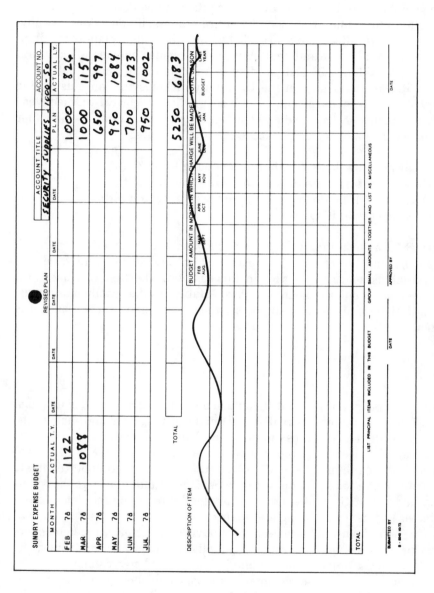

Figure 15.6 Security Supplies budget, showing actual expenses for two-month period.

175

achieve those objectives. *The objectives should have been established by management and security, jointly.* This is another illustration of the top-down and bottom-up process. Management initially sets operating and expense guidelines, and Security, after doing its homework, comes back with plans, alternatives and priorities. The entire process, if honest and healthy, is a mutual effort rather than a struggle by one side (Security) for recognition or survival. That honest and healthy process includes, incidentally, the absence of old-fashioned budget padding in anticipation of budget cuts.

Dr. R. Paul McCauley of the University of Louisville, an outstanding scholar of security management, has a theory called "security by Objectives" which is exciting in its simplicity.[1] In an abbreviated form, his first four steps in security management's approach to a task are:

1. What must be done (or what do we have to do)?
2. How must it be done (or how are we going to do it)?
3. When must it be done (or when are we going to do it)?
4. How much will it cost?

Dr. McCauley's theory forms a sound basis for a practical approach to planning and budgeting. It incorporates, in slightly different form, the three variables suggested earlier in this chapter. The first two questions define the operation or projects; the third establishes the schedule or timing; the fourth determines estimated costs. In essence, this is what a budget is all about.

SUMMARY

Planning and budgeting go hand-in-hand; a budget is a plan stated in financial terms. Budgeting requires a realistic estimate of programs and their costs, and an allocation of resources to achieve planned objectives.

Because budgets are prepared well in advance, effective budget management requires thinking ahead, anticipating needs based upon relatively predictable conditions. The budget then becomes a tool to ensure that plans are carried out. It gives direction to planning by requiring the definition of specific programs, their timing and their costs.

The "top-down and bottom-up" approach to budgeting is recommended. In this process senior management establishes goals and guidelines; the Security Manager provides the detailed planning and cost estimates; senior management reviews these recommendations, establishes priorities, and allocates funds. Where budgeting reflects this interaction of senior and middle

---

[1] McCauley, R. Paul, "Zero-Based Security," *Security World* magazine, Vol. 14, No. 7, July 1977, pp. 40–41.

management, the protection program will be "presold," based upon a mutual understanding of company goals and departmental objectives.

Budget costs are generally broken down into capital expenses, salary and sundry expenses. The first category of costs are generally fixed or easily determined. The use of detailed records from month to month and year to year makes it possible to arrive at realistic salary and sundry projections. In the area of sundry expenses, such factors as the volume of expenditures in a given category and the distinctive nature of given costs can be used to establish categories. It is generally more efficient to manage a number of smaller sundry accounts than to rely upon large, "catchall" accounts.

REVIEW QUESTIONS

1. What are the five elements in the definition of a budget?

2. What are the three variables in a budget?

3. Briefly outline the steps in the "top-down and bottom-up" approach to budgeting.

4. Give an example of each of the following: a capital expense; a salary expense; a sundry expense.

5. Discuss the approach to setting up a salary expense budget. How should overtime expenses be handled?

6. Give four examples of sundry accounts that might be set up for a Security Department.

16

Program Management

The Security Department of any company provides a protection program addressing itself to the security needs of the company, based on the presence of known risks. The protection program is comprised of many lesser programs, all somehow interrelated and coordinated to form the entire protective blanket.

Because companies are living, dynamic entities, they constantly change, requiring the security programs to change also. Failure to adjust to the company's constant shifting and movement puts the security efforts out of focus. Example: a firm changes its policy and commences paying its employees on payday with bank checks instead of cash in pay envelopes. The Security Department's "program" for protecting the large cash payroll and everything surrounding that responsibility, including the arrival of the armored car in the morning, filling pay envelopes and disbursement of envelopes, must change.

The need for change in this case may be most evident, but in reality there is a phenomenon of resistance to change. Long after the change is made to payment by check, there is a chance that part of the Payroll Department's program *and* the Security Department's program will still be in place, functioning inefficiently and at an unnecessary cost. Notice that the Payroll Department is included in this program failure. Program failures are not limited to security but occur everywhere in organizational life, particularly in large organizations, with the chance increasing in direct relationship to the increased size of the organization.

With change come new risks, hazards that were not necessarily present prior to the change. The new risk in the example above might well be the vulnerability of the blank payroll checks to misuse. Thus a new security program is needed.

THE INSPECTION PROCESS

Inspection is an important part of the security management process which ensures that risks are recognized and covered in security programs, and that programs are necessary and cost-effective. The assessment of what is happening from a security point of view is made through an inspection program. Such an inspection program

1.   Must have full support of senior management to bring about necessary change if change is needed.
2.   Must be continuous in nature.
3.   May be formal or informal.
4.   May be structured or unstructured.

Support of Senior Management

If the inspection, which is a close and critical examination or scrutiny, reveals the need for change, then change *must* occur. More often than not the change requires money. Again using the payroll example, safe storage for the blank payroll checks requires a secured storage room or vault. If management fails to provide the necessary funds to construct, modify or otherwise secure a storage area, and refuses to allow the purchase of an adequate vault, the inspection process is compromised. Such an occurrence is not uncommon: a security inspection will reveal a need, but management decides to incur the risk (gamble that the risk factor is not worthy of the expense) and withholds the required dollars.

In the case of the blank payroll checks, to secure or not to secure is the issue. There is no empirical way of determining the extent of the risk; it is judgmental. Management personnel in the finance division could say that the risk is minimal because the checks must be processed through a check-making machine that imprints the amount as well as affixing the indicia-signature, and the machine is always under lock and key. Security's position could be that an employee intent on defrauding the company by means of the blank checks will bide his time until security on the check-making machine becomes lax (and it will). Or Security may point out that check-making machines are available on the market (as well as underground) and the indicia-signature is easy to counterfeit.

Because company management and security management do not concur on the level of risk or the probability of loss does not necessarily mean that company management lacks confidence in its security management; on the contrary. Company management, which is ultimately responsible for the welfare of the organization, is functioning not ill-advisedly or ignorantly, but fully advised by protection professionals of the whole spectrum of risks. Company management makes the final decision as to the dollars they are willing to spend to prevent losses, and the chances of loss they are willing to take by investing those dollars elsewhere in the business. After all, simply being in business is a large risk in itself.

Ideally, security must have the full support of senior management to bring about change if change is needed. The "if needed" should be the only opposing issue between security and management. The good security executive more often than not will obtain management's agreement that the change he recommends is, in fact, needed.

Continuous Inspections

To keep pace with the constant changes in the organization, changes in our society in terms of attitudes, life-styles and moral values, and the rapidly advancing technological modifications all around us, the inspection process must be an ongoing, never-ending activity. The larger the organization, the more reasonable that statement sounds; the inspection task never seems to be finished. For smaller organizations, however, down to the one-man operation, the continuous inspection process appears less reasonable. Yet even the smallest security department has a host of internal (security department) and external (company) areas to inspect—and inspect in great detail, too. The added advantage in the smaller firm is that the security inspection may also serve the purpose of an internal audit, which is usually conducted in a large company by internal auditors from a sub-unit within the finance division.

Inspection is one area where it is fair to say that one's work is never done.

Formal or Informal Inspections

A *formal* inspection is one to which some fanfare is attached; it is usually preceded by an announcement, and the unit under inspection "prepares" for the event, including some extra housekeeping activities that would not otherwise happen at that point in time. To add to the importance of the occasion, a senior executive may accompany the security executive on the inspection, thereby encouraging total cooperation on the part of the unit management.

For the company which has just upgraded the security function, hired a new security administrator, or initiated a security department and program with a new security chief, the formal approach to inspections is most desirable, primarily because it tells the company how senior management feels about protection, and thus establishes the desirable climate.

Informal inspections are usually the result of a long and firmly entrenched inspection program, understood by all and accepted as part of the organizational life. The inspections have been stripped of all the external trappings of importance, but their functional importance has not been lessened in any manner. They are seriously and quietly executed in a spirit of understanding and cooperation.

Structured or Unstructured Inspections

A *structured* inspection, as opposed to an unstructured inspection, is one that moves systematically, perhaps even rigidly, from one designated inspection area to the next and from one inspection point to the next. The following could be part of such a structured inspection:

Warehouse Exterior
1. Fencing
   a. vegetation growth
   b. general conditions
   c. additions or deletions?
   d. evidence of penetration?
2. Gates
   a. gate schedules
   b. inventory locks
   c. lock schedules
   d. key controls
   e. gate assignments
   f. gate traffic logs
      1. train
      2. truck
      3. personnel

Two examples of checklists for use in a structured inspection are included as appendixes to this text. Appendix B is a more comprehensive example of a structured inspection or security survey. Appendix C is another structured "checklist" approach to inspecting a retail operation.

The *unstructured* inspection, in contrast, would approach the warehouse unit in a more random manner, with less methodical attention to small specifics. The experienced eye of a top security professional would note at a glance, without following a checklist, that weeds and other vegetation against the fence needed clearing.

It stands to reason, then, that the decision as to which type of inspection format is needed depends a great deal on the expertise of the security executive who is involved.

Who Conducts the Inspection?

Ideally the Director or Manager should conduct the inspection, along with, *in every case possible,* the next-ranking man in his organization. For example, in a very small department, with a chief and a uniformed staff of six men, including a sergeant, the sergeant should accompany his chief.

Why should the manager himself conduct the inspection? It would seem that a subordinate could easily follow the structured inspection and its checklist.

Certainly any number of security officials, down to supervisors, can conduct inspections. But the lower in the ranks the function is delegated, the less important the event becomes in the eyes of the management area under inspection. This is one reason why the head of security should conduct inspections. A second reason is that company management looks to its security manager for *his* expertise and wisdom when it comes to protecting the company. His involvement in assessing risks and countermeasures assures them of the *best* assessment.

Why have a second man along on the inspection? There are three reasons. First, the experience itself is an outstanding training activity. After accompanying the manager on a number of inspections, the second in command—the lieutenant, for example—could move into that function easily and confidently. Second, besides gaining valuable information about the entire process of risk assessment and program evaluation, the lieutenant gains stature in the organization because of his relationship with the manager, who invariably holds great respect by virtue of responsibility and position in the company. Finally—and this is particularly true in small security organizations where the next in command is not necessarily the heir apparent—he becomes increasingly "sensitized" to conditions he never recognized before and conditions that never occurred to him. This reason, like the first, is a form of training. In the former example, however, the purpose of the training was to prepare the lieutenant to move up to the top; here the purpose is more to increase the level of awareness of a line-type supervisor and improve his efficiency on the job.

Another dimension can be added to the inspection process by having appropriate security supervisors quietly make an inspection in advance of the real one, using the structured format as a guideline and letting them subsequently compare their results with the manager's. The manager had better be thorough, however, because if he overlooks areas which the supervisors found to require change or correction, his failure tends to discredit his ability in the eyes of those subordinates.

In a large organization in which the warehouse is to be inspected, the following would probably comprise the inspection party: Security Manager, Assistant Security Manager, Security Supervisor whose area includes the warehouse, the warehouse superintendent and his assistant.

In some situations, particularly in the establishment of new programs or a comprehensive re-evaluation of an existing program, it may be necessary or advisable to engage the services of an outside security consultant to conduct a security survey. In such cases the security manager or director will, of course, work closely with the security consultant and with company management.

Wise indeed is the security executive who has the foresight and professional confidence to utilize an outside consultant. And why shouldn't he? Other executives in the corporation call on that kind of resource in their efforts to maximize efficiency. Data Processing frequently calls in computer consultants, Human Resource people call in training consultants, and so it goes across the organization. Yet I've heard from our industry some say such things as, "If I asked my boss for a budgetary provision for a security consultant he would only laugh and say 'That's what I hired you for.' " That's fine, as long as that security executive knows everything and always has all the answers to all the problems. A qualified, professional security consultant could do the following:

1. Reduce security costs
2. Recommend alternative approaches, one of which could solve a long-standing problem or budget obstacle
3. Strengthen your position on a given stand or project resisted or rejected by senior management
4. Obtain concessions from management
5. Overcome management doubts about the protection program and its expenses
6. Offer new ideas and insights that can be implemented after the consultant's work is concluded

In the sixties and seventies many security managers and directors were intimidated by consultants and viewed their retention by management as a threat to their personal security. Today, in the eighties, enlightened security administrators recognize that consultants can be an important resource.

The entire inspection program, again, has as its objectives (a) the assessment of risks, and (b) the assessment of their counter-measures, usually security programs. We will examine both aspects of this assessment.

ASSESSMENT OF RISKS AND COUNTERMEASURES

Risk Assessment

Inspection reveals conditions brought about by any number of things, such as the company's decision to pay by check instead of pay envelopes, which may pose a security risk. The possibility and probability of the risk resulting in a loss, and the magnitude of the loss, depend on the risk itself.

The Risk	Is It Possible to Have Loss?	Probable?	What Would Be Probable Loss?	How Much to Counter- measure?	Cure Risk?
Open petty cash fund	Yes	Yes	$15	$4.50	Yes
Blank pay- roll checks	Yes	Yes	Many thousands	$385	Yes
Unprotected skylights in grain warehouse	Yes	No	Under $3,000	$5,000	No

For example, every security executive would agree that finding a cigar box used in the purchasing department as a repository for a petty cash fund represents a risk. If the fund amounts to $15, the loss would be $15. That is clear. And to "cure" that risk or provide a countermeasure (perhaps in the form of a lockable tin box with the keys in the possession of the accounts payable manager) is a relatively easy and inexpensive thing to do. In the case of the blank payroll checks, on the other hand, the possibility of loss, the probability of loss, the potential of loss, and the cost to cure the risk form a more difficult equation.

It is not within the scope of this text or chapter to delve deeply into the exacting science of risk management, a subject in itself. The key point to be made is that from the discovery of what appears to be a risk, to the decision as to what action to take (i.e., cure it, minimize it, or live with it), there is a close interaction between security management and company management. This interaction takes place in the office of the security head's superior, where the final decision is made, particularly if the countermeasures involve capital or expense funds.

Selection of Countermeasures

There are four possible cures or countermeasures for every risk: procedural controls; hardware (fences, gates, locks, keys, etc.); electronic systems (alarms, access controls, CCTV, etc.); and people.

In the case of the petty cash fund, the countermeasure was hardware, in the form of a lockable tin box. In the case of the payroll checks, not only would hardware (vault or vault-type room) be a countermeasure, but so would a control procedure such as the accounting for checks by check serial numbers, withdrawal of checks from the vault by number (by batch) and the signing for such withdrawal by the appropriate employee, a prompt check reconciliation program after return from the bank, etc. The unprotected skylights might require hardware (an inside latch or an outside lock or padlock) and/or electronics (an alarm).

One of the important ongoing responsibilities of the Security Director or Manager will be to evaluate, select, and recommend appropriate deterrents for each significant risk from these four categories of countermeasures.

Procedural Controls

Policy tells us *what* we must do, whereas a procedure tells us *how* we are going to do it. Procedural controls are intended to define how any activity is to be carried out in such a way as to prevent or expose any violation of policy (and attendant potential for loss).

For example, a gambling casino's policy is to ensure that changegirls are accountable for their individual "bank." To make them accountable, which in and of itself contributes to the prevention of theft, they must follow a structured procedure—a procedural control. This procedure might spell out the specific amount of the changegirl's fund or "bank." It would then require that she check out her bank from the head cashier upon reporting for work, count it to ensure the full amount is there, and sign a designated form that she did receive the fund and the amount recorded was therein. Such a form should also be countersigned by the head cashier and placed in a certain part of the vault, to be removed only when the fund is returned at the end of the shift, at which time the fund is then counted by the head cashier, signed off by same, and countersigned by the change girl. The procedure might additionally require that the form be filed and retained for ninety days. Each of these steps is designed to establish accountability for valuable assets (in this case, cash) and verification of activity by more than one source.

Since it is often just as easy and involves little or no additional expense to establish a controlled procedure as an uncontrolled one, this type of countermeasure is generally the least expensive. (It should be noted that procedural controls in some situations may be automated, as when a computer is programmed to control and monitor the issuance of purchase orders, shipping invoices, bills of lading, receipts and other paperwork involved in a transaction. In this circumstance the procedural controls have become *electronic,* moving into a higher category of expense.)

Hardware

Many loss risks can be significantly reduced by the relatively simple application of some form of hardware, from a padlock on the company's gasoline pump to a perimeter fence with adequate lighting. Hardware is most common in the average person's defensive strategy in his private life. Lockable suitcases, chains and locks to protect bicycles, bars or decorative screens on residence windows, front door peekholes, night latches, outdoor lighting—all of these constitute hardware. In the business environment such physical protective measures may become more sophisticated, progressing to security containers (safes, lockable file cabinets and vaults) and other equipment or devices. Still, hardware is the second least expensive among the four basic countermeasures.

In modern applications security hardware is often combined with electronics; for example, a CCTV-monitored truck gate that is electronically (and remotely) controlled, or a fence whose protection as a physical barrier is supplemented by an intrusion alarm.

Electronics

In addition to closed circuit television, electronic countermeasures include such devices as automated access control systems and the whole spectrum of alarms. These include intrusion alarms, motion detection alarms, sound or vibration detection alarms, smoke detectors, heat detectors, waterflow alarms and others. Electronic devices constitute the fastest growing category of security countermeasures. While more expensive both to install and to maintain than procedural controls or basic hardware, they have become a fact of life for almost all businesses, large or small.

Alarms in particular were originally designed to replace the people who were previously deployed and utilized to provide precisely the same kind of "alarm" or warning service. Electronic alarms have proved to be better than people for a number of reasons. They are less costly (when compared to the annual salaries of personnel required to perform the same function); they will not fall asleep; they are always on the job despite deep snow, slippery streets, or a death in the family; and they are honest.

Personnel

Ironically, the utilization of people as a security countermeasure can be the most efficient and effective strategy or, depending upon the circumstances, the poorest.

Because of the ongoing expense of personnel (not only for salaries but also for fringe benefits, vacation and sick leave, supervision and replacement), every effort should be exercised to cure risks whenever possible by every means other than by utilizing people. The rule of thumb is: use people only in those areas where procedural controls, hardware or electronics cannot be employed more efficiently.

Obviously, there are security functions for which people are the best and sometimes the only countermeasure. The greatest attribute of people, one which can never be replaced, is their ability to exercise *judgment.* In that capability lies a critical factor in the decision to use people. Wherever judgment is essential in carrying out a security function, people should be utilized. A common example might be the job of overseeing employees as they leave work in a production plant, in terms of inspecting lunch pails and other containers. Personnel are essential for a variety of other roles which cannot be effected by procedures, hardware or electronics. Among these functions are guard posts and patrols, inspections, investigations, prevention of criminal attacks, maintaining order, crowd control, etc.

Assessment of Countermeasures

The other side of the inspection coin is the examination of existing countermeasures, usually protection programs and activities, originally set into motion to cure the known risks. Whereas the discovery of risks usually comes from conditions that are observable or comprehensible by virtue of what has happened, what is happening and what could happen, countermeasures are best assessed through an analysis of the countermeasure activity itself. This analysis is usually accomplished by asking questions. *The primary and most devastating question is "why?"* Every countermeasure, every security program, should be subjected to the following questions:

> Why are we doing it?
> Must we do it at all?
> If we must, is there a better way?
> Is there a less expensive way?

In one organization, for example, the new Security Director asked the supervising agent of the main complex what the guard on the back side of the complex was doing there. The Director was told it was a necessary post because the guard logged all trucks coming through that gate, opened the gate in the morning, locked the gate later in the morning, logged trucks coming from the main entrance that serviced the far side of the complex, and opened the gate late in the afternoon to accommodate employee vehicles. Additionally, the guard controlled traffic when the railroad brought in freight cars and took out the emptied ones. Besides, the Director was told, "We've always had a man on that post. That's why we built him a guard shack and installed a telephone."

By holding this particular assignment up to the four questions above, it was discovered that the guard was a holdover from a former procedure and that his work, such as logging trucks, was a total waste. No one ever checked his logs, and they contained no more information than that gathered at another location. The roving patrol officer could open and close the gates according to schedule, and the railroad's brakeman stopped what little traffic

there was when the box cars were being moved. Thus the company eliminated one guard, as well as the expense of one telephone, and was able
to tear down one guard house that consumed energy needlessly with its
electrical service.

Elimination of functions is obviously the ultimate in reducing costs,
but the opportunity for such action proves to be rare. By persistent application of the *why* test, however, limited opportunities will constantly present
themselves. Another outside guard operation was modified, for example,
by replacing weekend guard coverage with an electrically controlled gate,
CCTV and communication phone. The guards had been poorly utilized during
this slow period and were not only unproductive but unhappy with that
assignment because it was boring. These hours were eliminated from the
salary budget. The capital expense for the hardware amounted to less than
the annual cost of one 40-hour man unit. Thus in one year the equipment
paid for itself and thereafter effected a cost savings to the company.

There is absolutely nothing within security's spectrum of programs
that should be immune from this inspection. The difficulty is not so much
in the application of the inspection as it is in getting managers and supervisors at every level in the security pyramid to ask themselves and their
respective subordinates, "Why are we doing it? Must we do it at all? If
we must, is there a better way? Is there a less expensive way?"

Interestingly enough, whereas managers and supervisors for some reason tend not to question their pyramids (and programs therein), line security
people do see better ways. The effective security manager will encourage
employees to come to him with their ideas. Too often they have already
suggested improvements that were ignored or rejected by their supervisor;
to make the suggestions to the manager might be misconstrued by the line
supervisor as insubordination. If an open climate of communications is established, however, as discussed in Chapter 13, there will be a constant flow
of new ideas.

Inspecting for Compliance with Procedures

Whereas our discussion of inspections up to this point has focused on finding
new risks, primarily brought about by change within the organization, there
is another very important dimension to the inspection process. Inspection
provides the additional benefit of determining *compliance* with already existing countermeasures which are known to be sound. This type of inspection
is executed at the line or first line supervisory level.

We may be satisfied, for example, that the locks on the gates are proper,
and the control of keys is properly spelled out, and the gates are scheduled
to be locked and unlocked at the right time—but *are these things happening*

as they should? As we observed in an earlier chapter, "people do not do what you expect, they do what you inspect."

The Security Director may set up a procedural control that requires the payroll department to secure the blank checks behind locked doors at the end of the day. But do they? The Security Director's inspection of the payroll area does not ensure compliance later on. But inspection by his people will tell him whether the payroll department is ignoring or forgetting the procedure or in some other way still contributing to the original risk. How security management responds (or reacts) to such information is absolutely vital, for two reasons:

1.   If security management fails to act on the information that the procedure is not being followed, they permit the risk to exist, which is counterproductive and inexcusable.
2.   The line people who make the discovery of noncompliance and consequent risk, and see their management's failure to take prompt corrective action, become discouraged and say "what's the use?" The downstream result is that the line employees lose interest and risks increase everywhere.

If security management is not going to follow up on inspection deficiencies, then it should not ask line employees to make inspections. Further, compliance inspections come to the attention of employees who work in the area being inspected, and if they come to realize nothing is going to happen because of compliance failures, they will laugh at the inspection as nothing more than an exercise.

If a condition or procedure is worthy of being inspected, it is worthy of a prompt follow-up by management. Many security programs, always aimed at reducing risks, often make non-security people's work more difficult—requiring them to keep certain doors locked, for example. It is inconvenient for them to lock and unlock a given door, so human nature steps in and they leave it unlocked. Security finds the unlocked condition in its inspection and reports it. Prompt action corrects the offender, improves security by reducing the original risk, and brings a degree of respect to the inspector. If the line employee believes, based on fact or fiction, that his inspection report will not be acted on, he will ignore the very security risks he is there to detect.

STATISTICS IN PROGRAM MANAGEMENT

Statistics constitute another tool in managing security programs. To be an effective and meaningful tool the statistics must be designed to reflect what a given program is or is not doing—month by month, this year compared to last year by month, and cumulative year to date. If improperly designed, the quantitative figures will either be meaningless or deceptive. Once the statistical format is in place, it too should be inspected on an ongoing basis to ensure it has not outlived its original purpose, that it accurately reflects current activities and programs.

Not only must the statistical presentation reflect desired and necessary information and currently reflect activities of an in-place program, but it must be *used,* otherwise the value of the statistics is lost.

Figure 16.1 is an important management tool in determining how effective the detection program is in one large security organization located in many cities, divided into districts. Reflected in the chart are the number of dishonest employees (DE) apprehended this month (TM), year to date (YTD), against last year to date (LYTD), miscellaneous detections (MIS DET) this month, year to date against last year to date, total detections (TOT DET) this month, and detections made by undercover agents (UC DET) year to date against last year to date.

In designing this statistical form, security management was concerned not only with totals, but specifically with detection activity in every single unit by district, by time (month, year to date, and last year to date), by employee and by other (misc.). It was also interested in one sub-classification or technique—that is, apprehensions of dishonest employees by the use of undercover agents.

The undercover data are an excellent example of designing statistics to serve a purpose. In this case the statistics do demonstrate the effectiveness of that particular technique when compared to the budget dollars spent for undercover agents. The last two columns alone tell us a great deal; i.e., the undercover program has improved on the whole, as reflected by the increase in detections for the same number of budget dollars (not reflected in the chart but known to management). They also reflect a problem in the East District and a lesser problem in the South District. What is the problem? Is it poor security supervision in those districts? Are personnel managers in those districts disclosing the identity of the undercover agents, thus defeating the program? Is it improper tabulation of statistical data? Whatever the cause, the statistics have waved a red flag that can lead to discovering and solving the problem.

These statistics also reflect another interesting story behind the sharp increase in apprehensions of dishonest employees. The Security Department pulled together, at an increase in the salary budget, a special detection unit of highly skilled security people to form an elite squad. Their impact on the department's overall effectiveness in detecting internal dishonesty is clearly seen in these statistics. Not only can such statistical tools tell the administrator his programs are working, but they also tend to serve as cost justifications.

	DE TM	DE YTD	DE LYTD	MIS DET TM	MIS DET YTD	MIS DET LYTD	TOT DET TM	UC DET YTD	UC DET LYTD
N-1011	1	4	2	0	0	0	4	0	0
N-1012	1	4	2	0	0	0	1	0	0
N-1013	3	8	3	1	3	3	9	1	0
N-1014	1	4	0	0	4	2	2	0	0
N-1015	0	9	6	0	2	0	1	0	2
N-1016	6	41	25	0	3	5	7	7	4
N-1017	1	27	0	0	1	0	8	4	0
N-1018	0	0	1	0	0	0	1	0	0
N-1019	0	2	3	0	0	0	3	0	0
N-1020	0	1	5	0	3	0	3	0	0
N-1021	0	2	0	0	1	0	0	0	0
NORTH DISTRICT TOTALS	13	102	47	1	17	10	39	12	6
S-1111	1	5	2	0	0	3	4	0	0
S-1112	0	5	1	0	0	0	0	0	0
S-1113	0	4	2	0	0	0	2	0	0
S-1114	1	4	2	0	0	0	1	0	0
S-1115	1	8	7	0	0	0	2	1	2
S-1116	0	2	1	0	0	0	0	0	0
S-1117	0	1	3	0	0	0	2	0	0
S-1118	2	3	6	0	0	0	3	0	2
S-1119	0	0	0	0	0	0	0	0	0
SOUTH DISTRICT TOTALS	5	32	24	0	0	3	14	1	4
C-1211	0	10	12	3	4	3	3	1	0
C-1212	1	4	7	1	2	1	2	0	0
C-1213	2	4	3	0	0	1	2	0	0
C-1214	0	1	2	0	0	0	0	0	0
C-1215	0	2	1	0	2	0	0	1	0
C-1216	2	12	19	0	0	5	2	1	0
C-1217	0	5	5	0	0	0	0	1	2
C-1218	0	2	1	2	2	0	2	0	0
C-1219	0	0	0	0	0	0	0	0	0

	DE TM	DE YTD	DE LYTD	MIS DET TM	MIS DET YTD	MIS DET LYTD	TOT DET TM	UC DET YTD	UC DET LYTD
CENTRAL DISTRICT TOTALS	5	40	50	6	10	10	11	4	2
E-1311	0	5	12	1	1	6	5	0	0
E-1312	0	5	10	0	2	0	0	0	0
E-1313	0	6	1	1	2	1	3	0	0
E-1314	0	1	1	0	0	0	0	0	0
E-1315	0	0	0	0	1	0	1	0	0
E-1316	0	0	0	2	5	0	3	0	0
E-1317	0	14	1	2	5	0	3	0	0
E-1318	5	13	4	0	0	0	7	0	0
EAST DISTRICT TOTALS	5	44	29	6	16	7	22	0	0
W-1411	4	26	13	0	0	3	9	4	0
W-1412	0	21	9	0	0	4	8	2	0
W-1413	1	15	5	0	0	2	4	3	1
W-1414	2	2	2	0	0	0	2	0	0
W-1415	0	4	4	0	0	0	3	0	0
W-1416	0	4	7	0	0	0	0	0	0
W-1417	1	5	6	0	0	0	1	2	0
W-1418	1	4	5	0	0	0	1	0	1
W-1419	0	14	12	0	5	0	0	0	9
W-1420	4	8	0	0	0	0	7	2	0
WEST DISTRICT TOTALS	13	103	63	0	5	9	35	13	11
GRAND TOTAL	41	321	213	13	48	39	121	30	23

Figure 16.1   Statistical record of detection activity in different units of a large organization.

SUMMARY

As organizations change, so do security needs. *Inspection* is the ongoing process which ensures that new risks are recognized and that established deterrents remain necessary and cost-effective.

To keep pace with organizational change, inspections must be continuous. The inspection process must have the full support of company management and the active participation of security management. Such inspections may be *formal* or *informal, structured* or *unstructured*. The structured inspection moves systematically from one area of exposure to another, following a detailed checklist.

Risk assessment evaluates the probability and cost of potential loss. From this evaluation comes a decision to adopt deterrents. Countermeasures may involve procedural controls, hardware, electronics or (the most costly) security personnel.

The inspection process also includes *assessment of existing counter-measures.* Every security program or practice must be subjected to the basic challenge: Why are we doing this?

Inspection also verifies *compliance* with protection programs. Are they being carried out as planned? Such verification comes at the supervisory and line employee level as well as from management; the effective manager will be responsive to this input.

Statistics offer another tool for ongoing evaluation of protection programs. Statistical information, too, must be subject to inspection to ensure that it is up-to-date, and it must be *used* if it is not to be a meaningless exercise.

REVIEW QUESTIONS

1. Define a structured inspection as contrasted with an unstructured inspection.

2. Ideally, who should conduct the inspection? Why?

3. What are the four types of countermeasures? Give an example of each type. How do the costs of each compare?

4. Discuss the possible consequences of security management's failure to follow up on inspection deficiencies.

5. Discuss the role of statistical tools in program management.

17

*Risk Analysis**

WHAT IS RISK?

Risk is associated with virtually every activity one can think of, but for the purpose of this text I shall limit the meaning of the word *risk* to the uncertainty of financial loss, the variations between actual and expected results, or the probability that a loss has occurred or will occur. In the insurance industry, the term *risk* is also used to mean "the thing insured," for example, the XYZ Company is the risk. Risk is also the possible occurrence of an undesirable event.

Risk should not be confused with *perils,* which are the causes of risk and are things such as fire, flood, and earthquake. Nor should risk be confused with *hazard,* which is a contributing factor to perils. Almost anything can be a hazard—a loaded gun, a bottle of caustic acid, a bunch of oily rags, or a warehouse used for storing paper products, for example. The end result of risk is loss or a decrease in value.

Risks are generally classified as "speculative" (the difference between loss or gain, for example, the risk in gambling) and "pure risk," a loss or no-loss situation, to which insurance generally applies.

For the purposes of this section, the divisions of risk are limited to three common categories:

- Personal (having to do with people assets)
- Property (having to do with material assets)
- Liability (having to do with legalities that could affect both of the above, such as errors and omissions liability)

WHAT IS RISK ANALYSIS?

Risk analysis is a management tool, the standards for which are determined by whatever management decides it wants to accept in terms of actual

---

* Reprinted from James E. Broder, *Risk Analysis and the Security Survey.* (Boston: Butterworth Publishers, 1984), pp. 1–11.

loss. In order to proceed in a logical manner to perform a risk analysis it is first necessary to accomplish some basic tasks:

- Identify the assets in need of being protected (money, manufactured product, and industrial processes to name a few).
- Identify the kinds of risks that may affect the assets involved (internal theft, external theft, fire, or earthquake).
- Determine the probability of risk occurrence. Here one must keep in mind that such a determination is not a science but an art—the art of projecting probabilities.
- Determine the impact or effect, in dollar values if possible, if a given loss does occur.

I will discuss these subjects in detail in a later section in this chapter titled "Risk Exposure Assessment."

WHAT IS A RISK ASSESSMENT ANALYSIS?

A risk assessment analysis is a rational and orderly approach and a comprehensive solution to problem identification and probability determination. It is also a method for estimating the anticipated or expected loss from the occurrence of some adverse event. The key word here is *estimating,* because risk analysis will never be an exact science. Nevertheless, the answer to most, if not all, questions regarding one's security exposures can be determined by a detailed risk assessment analysis.

WHAT CAN RISK ANALYSIS DO FOR MANAGEMENT?

Risk analysis provides management with information on which to base decisions, such as: Is it best always to prevent the occurrence of a situation? Should the policy be to contain the effect a hazardous situation may have? Is it sufficient simply to recognize that an adverse potential exists, and for now do nothing but be aware of the hazard? The eventual goal of risk analysis is to strike an economic balance between the impact of risk on the enterprise and the cost of protective measures.

A properly performed risk analysis has many benefits, a few of which are:

- The analysis will show the current security posture (profile) of the organization.
- It will highlight areas where greater (or lesser) security is needed.

- It will help to assemble some of the facts needed for the development and justification of cost effective countermeasures (safeguards).
- It will serve to increase security awareness by assessing the strengths and weaknesses of security to all organizational levels from management to operations.

Risk analysis is not a task to be accomplished once and for all time. It must be performed periodically in order to stay abreast of changes in mission, facilities, and equipment. And, since security measures designed at the inception of a system have generally proved to be more effective than those superimposed later, risk analysis should have a place in the design phase of every system. Unfortunately, this is seldom the case.

The major resource required for a risk analysis is manpower. For this reason the first analysis will be the most expensive, as subsequent ones can be based in part on previous work and the time required will decrease to some extent as experience is gained.

The time allowed to accomplish the risk analysis should be compatible with its objectives. Large facilities with complex, multishift operations and many files of data will require more time than the single shift, limited production locations. If meaningful results are expected, management must be willing to commit the resources necessary for accomplishing this undertaking.

THE ROLE OF MANAGEMENT IN RISK ANALYSIS

The success of any risk analysis undertaking will be strongly contingent on the role top management takes in the project. Management must *support* the project and express this support to all levels of the organization. Management must *delineate* the purpose and scope of risk analysis. It must *select* a qualified team and formally *delegate* authority. And management must *review* the team's findings.

Personnel who are not directly involved in the analysis process must be prepared to provide information and assistance to those who are conducting the analysis and, in addition, to abide by any procedures and limitations of activity that may ensue. Management should leave no doubt that it intends to rely on the final product and base its security decisions on the findings of the risk analysis team. The scope of the project should be defined and the statement of scope should specifically spell out the parameters (limitations) of the analysis. It is oftentimes equally important to state specifically what the analysis is *not* designed to accomplish or cover. This will serve to eliminate any misunderstandings at the start rather than at the conclusion of the exercise.

At this point it may be well to define and explain two other terms that are sometimes used interchangeably with risk. They are: *threats*—anything that could adversely affect the enterprise or the assets, and *vulnerability*—weaknesses, flaws, holes, or anything that may conceivably be exploited by a threat. Threats are most easily identified by placing them in one of three classifications or categories: natural hazards, accidents, or intentional acts. Vulnerabilities are most easily identified by collecting information from interviewing persons employed in the facility, by field observation and inspection, by document review, and, in the case of hardware or electronics, by conducting tests designed to highlight vulnerability and expose weaknesses or flaws in the design or the system.

Threat occurrence rates/probabilities are best developed from reports of occurrence or incident reports whenever this historical data exist. Where the data do not exist it may be necessary to reconstruct them by conducting interviews with knowledgeable persons.

RISK EXPOSURE ASSESSMENT

Before any corrective action can be considered, it is necessary to make a thorough assessment of one's identifiable risk exposure. In order to accomplish this it is essential that three factors be identified and evaluated in quantitative terms. The first is to determine the types of loss or risk that can affect the assets involved. Here examples would be fire, burglary, robbery, or kidnapping. If one of these were to occur (for the sake of this portion of the text we will consider only single, not multiple, occurrences) what effect would the resulting disruption of operations have on the company? For example, if vital records were destroyed by fire or flood, what would the effect be on the ability of the company to continue in operation? There is a saying common to protection professionals, "One may well survive a burglary, but one good fire can put you out of business forever." If the chief executive officer, on an overseas trip, were to be kidnapped by a terrorist group (or even suffer a serious heart attack), who would make the day-to-day operating decisions in his absence? What about the unauthorized disclosure of trade secrets and other proprietary data? After all (or as many as possible) of the risk exposure potentials are identified, one must then proceed to evaluate those threats that should they occur would produce losses in quantitative terms—fire, power failure, flood, earthquake, and unethical or dishonest employees, to name a few factors worthy of consideration.

To do this we proceed to the second factor: estimate the probability of occurrence. What are the chances that the identified risks may become actual events? For some risks estimating probabilities can be relatively easy. This is especially true when we have documented historical data dealing with identifiable problems. For example, how many internal and external theft cases have been investigated over the past year? Other risks are more difficult to predict. Sabotage, industrial espionage, kidnapping, and civil disorder may never occur or may occur only on a one time basis.

The third factor is quantifying (prioritizing) loss potential. This is measuring the impact or severity of the risk, if in fact a loss does occur or the risk becomes an actual event. This exercise does not become final until one develops dollar values for the assets previously identified. This part of the survey is necessary to set the stage for classification evaluation and analyzation of the comparisons necessary to the establishment of countermeasure priorities.

Some events or kinds of risk with which business and industry are most commonly concerned are as follows:

- Nuclear attack or accident (Three Mile Island)
- Natural catastrophe (tornado, hurricane, earthquake, volcanic eruption, and flood)
- Industrial disaster (explosion, chemical spill, structural collapse, and fire)
- Civil disturbance (sabotage, labor violence, and bomb threats)
- Criminality (robbery, burglary, pilferage, embezzlement, fraud, industrial espionage, internal theft, and hijacking)
- Conflict of interest (kickbacks, trading on inside information, and unethical business practices)
- Miscellaneous risks, threats, or loss factors (bookkeeping errors, unaccounted for inventory losses, traffic accidents, alcohol and drug abuse, absenteeism, gambling, and improper leave or time clocking)

The author recognizes that some of the above events (risks) are unlikely to occur. Also, some are less critical to an enterprise than others if they do occur (fire versus burglary). Nevertheless, *all* are possibilities and are thus deserving of consideration.

RISK IDENTIFICATION

In systems security, the primary purpose of vulnerability identification or threat (exposure) determination is to make the task of risk analysis more manageable by establishing a base from which to proceed. When the risks associated with the various systems and subsystems within a given enterprise are known, then the allocation of countermeasures (resources) can be more carefully planned. The need for such planning rests on the premise that security resources, as with all other resources, are limited and therefore must be allocated wisely.

Risk control begins, logically, with identification and then classification of risk. To accomplish this task it is necessary to examine or survey all of the activities and relationships of the enterprise in question and develop answers to these basic considerations:

- Assets—What does the company own, operate, lease, control, have custody of or responsibility for, buy, sell, service, design, produce, manufacture, test, analyze, or maintain?
- Exposure—What is the company exposed to that could cause or contribute to damage, theft, or loss of property or other company assets or that could cause or contribute to personal injury of company employees or others?
- Losses—What empirical knowledge is available to identify the frequency, magnitude, and range of past losses experienced by this and similarly located companies performing a like service or manufacturing the same or a similar product?

Obviously, the answers to these questions and any additional questions that may be raised when conducting initial inquiries will be the basis for the risk identification and eventually risk evaluation as it specifically relates to the enterprise in question.

Security professionals use many techniques to develop data for risk identification. They may review company policies, procedures (or their absence), organization, and activities to ascertain what risks have been identified and how they are perceived as management responsibilities. They may review insurance and risk related files, including claims and loss records. Interviews with the heads of departments that have experienced loss exposures develop information on the organization and functioning of loss control procedures, if in fact any exist. Conducting inspections and interviewing management and other personnel in enough locations and activities develops a complete picture of the company's risk exposures as a basis for later evaluating loss control procedures and their effectiveness.

The tools necessary to accomplish the above are the ability to conduct comprehensive interviews; the ability to conduct inspections and field observations of operations, procedures, manpower, and electronics applied in security systems; and the ability to identify, obtain, and analyze pertinent records.

Another technique is to develop asset data. To do this one completely identifies all company assets, tangible and intangible, in terms of quantity and quality. Then one identifies the location of all company assets as well as obvious exposures that may exist at these locations. Next one must determine the value of these assets in terms of actual dollars. This should be broken into the following three categories:

- Owned assets $ _____
- Leased assets $ _____

- Facility losses $ _____
  Total tangible assets $ _____
  Total intangible assets $ _____
  Grand total $ _____

The identification of all company assets, coupled with a history of loss exposure for this company and companies similarly located and engaged, will normally be sufficient to identify most of the major risks involved.

After this identification procedure, the security survey or inspection can be limited to those risks or exposures that specifically relate to the enterprise in question. These risks will usually include most, if not all, of the following:

- Crime losses, such as burglary, theft (internal and external), fraud, embezzlement, vandalism, arson, computer abuse, bomb threat, theft of trade secrets and industrial espionage, forgery, product forgery and trademark infringement, robbery, extortion, and kidnapping, to name the most common crime risks encountered by business and industry.
- Cargo pilferage, theft, and damage
- Emergency and disaster planning
- Liability of officers and directors
- Environmental controls as directed by occupational safety and health codes
- Damage to property from fire, flood, earthquake, windstorm, explosion, building collapse, falling aircraft, and hazardous processes
- Comprehensive general liability arising from damage caused by any activity for which the entity can be held legally liable
- Business interruption and extra expense. An evaluation of this type of risk may require a detailed study of interdependencies connecting various segments of the entity and outside suppliers of goods and services. It may indicate the need for extensive disaster planning for reduction of the risk
- Errors and omissions liability
- Professional liability
- Products liability and completed operations

As can be seen from even a cursory review of the above identified risks, the scope of risk identification alone, separate from risk evaluation and risk control, presupposes a degree of education and practical knowledge not often possessed by the individual security manager. This proposed knowledge implies that the person who is charged with this responsibility has the education, training, and practical experience necessary to seek out, recognize, and thus identify not only the risk involved but also its applicability to the enterprise in question. It goes almost without saying that the process of risk identification, evaluation, and control in any dynamic organization, public or private, requires constant attention by professionals who possess the necessary knowledge and tools to accomplish the task.

EXAMPLES OF THE PROBLEMS
OF IDENTIFICATION

The author was given the assignment of conducting a security survey for a chain of fast food restaurants. At the initial meeting with the management staff of this chain, reports from the company's internal audit division were furnished for our review. These reports showed all crime-related losses for a twelve-month period. These reports contained statistics that showed a disturbingly high incident rate for "robbery." One of the firm's top management people stated that he had a growing concern that one of the part-time high school cashiers working in their restaurants might get shot in the course of a robbery because of the absence of procedures instructing cashiers in how to deal with this problem.

Field inspections of a representative number of these restaurants produced evidence that their principal problem was burglary, followed closely by internal theft. "Armed robbery" or just plain robbery, as perceived by management, while admittedly always a dangerous problem, was not as frequent or as serious as management had been lead to believe by the statistics in the audit reports. Further inquiry revealed that the terms *robbery* and *burglary* were being used indiscriminately and, in many cases, synonymously.

It was only after properly identifying the real problem that we could then proceed to develop the necessary procedures and allocate the necessary resources to address and then solve management's concern.

In another case, the author met with the management of a national corporation that, among other things, printed negotiable instruments. The purpose of the meeting was to develop a mutual agreement regarding the scope of a security survey to be conducted at one of their West Coast plants. At the outset, one of the management representatives asked the question, "Have you ever conducted a security survey at a plant that prints negotiable instruments?" The simple fact of the matter then was that I had not. Nevertheless, the answer I gave was, "No, I haven't, but that really doesn't matter. It is immaterial to me if your plant manufactures widgets or prints negotiable instruments. You will either have a security program or you will not. If you do it will either be functional, or it will not. In either event, it can be evaluated and we can determine if the state of the security in existence at the plant is adequate, given the unique requirements for protection that this type of production requires. If we feel the system is not functional, we will make recommendations to upgrade the quality and the quantity of the security safeguards necessary to accomplish the goal.

If you have no program for security, we will design one for your consideration to meet the above requirements."

In security, as with many other disciplines, we deal in standards and principles. These remain relatively constant, regardless of the product involved. The end result is loss control. This means one either has or does not have an adequate security system. One way to find out is to conduct a survey and identify those harmful events that may interfere with the ultimate objectives, as they may be defined by the enterprise in question.

SECURITY CHECKLIST

Until now I have been discussing the techniques and tools that the security professional needs in order to develop data for risk identification. Very often, security checklists are used to facilitate the gathering of pertinent information. These checklists take many forms. They can be a simple list of questions asking for only a yes or no response, or they may ask open-ended questions requiring narrative responses. They may be brief and narrowly focused on the specific operation or activity in question, or they may be broader in scope and cover security concerns common to all of the company's operations. No matter what the appearance, the purpose of a security checklist is to provide a logical recording of information and to assure that no important questions go unasked.

The checklist is usually the backbone of the security survey or audit. A general security checklist that is designed for company-wide use can be found in Appendix B at the end of this book. It may include many items that are appropriate in some situations but not in others.

REVIEW QUESTIONS

1. What is "risk" and why is it important to the security manager?

2. What are the four basic tasks involved in risk analysis?

3. What can risk analysis do for management? Explain using examples.

4. Define "threat" and "vulnerability."

5. What are some of the techniques used in developing data for risk identification?

6. Name some of the risks with which business and industry are most concerned.

7. What is the purpose of a security checklist?

18

THE SECURITY SURVEY*

The goal of risk management—to manage risk effectively at the least possible cost—cannot be achieved without reducing, through a total management commitment, the number of incidents that lead to losses.[1] Before any risk can be eliminated (or for that matter, reduced) it must be identified. One proven method of accomplishing this task is the security survey. R. M. Momboisse has defined the security survey as: "A critical, on-site examination and analysis of an industrial plant, business, home, or public or private institution to ascertain the present security status, to identify deficiencies or excesses, to determine the protection needed, and to make recommendations to improve the overall security."[2]

WHY ARE SECURITY SURVEYS NECESSARY?

The latest available reports estimate that the cost of crime to American business is in excess of $40 billion per year and rising. Perhaps the biggest problem is that most corporate managers do not even know if they have a problem. They do not know how to find out if they have a problem or even if they want to know whether or not they have a problem. Some managers seem to prefer to keep things as they are and to regard any suggestion of increased security as direct or indirect criticism of their ability to manage the operation successfully. Nevertheless, most general business security surveys result in the conclusion that crime loss to any given business concern is between 3 percent and 4.5 percent of total sales. Sometimes surveys conclude that losses attributable to theft are equal to or exceed profit. This is especially true for chain store operations where each individual store is regarded as a separate profit center and records for inventory shortage are kept for each location.

---

* Reprinted from James E. Broder, *Risk Analysis and the Security Survey*. (Butterworth Publishers 1984), pp. 41–48.
[1] The field of risk management encompasses more than security and safety. These two subjects, however, are the cornerstone of most effective risk management programs.
[2] Momboisse, R. M., *Industrial Security for Strikes, Riots and Disasters*. (Springfield, Ill.: Chas. C. Thomas, 1968), p. 13.

Crime losses far exceed the losses to business caused by fire and industrial accidents. One security expert estimates the annual loss to business from crime as being twice as great as the combined total of all business losses due to fire and accident!

Are you really concerned about how crime may affect your business? asks the American Management Association. Then take a moment to read the following documented facts:

- White collar crime has doubled since the early 1970s and is currently estimated to exceed $44 billion annually. (The key word is "estimated.")
- Employee pilferage—$5 to $10 billion per annum.
- Embezzlement and computer fraud—$4 billion per annum.
- Commercial bribery and kickbacks—$3.5 to $10 billion per annum.
- Security theft and fraud—$5 billion per annum.

In addition, the U.S. Chamber of Commerce estimates that up to 40 percent of all business theft may involve employees. In some industries (cargo shipping, transportation) 85 percent of loss due to theft is attributable to employees.[3,4,5]

WHO NEEDS SECURITY SURVEYS?

A Stanford Research Institute report titled "Business Property Security," says, when discussing business vulnerability to crime loss, "Likely victims are growing businesses where expansion occurs faster than control systems are set up and large companies where close control over branches and divisions is not feasible." And while this fact has been experienced by many professional security consultants with whom the author has discussed this subject, every business entity, no matter how large or small, could profit from having an objective survey of their security protection.

Most surveys show that the majority of business security is directed toward the problems of external theft—burglary and robbery—as a first and most immediate priority. This situation reflects the development and growth of security from an historical perspective. It was once thought that most, if not all, problems concerning theft from a company were external in nature. Prior to that period during and just after World War II, before the large scale expansion of U.S. and Canadian industry and the development of the multinational corporation, many companies located in North America

---

[3] Background, Findings, and Recommendations." Crimes Against Business Project, American Management Association, 1977.

[4] "The Cost of Crimes Against Business." (Washington, D.C.: U.S. Department of Commerce, 1976).

[5] "White Collar Crime: Everyone's Problem, Everyone's Loss." (Washington, D.C.: U.S. Department of Commerce, 1974).

were at the stage of development we now regard as relatively small to medium industry and business. Many commercial enterprises were of the "Mom and Pop" variety. Because of close supervision and the personal identification that existed between management and labor in these companies, internal theft by "trusted" employees was seldom considered, much less planned for. Hence the development and proliferation of the burglar alarm business to protect these enterprises and combat external theft.

With the growth of the national and multinational corporations and the almost total demise of the "Mom and Pop" commercial and variety stores, we saw a parallel change in business ethics and standards. These changes also affected society as a whole. As an example, in the so-called turbulent 60s, a new term was coined: "The Establishment." Crimes against The Establishment were then, and still are, perceived by many to be permissible, in fact, not crimes at all.

The lack of personal identification within a company by its employees and the dramatic dilution of ethical and moral standards on the part of business combined to make internal theft by employees a simple process of rationalization. After all, who is Standard Oil, ITT, Safeway? "They" make gigantic profits by "ripping off" the general population (read *us*). "They" won't miss one little screwdriver I need for my workshop at home." Thus does the theft of one small item, multiplied 10,000 times each year in many large companies by many similarly motivated employees, add up to a combined annual loss that can far exceed the total loss by a given company from external theft over the entire period of its corporate existence!

Enlightened students of criminology now understand that the most predominant and certainly the most prevalent form of business crime is employee theft in its various forms. So widespread a problem is business crime that a U.S. government survey[6] estimates that 25 percent of business failures are attributable to employee dishonesty.

According to the same government source, the smaller the business, the more likely it is to be the victim of crime. Businesses reporting $1 million of revenue per year are particularly hard hit by crime loss. This is especially true for a retail enterprise that operates on a 2 percent profit margin or a grocery store that has a 1 percent profit line. As serious students of this problem have come to realize, losses due to crime can and do have a dramatic impact on net profits.

Shoplifting, employee theft, and vandalism all cost American business billions of dollars annually. Based on a company's percentage of net profit, Figure 18.1 illustrates how much more a company needs to sell to offset losses in stolen merchandise, equipment, and supplies. The theft of one $500 electric typewriter from the premises means the company must sell $25,000 worth of merchandise to break even if the company or organization is in the 2 percent net profit category, $8,333 if it is in the 6 percent category.

---

6 "Crimes Against Small Business." Small Business Administration, 1969.

Actual	If Company Operates at Net Profit of:				
Loss of:	2%	3%	4%	5%	6%

These additional sales are required to offset an
actual loss:

$ 50	$ 2,500	$ 1,666	$ 1,250	$ 1,000	$ 833
100	5,000	3,333	2,500	2,000	1,666
200	10,000	6,666	5,000	4,000	3,333
250	12,500	8,333	6,250	5,000	4,166
300	15,000	10,000	7,500	6,000	5,000
350	17,500	11,666	8,750	7,000	5,833
400	20,000	13,333	10,000	8,000	6,666
450	22,500	15,000	11,250	9,000	7,500
500	25,000	16,666	12,500	10,000	8,333

Figure 18.1   Loss to Sales (Profit) Ratio

Worse yet, it is still without one electric typewriter. Figure 18.1 is an example
of the impact of loss versus net profits.

ATTITUDE OF BUSINESS TOWARD SECURITY

In general we find that most businesses will protect themselves against
the entry of burglars and robbers onto their premises. Most will also give
protection to high value areas, such as computer centers, vaults, precious
metal storage areas, and any location where money is the principal product,
such as in banks and casinos. Most businesses, however, do not concern
themselves with protection against unauthorized personnel and visitors. Yet,
75 percent to 85 percent of external theft is directly attributable to this
source.

Likewise, if security protection is paid for by a facility where it is
regarded as a capital expense or a yearly expenditure and where it is regarded as reducing the profit line of that particular unit or entity, we can
expect the person in charge of that facility to authorize only the minimum
and least expensive security protection with which he can get by. If, on
the other hand, security is required by corporate management or mandated
by one's client or the various governmental agencies for industries engaged
in sensitive government contracts, we see plant managers installing security
protection without regard to costs.

This latter proposition presupposes another problem. Most plant managers do not have the foggiest idea what kind of security they must have for adequate protection. Granted, with regard to sensitive government contract work, security guidelines are made available. Nevertheless, many are the managers who have fallen prey to the security manpower and hardware salesmen, each of whom proposes a package deal for security protection guaranteed to solve all problems and each of whom operate to the mutual exclusion of the other's service. As a result we constantly encounter security programs that overemphasize manpower (guards) or hardware (alarms or electronics) when the proper solution to the problem is usually an effective marriage of the two, coupled with adequate written procedures to deal with the most common occurrences or eventualities encountered in the real work-a-day world.

WHAT CAN A SECURITY SURVEY ACCOMPLISH?

One approach to determining whether or not there is a need for a security survey is first to examine what services an experienced security expert can provide and then to seek information on security (crime) -related losses being incurred by the particular business or company. The security expert can either be in place, that is to say a member of the staff of the enterprise, or an outside consultant, or both.

Security-related problems might include any or all of the following: theft, fraud, forgery, arson, burglary, robbery, malicious damage, personnel screening and investigation, theft of trade secrets, industrial espionage, executive protection, kidnap, extortion, bomb threats and bombings, and emergency and disaster planning, to name but a few of the more common problems encountered.

If the company or facility being considered has a security plan, the survey can establish if the plan is up-to-date and functional in every respect. Experience has shown that many security plans were established as the need dictated, without regard to centralization and coordination. Upon review, many such plans resemble a crazy quilt affair. More often than not these plans need to be brought together in such a manner that the component parts complement instead of contradict one another.

If the facility has no security plan, then the survey can establish the need for one and develop some or all of the following security services, most of which are commonly found in an industrial setting. By conducting a comprehensive survey of the entire facility—its operations and procedures—one can identify critical factors affecting the security of the premises or operation. The next step is to analyze the vulnerabilities and recommend cost effective protection. This will assist the client in developing policies and procedures to do the following:

- Protect against internal and external theft, including embezzlement, fraud, theft, burglary, robbery, industrial espionage, and the theft of trade secrets.
- Develop access control procedures designed to protect the facility perimeter as well as computer facilities located internally.
- Establish lock and key control procedures.
- Design, supervise, and review installation of anti-intrusion detection systems.
- Establish an executive protection program for corporate personnel here and abroad to deal with extortion and kidnap problems.
- Provide control over the movement and identification of employees, customers, and visitors on company property.
- Review the selection, training, and deployment of security personnel, proprietary or contract.
- Assist in the establishment of emergency and disaster plans and guidelines.
- Identify the internal resources available and needed for the establishment of an effective security program.
- Develop and present instructional seminars for management in all of the above areas.

The above list is by no means all inclusive. It does set forth some of the most frequently encountered programs and systems reviewed or developed as a result of a security survey.

WHY THE NEED FOR A SECURITY PROFESSIONAL?

Losses due to all factors continue to represent problems of major proportions for business and industry. To the extent that the services of a security professional can help in eliminating, preventing and controlling a company's losses, he is needed. In answer to this question Charles Sennewald stated, at the "Security World" Expo 82 Conference on Security Management, that:

> Crime prevention, the very essence of a security professional's existence, is another spoke in the wheel of total loss control. It is the orderly and predictive identification, abatement, and response to criminal opportunity. It is a managed process which fosters the elimination of the emotional crisis response to criminal losses and promotes the timely identification of exposures to criminality before these exposures mature to a confrontation process.
>
> The proper application of protection techniques to minimize loss opportunity not only promises the capability to improve the net profits of business but also functions to reduce to acceptable levels most disruptive acts, the consequences of which often exceed the fruits of the crime.

HOW DO YOU SELL SECURITY TO MANAGEMENT?

As I mentioned earlier in this chapter, some managers, for a variety of reasons, are reluctant even to discuss the subject of security. In the aftermath of an unsuccessful attempt to burglarize a bank vault, the bank operations manager learned that the anti-intrusion system was ten years old and somewhat antiquated. "Why didn't the alarm company keep me advised of the necessity to upgrade my system as the state of the art improved?" he asked. The answer he received was, "The alarm system functioned adequately for ten years with no problem. Would you or the bank have authorized an expenditure of $5,000 to upgrade the alarm system before you had this attempted burglary?" The bank representative reluctantly admitted that he would not. This case is typical of what we call the "knee-jerk reaction" to security. One security consultant with whom the author is acquainted describes it as locking the barn after the horse has been stolen. We all know that the only thing this protects is what the horse left behind.

Nevertheless it is not uncommon to find that management's attention is gained only after a serious problem pointing to the lack of adequate protection is brought to its attention. The first reaction is often one of overkill. The response pendulum swings from complacency to paranoia when the facts indicate that a proper response should be somewhere in between. Given this situation, an unscrupulous alarm salesman will prescribe an electronics system worthy of consideration by the manager of the bullion vault at Fort Knox.

There are some things a security director or consultant can do to convince top corporate management that security is worth spending some money to obtain. Some methods that have proven successful are listed below.

1. Establish a meaningful dialogue with the decision makers in the management hierarchy. First try to ascertain their feelings about security. What do they really want a security program to accomplish for them, if in fact they want anything? Do not be surprised to learn that some management personnel regard security as a necessary evil and thus worthy of little attention (that is, money and manpower). Marshal the facts. Research the history of security losses experienced by the company and use this information to develop trend projections.
2. When collecting data to support your position, deal in principles and not personalities. Use the technique of nonattribution for all unpublished sources of information. With published sources, such as interoffice memos, excerpt the pertinent data if possible. Avoid internecine power struggles at all costs. Maintain a position of objective neutrality.
3. Be as professional about security as you can. The better you are at your job, the greater attention you will command from your superiors. There are many avenues you can explore to develop the information

you need, such as developing contacts with other security professionals who share similar problems. Don't reinvent the wheel. Attend security seminars, purchase relevant books, and do research.

4. In making a proposal to management, hit the highlights and make your proposal as brief as possible. Save the details for later. In any proposal that will cost money make certain you have developed the cost figures as accurately as possible. If the figures are an estimate, label them as such and err on the high side.

5. It is a wise man who knows his own limitations. If you need outside help (and who doesn't from time to time) do not be reluctant to admit you need assistance. Such areas as electronics, computers, and sophisticated anti-intrusion alarm systems are usually beyond the capabilities of the security generalist. Do some study. Know where to go to get the help you need.

6. Suggest that management hire an outside consultant. Competent security professionals have nothing to fear by obtaining a "second opinion." Often, the "expert from afar" has greater persuasion over management than members of their own staff. More often than not the consultant will reinforce your position by reaching the same conclusions and suggesting the same or similar recommendations.

7. Use the right timing to present your position. Recognize that management's priorities are first and foremost the generating of profit. In order to capture management's attention one should wait for the right time and circumstances to present a proposal. It is difficult to predict when this may occur. Therefore, have your facts developed and be ready at a moment's notice to make your presentation. It will be too late to do the research when you are called before the board of directors without notice to explain just how a breakdown in security could have occurred and what you propose to do to solve the problem for the future.

8. Develop a program of public relations. Security represents inconvenience even under the best of circumstances. Once you have management thinking favorably about your proposal you will need to sell it to everyone in the organization in order for it to be successfully implemented. Most employees enjoy working in a safe and secure environment. Use this technique to convince employees that the program was designed as much for their safety and security as for the protection of the assets of the corporation.

Do your homework in a thorough manner and you can't help but impress management with your capabilities as a security professional. Remember, be patient. Few are those who have been able to sell 100 percent of their security program to management the first time out of the starting blocks.

REVIEW QUESTIONS

1.   Define the security survey and discuss its importance as a management tool.

2.   What can the security survey accomplish?

3.   How can the security survey help sell security to management?

19

Office Administration

In an efficient and well-managed organization, general security office administration has six distinctive functions, each of which plays an important role in the success of the total back-office effort (Figure 19.1). Irrespective of the number of employees available for office duties, the functions themselves are constant. People may change, but functions do not. Like the placement of stones in a pyramid, each office administration function is unique, critical to the whole, and conspicuous. The functions are:

1. Office supervision
2. Secretarial
3. Reception
4. Clerical

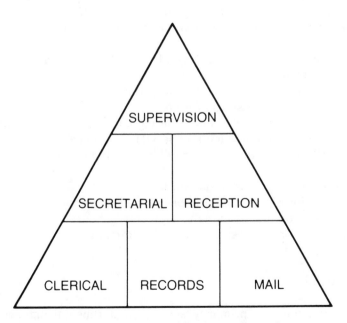

Figure 19.1 The six functions of Security office administration.

5.   Records (Data retention and retrieval)
6.   Mail

The functions obviously suggest the type of employee required to discharge each function—but that is not to preclude the possibility of joining two or more functions together under one employee, or, conversely, of having two or more employees assigned to the same function. And the interrelationship between functions is most important in the daily office effectiveness and orderly work-flow. Figure 19.2 illustrates possible compacting configurations, depending upon the size of the organization.

The problem with combining functions is that they tend to lose identity; the employee tends to focus or set priorities on personal preference or workload demands. As a consequence, less desirable tasks such as filing become backlogged. An understanding of the risks of combining functions is necessary to provide adequate training and supervision for employees who are handling multiple functions.

DESCRIPTION OF FUNCTIONS

Supervision

In addition to the traditional and necessary supervisory responsibilities such as performance evaluations, training, discipline and scheduling, the supervisor of the overall office activities would be responsible for the following:

- Monitoring the day-in and day-out work flow to ensure everything is following plan.
- Coordinating activity between the various functions.
- Assigning tasks and special projects.
- Projecting supply needs, then ordering and controlling supplies.
- Arranging for maintenance and servicing of office equipment.
- Personally overseeing special projects, including doing such projects himself.
- Ensuring security of records and files.
- Arranging for replacement of absent office personnel, reassigning their functions to others, or filling in temporarily himself.
- Inspecting work to ensure standards are maintained.

Secretarial

The secretarial function primarily services departmental management. In a large organization there may be an executive secretary (personally serving

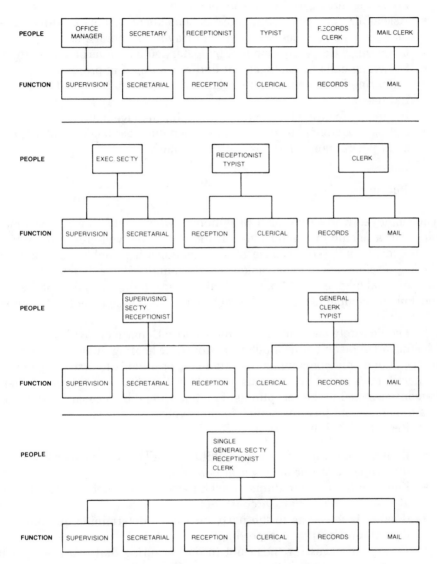

Figure 19.2 Possible configurations of functions and employees in office administration.

the Security Director or Manager) as well as an office manager. Secretarial service usually includes:

- Coordinating appointments.
- Preparing managerial correspondence.
- Assembling and presenting those documents requiring executive signature, such as invoices, expense and travel vouchers, etc.
- Gathering data as requested for budgetary submissions or explanations.
- Screening calls to management and re-routing if appropriate.
- Gathering files, reports and statistics as requested for specific managerial needs.
- Arranging for travel accommodations for management.
- Acting as a communication link between the organization and management when management is not in the office.

Reception

The employee who serves as a receptionist, whether it is a uniformed male officer or a female in regular office attire, should be well-groomed, perhaps even exceptionally so, because of the function's high public visibility and the impression that person makes on the public. If the function is more that of a telephone receptionist, telephone answering training (offered by local phone companies) should be required prior to assignment to the phone board or desk.

People rarely come to or call the Security Department with good news. Meeting a cold, somber or aloof receptionist or hearing an unfriendly voice on the phone only compounds the problems, or it tends to discourage future contacts, even if future contacts would be beneficial to the department. Persons assigned to the receptionist function should be pleasant and courteous in person and have a "smile" in their voices.

Receptionist duties may include:

- Knowing the names and responsibilities of all personnel in an investigative, supervisory or managerial position.
- Knowing the current status of such personnel throughout the day; i.e., at lunch, in a meeting, in court, etc.
- If caller is vague as to the party he wants, determining the nature of the call and routing it accordingly.
- Taking messages for those not in and ensuring that messages get to the proper party in a timely manner.
- "Matching up" visitors or callers with the appropriate party.
- Having guests sign visitor ledger and obtain badge, if required.
- Accomplishing sundry light tasks during slow periods, such as matching trailer security seal numbers against manifests, typing index cards, and so forth.

Clerical

The clerical function is normally filled by an employee who has a range of office skills up to and possibly including shorthand.* This person is the office "generalist," and as the chart in Figure 19.2 suggests, this is a fundamental office function. A sampling of clerical activities includes:

- Transcribing recorded field reports into typed reports.
- "Packaging" files or assembling the contents of a given file into the standard format.
- Logging incoming data on appropriate forms or charts for subsequent compilation.
- Converting compiled statistical data into typed charts or forms for duplication and distribution.
- Processing, sorting and distributing forms and documents as required.
- Operating a small computer in terms of inputing data as well as retrieval.
- Preparing index cards on all names processed through Security, with appropriate source reference.
- Typing memoranda, notices, instructions, orders, training materials for duplication and distribution.
- Acting as relief for secretary, receptionist, records clerk and mail clerk.

Records

Records and the records maintenance program may appear to be relegated to a low status, but in actuality the whole record function is the lifeblood of a security organization. To put it another way, the records of a security department really constitute the detailed diary or historical recordings of all security-related events up to the present. So that the reader may better appreciate the scope and importance of this function, the following list represents a sampling of the types of records that may be found in a security records section:

- Company arrest records of all non-employees.
- Company arrest records of employees.
- Employee security terminations.
- Open investigation files on current employees.
- Reports on all burglaries against the company.
- Reports on all arson attacks against the company.
- Reports on all vandalism or malicious mischief.

---

* In this computer age such employees may now have computer skills as a routine part of the clerical function.

- Reports on all bomb threats.
- Reports on all obscene phone calls.
- Reports on all major thefts.
- Reports on all suspicious circumstances.
- Reports on all intrusion, waterflow or other fire alarms.
- Reports on all daily patrol activities.
- Reports on all fraud, counterfeit, or impostor incidents.
- Security intelligence files (undercover reports . . . information received).
- Security attendance files.
- Construction, blueprints, etc. on company properties.
- Files on truck schedules and security seal numbers.
- Document files (usually exception or "authorized OK" forms).
- Files of training materials.
- Memo reference files.
- Correspondence files.
- Equipment and resource files.
- Contractor and supplier files.
- Special events files.
- Emergency procedure files.
- Fidelity bonding file.
- Master indices (main index file).
- Accident reports.
- Files on former security personnel.

The foregoing list in no way constitutes a necessarily complete records configuration, nor does it suggest that every security organization requires all such categories. It does illustrate the wide spectrum of possible categories a security department may be required to retain.

Record Filing Systems

There's no question that the computer is becoming a new and viable security management tool, not only in access control programs but also in capturing, storing, and retrieving important security data. However, the manual system is still the most dominant form of record retention in our industry and an in-depth analysis of how that system works can still serve as a format for computerized programs.

To bring order to the records is, of course, the challenge. "Order" means that any given record or file can be located promptly and pulled on demand. Delays or the excuse that "we can't find it" reflect, to some degree, disorder. Order means the material is filed in a systematic way and the system is logical and disciplined.

Figure 19.3   Sample of annualized alpha-numeric filing system.

There is no *one* correct filing system. The design of the system must serve the particular needs of the given organization. The simpler the system, the better. As an example, the entire list above could be filed in a basic alphabetic arrangement, where all burglary files would naturally be filed in the "B" section. An alternative would be to file burglaries under the "C" section for "Crimes" or "Criminal Investigations." For the sake of this presentation, the author will use the straight basic alphabetic system.

The alphabetic system provides the rough or first division of materials. It cannot stand by itself in every case, so a secondary alphabetic or numeric system is necessary. This can best be illustrated by the alpha-alpha system; in filing arrested shoplifters, for example, "S" for "Shoplifters" is the first alpha, and the names of each shoplifter (Abrams, Brown, Cole, Davidson, etc.) form the second alpha.

In the alpha-numeric system, on the other hand, burglaries would be filed under B (the alpha) and an individual case number assigned to each (B-1, B-2, B-3, etc.), the number constituting the numeric control. Depending upon the volume of activity, the system can be "annualized" for increased control and ready statistical information, as illustrated in Figure 19.3.

The difference between the alpha-alpha and alpha-numeric method is that the former readily identifies and stores *names of people* and the latter identifies and stores *incidents* in which people are not always known, arrested or identified. If the burglar is caught and known, the master index file (usually a 3×5 index card filed alphabetically) of suspect's name refers to the appropriate file, as shown in Figure 19.4.

Figure 19.4   Master index file card of suspect's name.

Control Card Ledger

The key to this system is discipline in the controls. A control card ledger must be maintained for all alpha-numeric systems. Usually the card is maintained in front of the controlled section and the next file number is assigned to each case as it occurs. What typically happens is as follows: The investigator is either dispatched to the scene of a reported or suspected burglary, or a security employee comes across the scene of such a crime and calls into the security headquarters for a file number. The records clerk pulls the control card for burglaries and gives the next unused number to the investigator, noting the assignment on the control card by date, location and investigator's name. That case is then an assigned and pending case. The investigation must be complete, "packaged," signed-off (approved by the appropriate supervisor) and filed. Once in file, the control card is checked-off by date and thus accounted for. If the file is then subsequently removed, a note is made on an "Out" card, filed behind the control card, as to who removed the file and on what date (Figure 19.5). If the file is not in its proper place, yet the control card shows it in and no entry is noted on the "Out" card, someone failed to follow the procedure.

The "Out" card is required for all alpha-alpha and alpha-numeric records, not for simple alpha files, such as correspondence records.

Master Index Cards

An extremely valuable tool in the area of records is the index card in the master index files. Not only is it an alphabetical locator reference card,

OUT

FILE #	DATE OUT	TAKEN BY	PURPOSE	DATE RETURNED
B-77-41	DEC. 6, 77	JONES	COURT	DEC. 9, 77
B-78-6	MAR. 11, 78	ALTON	SUPPLEMENTAL REPORT	MAR. 12, 78
B-78-6	MAR. 16, 78	ALTON	SUSPECT IN CUSTODY-TO P.D.	

BURGLARY

FILE #	DATE ASSIGNED	INVESTIGATOR	LOCATION	DATE IN
B-78-1	JAN. 1, 78	Morlock	Greenridge pump house	JAN. 4
B-78-2	JAN. 3, 78	Sutton	Crenshaw tire center	JAN. 8
B-78-3	JAN. 22, 78	Zeigler	Optometrist office	JAN. 24
B-78-4	FEB. 16, 78	Wagner	Montclair	
B-78-5				
B-78-6				

Figure 19.5   Sample control card and "out" card.

but it also can serve as a record in and of itself. Incidental information of a derogatory nature can be noted thereon, from a wide variety of sources, and filed for future reference. Local newspapers provide a wealth of information about individuals in the community involved in antisocial behavior or criminal activity. Such information can be extracted, noted on the card and filed away. If at a later time a person by the same name applies for work with the company, the automatic search of the master index (part of the new employee screening process) will disclose the derogatory information. An investigation can determine if the applicant is indeed the same person named on the card. Certainly the fact that the names are identical should never be the grounds for action against the person, but it does give direction to the background investigator.

File Control

Security files should never be pulled and released without supervision of the responsible records clerk or supervisor.

Mail

The humble task of processing mail, both incoming and outgoing, receives a lot of attention, and rightfully so. A great deal of business communications is by necessity reduced to the written word and dispatched by mail, whether in-house mail or the U.S. postal system. Queries, answers, instructions, notifications and a host of other written messages must move expeditiously between given parties. Failure to receive such communications can be costly, cause failures, or at the least be embarrassing. As a consequence, mail failures or undue delays can provoke emotional reactions. Therefore the mail function should include the following:

- One person, whether full-time, part-time or combined responsibility, should be clearly charged with that responsibility. There should be no confusion as to whose assignment it is.
- Periodic daily pick-up from the main company mail distribution room.
- Opening and date stamping of all mail except those envelopes marked confidential.
- Knowledge of who's who, past and present, in the security organization and the company as a whole (to expedite misdirected or improperly addressed correspondence).
- The capability to hand-deliver or hand-post special correspondence.
- Last but not least, an appreciation for the importance of the function. (This can only be achieved by management.)

OFFICE SECURITY

The security office is the repository of a vast amount of information, factual and otherwise (suspicious, not yet verified and still under investigation). All of this data must be categorized as highly confidential and demands security. There are two aspects of security in connection with this information. One is personnel and the other is physical. The people who are hired to work in the office administration area of a security department require precisely the same degree of thoroughness in the background investigation as does any other security employee. The sensitivity of information contained in the files, even in the kind of company not engaged in national defense or other highly sensitive activities, deserves maximum security, even if only from a company liability point of view. The release of information concerning a janitor's discharge due to writing obscene letters to a secretary in the blueprint office, for example, could bring serious and unnecessary repercussions from a civil lawsuit.

Proper physical security requires that all filing cabinets be equipped with a lock as well as a drop bar that runs vertically down in front of the drawers and is secured in place with a padlock during non-office hours.

Additionally, if the office area is in a separate security building, it should be protected by fire and intrusion alarms.

THE OFFICE ENVIRONMENT

The fact that a security department is not a profit-center, or is considered non-productive in terms of the industry or business it serves, in no way justifies hand-me-down equipment or furniture. The security office deserves the same quality of work environment as any other department in the organization, and it is the responsibility of security management to insist on that equality. Office personnel need a clean, fresh, open space in which to work, with good equipment, sufficient light, a place to relax and a general climate which fosters the concept that they too contribute to the overall success of the firm and, as a result, take genuine pride in their department generally and in their work specifically.

SUMMARY

Security office administration includes six key functions. Each is unique and critical. Although it is not always possible that they be performed by different people, it is essential that the specific functions should not lose their identity.

Supervision covers the day-to-day responsibility for the effective functioning of the security office, including planning, provision for supplies and equipment, coordination of work assignments and inspection.

The *secretarial* function provides internal secretarial services for departmental management. The *clerical* role is that of the office "generalist," including typing, filing, processing forms and documents, etc. The *receptionist,* as the department's first point-of-contact with outsiders, should project an image of courtesy and cooperation. The handling of *mail* is also a specific and important responsibility.

Records maintenance is a significant part of the security program. Examples include records of arrest, termination, investigation, crimes of all kinds, reference material, equipment and resource files, etc. Whatever filing system is used, it must provide disciplined control and accessibility of information.

Finally, it is important that principles of security be embodied in the hiring of office personnel and in the internal practice of physical security. The physical environment of the security office should reflect the importance attached to this function by the company.

REVIEW QUESTIONS

1. What are the six basic functions of security office administration? Give examples of several of the responsibilities that come under each function.

2. Describe the alpha-alpha and the alpha-numeric systems of filing records.

3. What is the purpose of the control card ledger in an alpha-numeric filing system?

4. What are the two aspects of security for the office administration area of the Security Department?

20

WRITTEN POLICIES AND PROCEDURES

The difference between a *policy* and a *procedure* is somewhat vague, yet I've been comfortable in defining the two as follows:

Policy: Management's position, statement, purpose, or direction (*what* management wants).

Procedure: The detailed steps management requires its employees to follow to achieve desired results (*how* management wants it done).

Policies and procedures (or operating practices) more often than not develop slowly, informally, in an unstructured fashion over a given period of time. This could range from months to years, depending on the nature of the organization. Of course, they evolve from the passing on of instructions—word of mouth communication. Sooner or later these policies and procedures are documented in writing.

Experience plays an important role in the formalization of policies and procedures. Consequently, you typically find new security organizations with few written policies and procedures; conversely, you find more established departments with sophisticated and comprehensive written policies and procedures.

THE HISTORICAL EVOLUTION

Let's examine a case study that should clarify the evolutionary process so common in the formalizing of policies and procedures.

Ron Mint recognizes the need for a quality guard service in his community. He has an outstanding guard dog who serves as his partner. He approaches a prospective client, with the dog. The client, owner and operator of a shopping center, is impressed by this unique team and gives Ron the task of securing the complex at night.

Ron does an outstanding job, resulting in another company asking for his service. Ron hires someone he knows who also has a trained dog. Now he has two clients.

After a while Ron has a staff of 20 security officers, 11 dogs, and a small kennel. As he continues to grow, he passes on his philosophy of "maximum protection with quality personnel that's unequivocally dependable" by informal discussions with his employees. Additionally, as each new employee joins the team, Ron, or now one of his supervisors, actually work alongside the novice to show him "the ropes" to ensure that the assignment meets the standards of Fort Patrol. Policies and procedures have yet to be written.

After a period of time and a variety of experiences, similar situations arise, such as an officer who's injured on duty and unable to perform his assignment for the balance of that particular shift. Some decisions regarding what should be done when such a situation arises were good—and some were not. Based on those experiences it becomes reasonable to devise a plan for the next similar eventuality. That plan is *the procedure to follow,* the step-by-step activities various employees will follow to deal successfully with the problem and effect a satisfactory resolution.

As the organization continues to grow, Ron can no longer personally share his philosophy with each and every new officer. So it's written down to be read and shared by all.

Part of Ron's philosophy finds its way into policies and procedures in the following fashion:

POLICY

To ensure that Fort Patrol provides quality personnel, all applicants for employment will be required to successfully pass the authorized psychological test and the personnel officer will require a background investigation verifying employment for the past seven years and ensuring that the applicant has not been convicted on any crime, other than a minor traffic violation.

PROCEDURE: PSYCHOLOGICAL TESTING

1. Advise an applicant at the time he submits the completed application for employment that candidates are required to take a psychological (paper and pencil) test and that the results are considered in the final employment assessment.
2. If the applicant agrees to take the test, provide him with the instruments and a place in a room which is quiet, well-lit, and ventilated.

PROCEDURE: VERIFICATION OF FORMER EMPLOYEES

1. The Fort Patrol employee responsible for verifying applicant's former employment first must examine the application for discrepancies of

dates in the applicant's employment history, e.g., any time not accounted for? Overlapping dates?

2. The employee must inquire into and require satisfactory explanations for any discrepancies or omissions.
3. If there are no discrepancies or if satisfactory explanations have been offered, then the employee should verify the existence of those former employers listed on the application by
    A. Telephone directory or information
    B. City business license or other governmental licensing bodies
    C. Listings in professional directories such as the American Society for Industrial Security
4. The employee should telephone the human resources office of the applicant's former employers, or the security department, if appropriate, and identify himself and the wish to verify the former employment of a candidate. Ask initially only for dates of employment and job title.
5. If that information is secured, the employee should inquire into the re-hireability of the candidate. If *yes,* so note. If *no,* inquire as to why.
    A. Document the phone conversation by noting on the application the date and time of the call and the name of the person with whom you spoke.
    B. Employee making the inquiry must sign and date the application.

BENEFITS

The benefits and logic of the written policy and procedure should be self-evident, yet they are worthy of examination in some depth, including such factors as consistency in performance, reduction of decision-making time, enhancement of controls, and provision for objective performance evaluation.

Consistency in Performance

The written procedure contributes to performance consistency because it requires each employee to do a given task or process the same way; thus we can predict the end results. If employees don't have a procedure to follow (and a procedure is like a road map), they'll do things in a way which we can't predict with any degree of certainty.

Reduction of Decision-making Time

The written procedure has most, if not all, of the necessary decisions built right into it; thus time to decide what to do, how to do it, where to do it, when to do it is eliminated.

Enhancement of Controls

Certainly an important function in the whole management process is the maintenance of control. The written procedure is a control because it controls behavior (action) before it occurs. Case in point: to ensure against a lawsuit for negligent hiring, certain pre-hire actions are most important in our society today.

A well-written procedure on how to conduct the background investigation protects the company because it *controls* all those necessary pre-hire steps. If there was no written procedure on how to "screen" new applicants, I guarantee that there would be as many ways to check the applicant's background (or not to check it) as there are individuals charged with that responsibility. In other words, no control.

Provision for Objective Performance Evaluation

The written procedure is simply another tool that can be used to objectively evaluate an employee's performance. It only makes good sense that if the procedure spells out what to do and an employee does otherwise, that deviation is a discussion point for correcting the performance.

COMPLIANCE

The question of how closely must one adhere to, or comply with, policies or procedures is a problem. A security executive may spend ten minutes emphasizing the importance of a given policy or standard operating procedure (S.O.P.) and conclude by saying something to the effect of, "On the other hand, we want some flexibility here." What kind of flexibility? Too often ranking executives will massage policies and procedures to meet particular circumstances, such as when security discovers an executive involved in some form of internal theft and the amount is not substantial. The policy of the company is to terminate all employees caught stealing. The procedure for terminating such employees, step by step, clearly defines the discharge process.

Yet a company officer or executive in a position of power may, for a variety of reasons, exert his influence and bypass the policy, i.e., the dishonest executive is not terminated but only warned. And a case can be made for exceptions such as:

1. The executive has been with the company for 25 years and has dedicated a great deal of his time and effort to the success of the company (and everyone agrees that's so).

2. The executive is known to spend many hours each week above and beyond the call of duty and deserves consideration.
3. The amount of the "indiscretion" is so small in contrast to the contribution that the executive has made that termination would be too severe.
4. All the other executives have done exactly the same thing—you want to fire everybody?

The list of reasons to not comply with company policies and procedures could go on and on. One more example: He didn't do it intentionally!

The question is whether flexibility should be permitted. The answer is of course. The dangers inherent in written policies and procedures, particularly procedures, are that they become inflexible and outdated and no longer viable. Yet some employees follow them religiously or follow them in *malicious obedience,* that is, following the rules to the letter knowing full well that the consequences could be counterproductive. On the other hand, unless "flexibility" is managed with great care and caution, it is easy to abuse this capability, and regrettably abuse still tends to be a prerogative of some managers.

To avoid conflicts over compliance with written procedures, some firms operate under "Guidelines," which lie somewhere between policies and procedures. Guidelines, by its very name, suggest direction but avoid any hint of absolute compliance. One would have to stray afar before being guilty of violating any of the guidelines—they're just that loose, or flexible.

Of course the looseness, or flexibility, leaves a lot of latitude for the operating manager—it allows wide variances in interpreting guidelines and, inevitably, permits inconsistencies in handling similiar situations. Until a company gets "burned," perhaps in a litigation regarding how a problem was handled, the guidelines are the easiest "rules" for everyone to live with. After all, compliance is a disciplinary problem, and with compliance issues removed from the scene, problems don't exist. Right?

COMBINING POLICIES AND PROCEDURES

Some organizations combine policy (the what) with their standard operating procedure (S.O.P.), or *standing* operating procedure, (the how). The following is an example of such taken from the contents in one firm's procedural manual; following that is the actual statement of policy and procedure.

Chapter 10.00 Safety
        10.01 Safety
              • Employee requirements
              • Health & Safety Committee
              • Accident Reporting
        10.02 Medical Services

Chapter 11.00   Security
     11.00   Statement of Security & Loss Prevention
     11.01   General Security Committee
     11.02   Employee Screening
     11.03   Security and Loss Prevention Awareness
        • New employee orientation
        • Loss Prevention Committee
     11.04   Security Incident Reporting
        • Known loss and incidents
        • Suspected activity
        • Annual Report
     11.05   Definition of Dishonesty
        • Definition of dishonesty
        • Other definitions
     11.06   Investigative and Security Interviews
     11.07   Security Methods and Practices
        • Acceptable security methods and practices
        • Unacceptable security methods and practices
     11.08   Security Miscellaneous
        • Lie detection examinations
        • Criminal history
        • Arrests for non-job related activities

Note the logical division of security activities/categories and how reasonable the codifying system is. Let's look at section (policy) number 11.06 to see what the policy statement says about interrogations (remember: this is an example of the combined policy and procedure).

11.06 INVESTIGATIVE AND SECURITY INTERVIEWS

Purpose

To define and establish standards for interviewing that will ensure maximum results, fair and consistent treatment, and that will protect the company against subsequent civil liability arising therefrom.

Scope

All employees.

Policy

It is the policy of the company to differentiate between investigative and security interviews. With respect to the latter, it is the policy of the company that they be conducted by specifically trained personnel and be handled in the most professional manner possible, and then only when there's reasonable evidence—direct or circumstantial—indicating that the employee is culpable.

Definitions

A. Investigative interview: The questioning of an employee seeking information and/or explanations. It is a fact-gathering process without challenges or accusations. The information gathered during such an interview is subsequently evaluated and may or may not lead to a security interivew.
B. Security interview: The security interview is an accusatory confrontation and is used only in cases of dishonesty or other extremely serious violations of rules, such as narcotics offenses.

Procedures

1. Employees being interviewed must be advised at the outset that they are not being forcibly detained and need not choose to submit to questioning.
    A. If an employee opts not to be interviewed, such a decision constitutes insubordination and the employee will be terminated. The matter may then be referred to local law enforcement authorities, if circumstances and evidence warrant same.
2. Security interviews must be conducted in the privacy of an enclosed office.
3. If a female employee is the interviewee, a witness is required, preferably another female.

FREE-STANDING POLICIES

Procedures invariably are related to a policy because they provide the detailed instructions for employees to carry out the intention of a policy. Conversely, there may be policies where procedures are not required—freestanding policies. The following is an example of a free-standing policy of one firm with respect to applicants:

CRIMINAL HISTORY

1. An applicant will not be refused employment solely based on the fact that he has been convicted of a criminal offense unless said applicant deceived the firm about such history and falsified employment application forms or bonding forms.
2. A criminal record may disqualify an individual from being hired or promoted to assignments such as, but not limited to, management, security, personnel, or positions of fiduciary trust.

Such policy statement obviously stands by itself, and no particular procedure is required to carry it out.

THE IMPORTANCE OF THE WRITTEN POLICY

In our litigious society where major employers are deemed desirable targets for lawsuits, the existence, or absence, of a written policy could be a significant factor in the final litigation outcome. An example is the aforementioned policy of the hiring of applicants with criminal backgrounds. If by chance an applicant was denied employment for some reason other than the fact that he had a criminal arrest and conviction record, and if there were no written policy stating that convictions are not a bar to employment, an applicant could conceivably instigate and successfully pursue a cause of action based on criminal conviction discrimination. The written policy, however, would be an important defense in this case.

POLICIES, PROCEDURES, AND THE SECURITY MANUAL

In the security industry, departmental as well as corporate policies and procedures would all come together in a main and central source of reference—the security manual. The following is the table of contents from the manual of a major retailer in the United States. Retail personnel arrest literally thousands of customers and employees each year and have, over the years, evolved into a highly sophisticated and professionally managed organization, as evident from the manual's detail.

LOSS PREVENTION MANUAL
Table of Contents

Chapter 1   Loss Prevention Program
    1.00 Purpose
    1.01 Organization
    1.02 Responsibility
    1.03 Authority
    1.04 Ethics and conduct
    1.05 Complaints against loss prevention personnel
Chapter 2   Shoplifting
    2.00 Shoplifting
    2.01 Prevention
    2.02 Shoplifter's equipment and methods
    2.03 Legal foundation for detentions, investigations, and searches
    2.04 Apprehension of shoplifters
    2.05 Processing shoplifters
    2.06 Prosecution of shoplifters
    2.07 Shoplifting reports
    2.08 Improper detentions
    2.09 Unusual dispositions

Chapter 3   Investigations
  3.00 The investigative process
  3.01 Authorized investigative aids and strategies
  3.02 Unauthorized investigative aids and strategies
  3.03 Interviews and interrogations
  3.04 Written statements of admission
  3.05 Investigative reports
Chapter 4   Frauds and forgeries
  4.00 Fraud generally defined
  4.01 Check fraud defined
  4.02 Check fraud investigations
  4.03 Credit card fraud defined
  4.04 Credit card fraud investigations
  4.05 Refund fraud defined
  4.06 Refund investigations
  4.07 Forgery defined
  4.08 Forgery investigations
  4.09 Counterfeiting
Chapter 5   Miscellaneous crimes and incidents
  5.00 Arson, arson attempts, and fires in stores
  5.01 Malicious mischief

The Security Manual then is the repository of all written policies and standard operating procedures that pertain to the security function. The Security Manual of course contains other material and information, such as job descriptions for all security classifications, training materials, reports, forms used by security personnel, but the main contents of the manual include written policies and procedures.

FORMAT AND MECHANICS

Written policies and procedures deserve a special "look," a format that sets such important documents apart from more routine documents. Figure 20.1 is an example of the format I recommend.

1.   Each page should reflect the name of the particular procedure.
2.   Each procedure and the contents therein should be codified for easy reference. In Figure 20.1 the General Security Committee procedure is Security Procedure # 11.01, and bomb threat incidents reported to that committee are 11.01.2.a.
3.   That "special look," in this case a vertical line margin with company logo on the lower left bottom.
4.   Logo identifies the company. This procedure is unquestionably an SSI Corporation procedure.

①

GENERAL SECURITY COMMITTEE   ② 11.01

Typical incidents will include, but not be limited to:

    a. known (or suspected) thefts
    b. incidents of break-in
③   c. attacks against employees' autos or personal property
    d. water flows or fires
    e. bomb threats
    f. vandalism
    g. unexplained breaks in the alarm system
    h. employee terminations for security reasons
    i. physical threats or attacks against fellow employees

3. Such reports will comprise part of the quarterly meeting agenda.

4. Committee members will submit requests or problems to the Chairman for inclusion on the agenda.

5. Minutes of the meeting will be distributed to all members of the Committee for subsequent distribution in each facility. Distribution will also include appropriate members of senior management.

④ **SSI**   **SSI CORPORATION**

⑤ Date issued: March 1, 1985   Page 2 of 2
                                                              ⑥

Figure 20.1   Format for written policies and procedures.

5. Each procedure should be dated. The presence of the date could suggest it's time to re-assess its viability or could reflect its absolute timeliness.
6. A two-page procedure noted.

SUMMARY

The difference between policies and procedures is best described as: a policy tends to be a guide to what management wants and a procedure specifically prescribes how it is to be accomplished. The development tends to be evolutionary from the spoken to the written word. Policies and procedures are tools for controlling and measuring performance. There's a degree of flexibility required when following procedures, and not all policies require procedures for implementation. Security policies and procedures tend to be the core of the department's operating manual.

REVIEW QUESTIONS

1. Define the difference between a policy and a procedure.

2. Guidelines are more stringent than a standard operating procedure. True or False? Why?

3. If the policy is to terminate employees for theft and the procedure spells out that process in detail, then every employee caught stealing will automatically be terminated. True or False? Why?

4. For every policy there must be a procedure. True or False? Why?

IV
PUBLIC RELATIONS

21

Selling Security Within the Organization

Good sense dictates that there is an ongoing need to "sell" the necessity and importance of the security function to the company as a whole. Employees at all levels of the organization must first be made aware of, then understand, and then come to appreciate the fact that the security function is a viable and integral part of the business, whatever that business or industry may be, and as such contributes to its overall success.

Why is there an ongoing need to sell security? Turnover of employees, including those in the managerial ranks, is one reason. A second is a result of the selling effect itself; that is, as security is understood and accepted, its role expands or takes on new internal dimensions (as discussed in Chapter 3) which require new selling.

A final reason is the ever-changing external factors which necessitate change in the security function. For example, race riots appeared on the American scene in the 1960s, followed in rapid succession by civil rights demonstrations, anti-war and general anti-establishment demonstrations, airplane hijackings, executive kidnaping and hostage ransoming, all having a dramatic impact on the private as well as the public sector. The impact in the private sector, of course, fell directly on the security forces. Shifts in security procedures and new security requirements to meet new challenges require selling.

Today, in the 1980s new threats, such as "hackers" accessing corporate computers, and terrorism and its impact on executive protection, are newer dimensions to protection responsibilities. Someone must convince EDP management that high school kids could conceivably secure the firm's payroll information or secure a copy of a valuable customer list. Someone must also convince the Chief Executive Officer that, today, he and his family have too high a personal and public profile and that overseas enterprise activities could provoke terrorist retaliation.

That someone is security management.

Selling security, then, is indeed an important security management responsibility.

HOW TO SELL SECURITY

Security First

The security executive cannot sell the necessity and importance of the security function to others if his own people do not understand it. More often than not, the average Security Department employee has a rather limited view of the security function, seeing it only as it relates to his or her particular assignment. They do not see the bigger picture. This "tunnel vision" has a predictable influence on one's attitude, and one's attitude affects one's job performance and relationship with others, in and out of the department.

The single most important aspect of retail security is *shrinkage* or *inventory shortage*. Inventory shrinkage, the difference between the inventory of merchandise on the books and the actual physical presence of goods confirmed by a physical count (inventory count), is the one very visible and tangible measurement of a security department's effectiveness in protecting assets.

In one retail organization, for example, the shrinkage percentage figure, causes of shrinkage, and goals are discussed on posters, in handouts, and in the Security Department's own publication. Yet, at a recent training meeting in the main office and warehouse facility for security officers assigned to that location, not one officer, including those with years of service, could explain the process whereby the company identifies the shrinkage percentage. And not one officer knew what the shrinkage percentage meant in terms of dollars. They were staggered when told that the company, like all major retailers, suffers an annual loss of millions of dollars. When they were told how important they were in the overall efforts to protect merchandise, the light of comprehension seemed to come on. The company's error was in *assuming* the employees understood shrinkage and *assuming* they knew how important their respective jobs were. Today these security officers are thoroughly convinced of the need and importance of the department as well as of their respective jobs.

New Employee Inductions

There is certainly no better opportunity to sell security than that afforded at new employee induction sessions. Not only is there a "captive" audience, but an audience eagerly receptive to information about their new work environment.

Some believe that the presentation on the security organization during the induction program should be made by a member of line management. Even with a prepared script, however, managers tend to deviate from the material, emphasizing those things *they* think are important (which may not be) and omitting information which they feel is better left unsaid because it is distasteful, such as the consequences of internal dishonesty.

Consequently, to ensure that new employees are exposed to the information deemed necessary and appropriate, it must be presented either by a security employee or by way of some form of audio-visual media.

The personal presentation is by far the better technique, *if*—and that is an important if—the security employee is a personable, interesting and effective speaker. The higher the rank of the employee making the presentation, the better. Ideally such presentations should be made by the Security Director himself. The further down the chain of command this task is delegated, the lower priority it will be given by the inductees. Thus the very objective of the exposure—to stress the necessity and importance of security within the organization—is defeated.

In a very large organization, spread over a wide geographical area, the Director's personal appearances may necessarily be limited to special events such as the opening of a new facility. Under such circumstances, use of audio-visuals is a good alternative.

Three of the most commonly used audio-visual formats are the slide/tape programs (35 mm color photographs projected on a screen with accompanying audio tape); a voice message on audio tape; and video tape. All three can be used effectively to orient, educate and sell security.

Slide/tape programs are inexpensive and relatively easy to put together. This particular medium can be used to explain to employees in a graphic and colorful manner what the Security Department does. Slide/tape programs can tolerably run eight to twelve minutes, long enough to develop an interesting message for general internal consumption as well as for new employee induction sessions.

Audio tape programs should be shorter, probably not exceeding four minutes. For this reason they are more practical for inductee consumption exclusively.

Video tape is unquestionably an exciting medium. One of its advantages is that it tends to personalize the guest or speaker so that people can identify with him or her—a feature not available in slide/tape or audio tape programs. Thus, video comes closest to a live personal appearance.

These media can, of course, be combined in a presentation. Slide/tape or audio programs might conclude with a video-taped interview with the Security Director for added personal impact.

More Audio-Visuals

The use of audio-visuals in selling security is not limited to new employee orientation presentations. One large hotel and restaurant chain uses the media described and, in addition, short motion pictures produced in-house to dramatize security and safety problems and procedures, ranging from the handling of bomb threats to fire prevention.

One retail organization has made effective use of an audio tape of an interview between the Security Director and a professional shoplifter, who consented to the interview in return for dismissal of a case pending against him in the local courts. The original tape was a high quality reel-to-reel recording, later reproduced many times on cassette tapes for wide distribution throughout the company.

The shoplifter responded frankly to questions about his trade and skills as they applied to the company. The crook was unquestionably a ham, but his precise answers, his obvious knowledge of the company's merchandising techniques, methods of presenting goods, use of fixtures, floor layouts of individual stores, exact location of stores, one store's laxity in following a given policy compared to another store, what he liked about stealing from this organization and what he feared—all had a hypnotic impact on employees listening to the tape.

"Capturing" this thief on tape has made the threat of shoplifting truly credible to the people who can do the most to thwart such activities. He has made literally thousands upon thousands of employees conscious of their role in preventing shoplifting. He has helped to sell the necessity and importance of security.

There are also a wide range of commercially produced 16mm motion pictures and video cassettes aimed at industrial and business consumers. Even films that do not specifically apply to the work scene and security's role there can help sell security—for example, a film on rape prevention presented by the Security Department for the education of female employees.

Executive Orientations

It is as important, if not more so, to deliver the security message to the management team as it is to the line employees. To ensure this, one organization requires all new incoming middle-management hires to come through the Security Department for a two-hour orientation (which contrasts with the average one-hour appointment in other departments). Their visit with Security, usually within their first month on the job, is part of an overall company orientation. The new Controller or Unit Manager thus becomes acquainted with department heads and their philosophies. This is certainly not an innovative practice, yet Security is not always included in this type of executive orientation, and it should be.

Consider the impression made on the new executive. He meets the Security Director in the latter's office, where, after light conversation, he is given an organizational overview of security. He is provided with an organizational chart on which he can fill in the names of key supervisors and their phone extensions for his future reference. He is asked about the security function of his previous employer and, using that as a comparison, the Security Director emphasizes the differences, pointing out the merits and virtues of the new company's program over what the new executive is accustomed to. Following that he is introduced to an assistant, who spends time discussing operational practices and problems. Then the executive is introduced to the balance of the department's staff personnel and is given a tour of the security offices.

These new managerial personnel are partially convinced of the importance of security when they arrive, due to the importance attached to the orientation schedule and the two hours devoted to security. There is no question in their minds when they leave the security offices that the security function is in the mainstream of the business and has its place in the sun.

Security Tours

Tours of the security facility are a dramatic way to sell security at all levels in the organization. The behind-the-scenes look is intriguing to most people, comparable to the fascination capitalized upon by the television and movie industry in "cops and robbers" entertainment.

To take a class of line supervisors out of their Supervisory Training School and give them a tour of the Security Department usually proves to be a highlight of their entire program. Seeing the proprietary alarm room, the communication center, the armory, the fraud investigators at their desks, the banks of files and indices referred to in background investigations— all this makes a lasting impression on employees.

Bulletins

An important aspect of selling is advertising. The power of a strong ad campaign is well known. Advertising copy has to be directed toward its market, must be interesting, and must have some regularity or consistency in terms of exposure. Given these criteria, the *Security Newsletter for Management* discussed in Chapter 13 constitutes part of the Security Department's ad program.

This four-page monthly publication not only keeps company management informed of what contributions the security organization makes, it is also used as a source document for meetings and loss prevention discussions.

This type of bulletin is a natural selling and communication tool. People are curious about crime and the unusual (look at your newspapers), and when such events occur in their neighborhood or workplace, their interest is intensified. Unless the dissemination of security events compromises security, why not share interesting aspects with other employees? Doing so highlights the necessity and importance of the security function.

Meetings

Visibility and the opportunity to speak and answer questions about security during company meetings is a powerful way to sell the organization. Because security usually has an impact, to some degree, on every aspect of company life, security has a message for whatever department of the company is holding a meeting.

The objective is to achieve visibility and a piece of the meeting agenda. As a rule the person who is calling or conducting the meeting is receptive to enlivening the agenda, and the change of pace and interest that a Security Department representative brings almost guarantees time. There is always an issue to speak to, depending upon the composition of the group; for example, at a meeting of Personnel Department employees, Security could talk about recent bond and application falsifications, and the importance of Personnel and Security working together to insure that only the highest quality of applicants be brought into the company.

The Security Director and Security Manager should participate in these meetings, but not exclusively. It is important to delegate this function down through all levels of the security organization to the first line supervisor. This not only helps security supervisors grow, it establishes an unofficial "speaker's bureau" and thus greater exposure. If there is reluctance to permit supervisors to speak for the department (usually due to fear they will say something that does not meet with management's approval), then prepare canned presentations and practice giving these talks in your own training session.

Security's involvement in company meetings can take many directions. In one retail organization, for example, that participation included the following:

- *Regional Store Managers Meeting.* Comprised of store managers and key staff personnel from one region of the company. During this meeting the Security Agent in charge of security within that region asked for and received fifteen minutes on the agenda, during which he reviewed the policy of scheduling fitting room checkers and budgetary considerations connected therewith. Questions and discussion revealed the topic was timely. The Security Agent left the meeting with a sense of accomplishment. Later feedback indicated that the Agent made an impressive presentation and there had been good dialogue.
- *Personnel Managers Meeting.* The Security Director asked for thirty minutes to discuss recent conflicts between Personnel and Security over employee disciplinary decisions. The essence of the message was: "By virtue of our different responsibilities, we are bound to find ourselves from time to time on collision courses. Why collide? Why must we have a Win-Lose relationship? Instead, if the matter cannot be resolved to the satisfaction of both sides, refer the issue up to the

next highest level for a decision." It was a positive and constructive meeting, and the Director's time was expanded to sixty minutes.

- *Department Managers Meeting.* The Security Manager met with department managers responsible for high loss areas in the business. He discussed contributing causes and suggested ideas on how they could combat such losses. The meeting was small and there was a great deal of attendee participation. The loss area under discussion was not due to theft but to "paperwork errors," yet Security's presence and interest was a plus; in the department managers' eyes, the Security Manager had stepped outside his traditional role and was assuming a different managerial dimension. He helped sell security because of that, as well as coming across as a pleasant and intelligent person, interested in their problems.
- *Dock Workers Meeting.* A Security Line Supervisor attended a meeting in the warehouse for dock employees. A video tape of a commercially prepared motion picture on internal theft was exhibited. The Security Supervisor answered questions following the film. This is a tough situation, to stand up and be willing to take any questions, and the dock workers knew it. Following is an exchange at one of those meetings:

  Dock Worker: Is it really true you use spies—undercover agents?
  Security Agent: That's true.
  Dock Worker: And you use them here?
  Security Agent: Yes.
  Dock Worker: Would you answer this then. How many you got? (tittering runs through the group)
  Security Agent: It fluctuates, but probably right now, somewhere in the neighborhood of six. (almost an audible gasp from the group)
  Dock Worker: Six. Wow! Would you answer this question then. What are their names?

Everyone, including the dock worker and the security agent, howled with laughter. That worker sat down and another stood up and changed the subject with an entirely different question. There was a good feeling about that meeting and it helped, again, to sell security.

Involvement Programs

Programs or activities that bring non-security people into personal contact with Security, with a common goal, tend to cement good relationships.

At one university, for example, students have worked with the Campus Security Department as volunteers. The volunteers are furnished a Security bicycle and two-way radio for shift patrol work. A similar program exists at another campus, where students voluntarily patrol wooded areas of a large Eastern university on their own horses. They provide this service to the security organization in exchange for the facilities for keeping their horses on campus.

Not only does the personal involvement have a positive impact on the individual, but his involvement, if visible to other employees of the company, serves as an example. The logic is simple: if students see other students patrolling areas of the campus, then they realize there *must* be a need for security, and if security is necessary, it is important.

Selling security within the organization sets and maintains a climate of understanding, appreciation, and support for the department's objectives. Some of that support comes in the form of budget dollars.

SUMMARY

There is an ongoing need to make all employees in the company aware of the importance of the security function. Security employees themselves should understand the importance of the security function and of their respective jobs.

Induction sessions for new employees offer an opportunity for presentations by the Security Director or another representative of the department. Audio-visual materials such as slide/tape programs, audio tapes, video tapes and motion pictures can be used effectively.

All newly hired middle-management personnel should undergo an *orientation session* with the Security Department. During this visit the new executive learns about the department's structure and function, meets the staff and tours the security facility.

Bulletins such as a Security Newsletter can be used to inform management of the Security Department's contributions to the company. *Company meetings* offer security representatives a chance to talk about their department's functions and answer questions. Security's relationship with other departments can further be improved by *involvement programs* which bring non-security personnel into contact with Security.

REVIEW QUESTIONS

1. Discuss the advantages of having new company managerial personnel come through an orientation session in the Security Department. What are some of the subjects that might be discussed in this session?

2. Discuss how each of the following can contribute to the task of selling security within the organization: new employee induction sessions; company department meetings; bulletins; audio-visual materials; tours of the Security Department.

22

Relationship With Law Enforcement

All law enforcement agencies are "security" organizations of one type or another, and many security departments (in the traditional sense) are actively engaged in the purest of law enforcement responsibilities, such as crime prevention, detection, apprehension and prosecution. The key difference between public law enforcement and private security is that law enforcement is a product of and serves the public sector, whereas security is a product of and serves a given segment of the private sector.

Policing, then, is a responsibility of both public and private police. The distinction between the two is found not so much in the organizational responsibility and objectives as it is in the master they serve. There is an absolute necessity for both—and a mutual dependency. The degree of harmony with which the two interface will be affected by many variables, but the relationship can and should be one of effective cooperation rather than friction or competition. In the words of the Report of the Task Force on Private Security, "Ideally, public law enforcement and private security agencies should work closely together, because their respective roles are complementary in the effort to control crime. Indeed, the magnitude of the Nation's crime problem should preclude any form of competition between the two. Rather, they should be cognizant and supportive of their respective roles in crime control. . . ."[1]

An interesting relationship existed between the private and public sectors in a mountain community in central California, a town inhabited by employees of a very large utility company headquartered many miles to the south. The company's Security Department was represented in the form of a "resident" Special Agent, affectionately referred to as "Sheriff" by residents for miles around (not only those who were employees of the utility company). The Special Agent was provided with a company car equipped with a radio for communication with the County Sheriff's Department based in the valley below the mountain range. Except for the summer months, there was an unwritten agreement that the "law" was represented by the

---

[1] *Private Security: Report of the Task Force on Private Security, op. cit.,* p. 19.

Resident Special Agent. In matters ranging from accidents to criminal offenses, the Agent responded and subsequently turned the matter over to the county. Although a representative of the private sector, he served the interests of the public sector as well.

Whether the line between security and law enforcement is fine or fuzzy, there is a great deal of movement back and forth over that line. There is a continual flow of retirees leaving the public sector and entering the security industry. There are law enforcement aspirants who launch their careers from the security industry. A growing number of "Security Degree" options are being offered in the Criminal Justice, Police Science and Administration of Justice programs at the community and state university level. All point up the simple fact that the two career paths run parallel.

The strongest link between the two factions is usually at the investigative and administrative levels, and the relationship there is one of mutual respect for the contributions each makes to the successful completion of the task, be it a stolen credit card case or plans for protecting a foreign dignitary. As a rule, the poorest or weakest relationship is at the lowest organizational end of both factions—the police patrolman placing the security officer at the bottom of the "pecking order" (the FBI is best, then Secret Service, State Trooper, City A Police over City B Police, etc.).

Focusing, then, on the relationship at the investigative and administrative levels, let us analyze what the public sector does to assist the private sector, and vice versa.

SERVICES OF THE PUBLIC SECTOR

Provides Information on Individual Criminal Histories

Formerly, this was the most actively pursued aspect of the relationship between the two sectors. The vital flow of intelligence has dwindled to a trickle today, because of right-to-privacy legislation.

The relationship was (and still is, to a lesser extent, today) one of many facets. Depending upon the jurisdiction in terms of state and local laws, and depending on the administration, the records of police departments might be wide open and accessible to security investigators, or "sealed" and officially unavailable. The process of obtaining criminal history information ranged from (1) making a phone call to the Police Records Division and asking for a name check, to (2) actually paying a police officer a preset fee for name checks, or (3) securing the necessary check through acquaintances or friends in the police department, or (4) having security investigators in the reserve or auxiliary ranks of the police department so that they had some access to criminal record files.

In the past, whatever was required to gain access to those records was provided, because of the need for the private sector to conduct its own background investigations. The fast food chain which is about to place an employee or prospective employee in a position of trust in their finance division cannot go to the local police and ask them to "clear" the applicant. They would be laughed out of the station. If the police did provide such services (which indeed would be a true service to the business community and certainly would reduce criminal conduct and white collar crimes that affect the community as a whole), they would soon be inundated with requests. So they could not provide such services even before there were legal privacy barriers.

Despite its limited access to criminal histories today, the private sector remains responsible for the consequences of its hiring decisions. For example, a hospital hires an orderly who will work in the children's ward. Local and state police records reveal that the orderly has a criminal history of sexually molesting children. Is it any wonder that security investigators are frustrated when denied information from police files? And in most cases the police are equally frustrated. They know why security investigators seek intelligence and they know how such information will be used, but the growing wall of protection around the offenders has stifled law enforcement's ability to work with the private sector.

The irony of this present condition is as follows: the public sector would not dream of hiring employees into positions of responsibility or trust without examining their backgrounds and assessing any records of criminal conduct—but the private sector is denied that prerogative. Yet the courts have held that the employer is responsible for the conduct of its employees. In a recent case, not yet adjudicated, a security guard raped an employee of the guard company's client. The guard had a criminal history of assaults against women but had never been convicted. There was no way the guard company could obtain that history. (In some states legislation now requires the licensing and fingerprinting of armed guards, but such remedy is limited and still falls short of being the solution.) The civil action brought against the guard company looks as though it will be fruitful. To protect the rights of the man who sought employment as a guard, then, others have paid and will pay a dear price.

The only possible hope this country has today in its efforts against criminal attacks lies in *preventing* crime, not in apprehending offenders after their criminal acts. One technique of prevention is to analyze risks. Without intelligence there is nothing to analyze.

Provides Information on Possible Criminal Attacks

Through their own system of informers, the police regularly gather intelligence that aids them in their work. It is not uncommon for police to pass on to a security organization information received that specifically affects a given firm or industry. For example, the police department in a large city may learn that the jewelry department of a department store chain with many local stores is targeted for a holdup within the next few days. The greater metropolitan area includes a multiplicity of police jurisdictions, and therefore no single agency could handle the case. Due to the large number of stores, police robbery surveillance teams simply could not be provided. Acting upon the intelligence gained from the police, the department store Security Department can provide its own surveillance.

On a more general basis, local law enforcement provides security with information on counterfeiting operations, check passing and fraud money order scams, the presence of professional boosters (shoplifters), credit fraud gangs, and a host of other similar intelligence that the security industry needs in its daily efforts to protect the industries it serves.

Provides Traffic Control Support for Special Events

The type of industry and its influence on vehicular traffic on dedicated streets will determine the relationship with local law enforcement in the area of traffic control. In some cases the only traffic impact may be predictable minor congestions when employees arrive in the morning and leave in the afternoon. This usually can be regulated with signals rather than manpower.

In other cases, such as the grand opening of a new shopping center, the anticipated traffic could be a major concern not only to the merchants, whose interests are defeated if traffic is snarled up and customers cannot get into the center, but to the police as well, who do not want a major traffic jam within their jurisdiction. Thus, the experienced security administrator, anticipating traffic problems at an upcoming opening, will sit down with the local police and outline the probable traffic control needs, usually based on his experience at a previous grand opening in another police jurisdiction. As a rule the police handle the traffic on the dedicated streets and Security provides the manpower for traffic control on the private roadways and on the parking lots.

Poorly coordinated efforts—and they do occur—result in monumental traffic jams (in one case the freeway off-ramp that serviced the street in front of a shopping center was backed up for over a mile and the Highway Patrol had to announce a "Sigalert"). Efficiently coordinated efforts move vehicles expeditiously into and out of the area.

Accepts and Processes Crime Reports

The police accept and process crime reports from firms that have security personnel and from those that do not, as well as from private citizens. Why, then, is this a special relationship with security? If there are no security personnel involved, the police will conduct some inquiry into the facts and details surrounding the alleged crime. Once the proper relationship with security is established, however, the police will accept, *on face value,* the report from a security department. In fact, they will usually accept the completed investigative report from the security department's report form and attach it to their own forms or have the information transcribed from the security report form onto their own form, word for word.

There are two reasons why the police will accept such security reports: (1) They recognize the professionalism (only of deserving organizations, of course) and respect that professionalism. (2) The report's content could be beyond the investigative expertise of the police (e.g., computer manipulation or a cycle variance in accounts receivable).

Coordinates with Security on Special Enforcement Projects

"Special enforcement" in this context means efforts directed against a general criminal problem, as opposed to investigation which concerns specific suspects.

When the proper relationship is established with the local authorities, a variety of joint projects of mutual interest and benefit may be undertaken. Such projects could include the following:

1. Because of a series of thefts of autos and auto parts, and thefts of packages from cars in a shopping center's parking lot, the security people can set up a surveillance from the roofs of stores and communicate by radio with plainclothes police down in the lot.
2. Because of complaints received that homosexual acts are being solicited in the public rest room at an amusement park or a hospital, a coordinated effort can be effected to detect and arrest such offenders.
3. Because of a series of indecent exposure incidents on the grounds of a local college, the campus security and police can set up stake-out teams as well as set "bait."

Coordinates with Security on Major or Important Investigations

There are occasions when a criminal case would be impossible to conclude successfully without a coordinated effort of both the private and public sectors. A dramatic example of such a case occurred in Los Angeles. Investigators for a chain of department stores learned that a large number of employees and non-employees were working together in a concerted effort to remove merchandise from the department store's warehouse. Most of the participants were identified, motion pictures were taken of some of the theft activity, and an undercover agent was successfully placed in the midst of the group to provide a flow of intelligence. The department store then went to the local authorities (in this particular case, the District Attorney's office) for assistance.

In a coordinated effort, the following occurred: A small electrical supply and service store was obtained about two miles from the warehouse. It was wired for voice recordings. A panel truck equipped with a 16mm motion picture camera was parked behind the store. Two D.A.'s investigators posed as employees in the store and one manned the camera vehicle. Department store investigators secretly marked the kind of merchandise the undercover agent had indicated would be stolen the next day. Through the undercover agent, word was passed to the thieves that there was a new "fence" in the area (the electrical supply store). The department store provided the money to buy the goods. In a short time regular trips were being made to the back door of the "fence," and investigators were buying stolen merchandise marked by other investigators the night before. The transactions were recorded visually by the hidden movie camera as well as audibly.

Results: a grand total of twenty-seven culprits were either indicted and arrested, arrested and referred to juvenile authorities, or, in those cases in which a public offense could not be established, discharged from the company.

A case of this complexity and magnitude could not have been resolved so successfully had it not been for the cooperation between private security and law enforcement. Criminal investigations provide frequent opportunities for this effective interface.

Provides Intelligence on Radical or Political Activists

Advance information about planned protest marches, demonstrations, rallies—in terms of location, time, who is gathering, their objectives, the route they will travel, their specific plans (such as tying up traffic)—is vital information to a security organization which is in the vicinity of these often socially disruptive activities. The intelligence can be even more crucial to a company which could be the object of attack—such as a major department store whose travel bureau sold excursion tickets to the Soviet Union. The Jewish Defense League demonstrated at the store, disrupting normal operations and blocking the doorways by sitting down and joining arms. Advance information allows time for planning a defensive strategy and course of action.

Good planning based on good intelligence pays off quickly. For instance, a major department store in Los Angeles was alerted to a planned Chicano rally at police headquarters, about a half mile from its downtown store.

The store's security force was beefed up. The rally was dispersed by police, sending hundreds of protestors (and hooligans, who tend to join such activities) fleeing down the main avenues leading away from the police facility. Groups of these youths broke hundreds of plate glass windows of stores lining the streets in their escape route. The department store lost five huge plate glass windows, but because its security personnel were in force, no merchandise was looted from the displays, and plywood panels (pre-fabricated for just such an event) were quickly erected for temporary security.

The absence of this type of intelligence from law enforcement agencies would put the security administrator at a marked disadvantage, if not in a hopeless position. And the flow of such information is directly related to the relationship of mutual trust and respect that has been established.

Provides Protection During Labor Disputes

Without question, the Security Department is the enforcement arm of management. As a consequence of that reputation and profile, its peace-keeping capabilities during a labor dispute are nil. Only the police can maintain any semblance of order on the picket lines, and even they have their grief because strikers tend to view them as protectors of management and management's property. Security's role is limited to a perimeter defense line on the company property. Police assistance is necessary in terms of keeping the peace, preventing or at least reducing violence against "scabs" or supervisory and managerial personnel, preventing the blockading of access roads, sidewalks and driveways. Without that type of regulatory order, dangerous situations might sometimes escalate out of control.

SERVICES OF THE PRIVATE SECTOR

The security industry's relationship with—or, perhaps more aptly stated, the industry's contribution to—the general law enforcement picture would include the following:

Contributes to the Local Criminal Statistical Data

The annual Uniform Crime Reports published by the Federal Bureau of Investigation are based on data generated at the local level. The statistical tracking of the number of various types of crimes in a community, the number of arrests, and the number of unsolved crimes serves a number of purposes, including possible budget justifications.

On first observation it might appear that the volume of criminal acts and arrests reflects police activity only. Yet the truth of the matter is that a percentage of these statistics reflect the activity of the security forces in the community—particularly in certain crimes such as larceny. The percentage could be quite small or substantial, depending on the community and the composition of the local police and security forces. The private security force responsible for maintaining order on a large college campus, for example, might often process as many offenders through the "booking" procedure as does the local police agency. In this circumstance, the community served by the private security agency might actually be larger than the one within the jurisdiction of the public law enforcement agency.

The published criminal statistics, then, reflect to some degree the joint effort, but more often than not the independent efforts, of *both* the public and private sector.

It should be pointed out that the Index reflects only "known" crimes; that is to say, crimes known to the police. Actually there is a great deal of crime known to the private sector but for a number of reasons never reported to the police—such as petty shoplifting cases and large internal larceny matters where the best interests of the company are served in a recovery of the loss instead of a prosecution, with its delays, costs, and doubtful outcome.

Provides the Community with "Tax-Free" Law Enforcement

The Security Department of a single department store in Los Angeles in one year will arrest and prosecute in excess of 2,000 offenders for such crimes as theft, burglary, forgery, credit fraud, counterfeit passing, indecent exposure, and others. Add up all department stores, plus chain stores; add all supermarkets and drug stores; add all the discount stores (including only those retailers who support security forces), and project their combined efforts. Such projection suggests a conservative figure of 50,000 arrests by security forces in the greater Los Angeles area each year, and the number is growing. Bear in mind that these figures apply only to the retail industry (which represents that segment of the private sector most actively engaged in crime/arrest activities). If the burden of that criminal behavior rested on the police, imagine what it would mean in terms of tax dollars!

Provides Liaison Between Law Enforcement and the Business World

The vast pool of intelligence and resources needed on a daily basis by the police is readily available through the various security organizations serving business and industry. In some cases the intelligence needed is

available within the Security Department by virtue of the type of organization—such as an investigator for a telephone company with high technical
skill levels needed in some police investigations. In other cases the need
can be filled only by a security investigator because the security man has
access to intelligence—for example, background information on a present
or former employee.

Public sector law enforcement personnel would be the first to agree
that many doors would never open without a court order if it were not
for the intercession of the security organization. Many companies, by written
policy, will not release any information to any governmental agency, but
will refer such agency to their Security Department. If the Security Department agrees to the release of information, it is released; if not, it is not
released.

Pages could be filled with examples of the relationship between the
public and private sector in this area of liaison. The following single example
will serve as an illustration, not only of this aspect of cooperative effort,
but of the thrust of this entire discussion of the complementary roles of
private security and public police.

A young police officer took an elective course in security while pursuing
his bachelor's degree in Police Science. A local Security Director taught
that class. Some years later, that officer was a homicide detective working
on a puzzling death. The only thing found in the deceased's pockets was
a cash register receipt. Recalling his earlier studies, the detective called
his former teacher. Examination and interpretation of the impressions on
that receipt provided a wealth of information that led to solution of the
case. The receipt was for the purchase of a specific classification of merchandise on the date of death. It provided information on where the purchase
was made in the city (by store identification number), when during that
day the purchase was made (by transaction count), and who sold the merchandise to the deceased (by employee ID code). Armed with that intelligence, and following an interview with the employee that was arranged
by Security, the detective resolved his case.

The relationship between the private and public sector in this case,
as in virtually all cases, served the professional interests of law enforcement
specifically, and the welfare of the community generally.

SUMMARY

The functions of private security and public law enforcement often overlap;
the two career paths run parallel. The relationship between security and
law enforcement is usually one of mutual respect and cooperation at the
investigative and administrative levels.

Law enforcement formerly provided the private sector with *criminal
history information* to assist in background investigations. In recent years,

legal decisions on the individual's right to privacy have restricted this service. Police often pass on to security organizations *intelligence concerning possible criminal attacks or civil disturbances.* The police can offer *traffic control support* for special events. The police accept *crime reports* from professional security organizations. The police may assist security in *special enforcement projects* concerning general criminal problems. *Major investigations* often require the coordination of police and security efforts. Police assistance is usually required in maintaining order during *labor disputes.*

The private sector assists law enforcement by contributing *criminal statistical data.* Private security departments arrest and prosecute many offenders each year, providing a form of *"tax-free" law enforcement.* Security departments can serve as *liaison between law enforcement and the business community,* providing intelligence and expertise as needed.

REVIEW QUESTIONS

1. Briefly explain six services which law enforcement can provide private security; and three services which private security can provide law enforcement.

2. Discuss the controversy surrounding law enforcement's providing of criminal history information to security investigators.

23

Relationship With the Industry

No matter how successful or effective a security function may be or appear to be, there is always room for improvement. There is always a better way. Only the manager isolated from the security community is satisfied with his operation. The need to grow, to reach out for ways to improve, is the mark of a progressive and enlightened security professional.

Where does one reach? The administrator must reach out into the security industry and its vast reservoir of resources and experience. Never before have we better understood the impact of today's shrinking world upon industry. It is a fascinating fact that one administrator's problems in New York City today may be identical to another's in San Francisco or Dallas tomorrow. And, perhaps more fascinating, one administrator's solutions to such problems may be better than the other's.

In the private sector, comparable industries or businesses are in a competitive mode, competitors in all things—with the exception of protection. In the case of neighboring universities, one institution competes with the other for academic standing, scholastic achievement within the faculty as well as the student body, athletic prowess, funding, enrollment, percentage of graduates continuing on in graduate studies, etc. Despite that climate of competition, the security heads of those same institutions meet and discuss common problems in a spirit of mutual cooperation, sharing ideas and information for the purpose of improving their efforts to protect their respective institutions.

A department store vigorously competes with its counterpart at the opposite end of the shopping mall in the timing, frequency, merchandise mix and price-points of sales, as well as other gimmicks to attract customers, such as in-store promotions around public figures and drawings for such prizes as new autos or ocean cruises. Competition is so fierce that if one store extends the hours it is open to the public, the other immediately follows suit. Yet, the security people work cooperatively, advising or warning one another of potential shoplifters, bad check passers, or credit card frauds.

The very nature of the security business demands communication and an effective relationship with the industry. The relationship can be divided into four categories: cooperation, participation, contribution, and education.

EFFECTIVE RELATIONSHIP CATEGORIES

Cooperation

The cooperative relationship within the industry can be divided into individual cooperation and organized (or structured) cooperation.

At the individual level, to establish and then develop personal contacts with peers is an important, if not vital, dimension of the security professional. Although selecting contacts is usually a highly subjective process, commonality of operations and respect for the individual are important. Once established, a professional kinship grows, allowing an honest exchange and sharing of ideas, opinions, and strategies, much to the mutual benefit of both parties. The key word here is *sharing*. How many times over the years does the typical security manager pick up the telephone and call a counterpart across the country or across town with a request for information or assistance! To be denied that capability would be crippling.

Despite the obvious reasonableness, let alone necessity, of maintaining such relationships with others in the business, some have voluntarily maintained very low profiles and could be called "isolationists." Such a posture is undoubtedly based on the false assumption that one must be a very outgoing, sophisticated and socially charming personality to make professional contacts and friends. Although a good number of professionals are socially comfortable in groups, a surprising number are shy or at least reserved. For many people it is an effort to approach a stranger, even if he too is alone, and strike up a conversation. But people in the security business do it, mostly because they feel compelled to for the very reasons discussed above.

Of course, the closest contacts are usually intra-industry—for example, hospital security people are in closer and more constant touch with others in their own area of specialization than with aerospace security people. However, there is a great deal of cross-industry cooperation. In a given period of time it is not at all unlikely that a retail security professional would be in touch with the utilities people for information on identity of possible subscribers at a given location; or with amusement park security for information on a former employee; or with airlines security for assistance in moving highly valuable negotiables between cities. If the two security counterparts are known to each other, cooperation (if legal and feasible) can be assured. If they are unknown, the degree of cooperation could be different.

The candid security administrator today who enjoys any degree of success will freely admit that his status is not the result of self-achievement, but rather the result of harmonizing all the input from many sources, including the influence of contemporaries in the industry. In sharing experiences, successes, failures and strategies, we change and grow.

There is a fine line between individual cooperation and organized cooperation, and one tends to weave back and forth over the line. Organized or structured cooperation comes about through associations, societies, or other organized gatherings or relationships of security professionals.

Perhaps an outstanding example of organized cooperation can be found in the retail industry's Stores Protective Association, serving the Southern California area. Comparable "mutual" protective organizations exist in other cities such as New York City and Washington, D.C.

SPA, as it is commonly referred to, is a non-profit corporation owned by a number of different department and specialty stores throughout the area which sustain the corporation through membership dues and charges levied for services provided. Services include "integrity" shopping, furnishing undercover investigators, furnishing some temporary security personnel, processing refund disbursements, bank check collections, and new hire screening.

The structured cooperation is best seen in the new employee screening operation. All membership stores contribute, on an ongoing basis, the names of all persons arrested for shoplifting and other related retail crimes, and the names of all dishonest employees, to the master index files of SPA. Names of new employees are researched against this immense file, with a predictable percentage of matchups.

This type of formalized industrial cooperation is obviously beneficial. At the time of this writing the northern part of California is exploring the possibility of joining Stores Protective Association, which would not only give stores there a vast resource of intelligence to draw on, but would add to the resources presently available to the companies in the south as well.

Another structured cooperative effort through SPA is their regular bulletin covering successful and attempted criminal attacks against member stores, including physical descriptions, names of suspects if known, methods of operation, vehicles used—all aimed at informing all stores to aid in future prevention or apprehension of the criminals. Additionally, SPA publishes what are called Special Bulletins, warning the various security departments about particular criminals, including their photographs. The bulletins are highly confidential.

The heads of the member stores' security departments meet monthly, usually for a luncheon hosted by one department, and there they discuss the problems of their industry. Their relationship is not restricted to the monthly meeting but is continuous in nature, one calling on the other when the need arises. Personalities always play some role, but the real relationship between these professionals is one of mutual respect and the willingness to share.

The high spirit of cooperation in the greater Southern California area is not uncommon among retail security organizations around the country (or around the world, as far as that goes). Many major cities have a similar, if not organized, retail cooperative relationship. The same is true in other industries.

Participation

The obvious advantage of participation, as evidenced by the Stores Protective Association, goes beyond the narrowly restricted and limited membership of one specialized field within a field (department and specialty clothing stores within the retail industry). Participation in other organizations has other advantages.

Organizations range from local to international, all offering the professional, at one time or another, something in the way of growth. Every security supervisor, manager, or director, irrespective of his particular industry, has a variety of professional organizations he may join as a member, visit, call on, or infrequently partake of—all aimed at enhancing his knowledge and his personal or departmental efficiency. A retail security executive in Los Angeles, for example, would have the following available to him:

1. Stores Protective Association
2. Special Agents Association of Southern California
3. Chief Special Agents Association of Southern California
4. National Retail Merchants Association
5. American Society for Industrial Security
6. International Association of Professional Security Consultants

This list excludes a variety of law enforcement associations (such as the State Peace Officers Association), training or educational organization membership, other national groups of limited interests (such as polygraph associations), the Atkins group (a number of department stores with a common interest), and corporate gatherings.

Participation in the groups at the top of the listing provides the greatest day-in and day-out impact on individual and departmental efficiency. As one moves down the list (inserting the excluded organizations where appropriate), the impact becomes proportionately less—but important nonetheless.

An overview of participation in those listed organizations follows:

1. *Stores Protective Association.* Discussed on preceding page.
2. *Special Agents Association of Southern California.* This is a local association of security people of all ranks, with an active associate membership of service and security supply people. The emphasis is on retail in general; i.e., not only department and specialty stores, but food, drug and discount as well. In addition to the fraternal interests, emphasis is placed on outside speakers discussing topics of mutual interest, such as opinions of the bench, pending legislation, governmental practices affecting the industry, and management practices. Concerns are local in nature, not national.
3. *Chief Special Agents Association of Southern California.* This group is restricted to security chiefs of major companies, with limited associ-

ate membership of number-two people. The association is fraternal, with emphasis on strong liaison with top local law enforcement officers. A significant and very noteworthy contribution to the security community is the publication every other year of a directory of all security and law enforcement organizations in the area and their key personnel. The directory is the only one of its kind and is coveted by all law enforcement as well as security personnel.

4. *National Retail Merchants Association.* This is a security group comprised of department, chain and large specialty store top security administrators who meet annually to exchange retail security problems and solutions, on the broadest possible basis. What is happening in New Orleans could happen in Seattle. Stores in Philadelphia, working with the Chamber of Commerce, are involved in a community-wide effort to reduce shoplifting. That program could work in San Francisco.

5. *American Society for Industrial Security.* This association serves the entire security industry in terms of membership and interest. Local chapters bring together professionals from all industries so that there is a cross-fertilization of ideas and experience. Emphasis is on upgrading the industry by establishing standards and educating members through professionally presented training seminars, workshops and annual national meetings.

6. *International Association of Professional Security Consultants.* This association is a forum for professional security consultants possessing disciplines concerned with identification, definition, and resolution of security-related problems. One objective is to establish standards of conduct and promote professional ethics for the security consulting profession as well as provide professional certification for security consultants.

The organizations named represent a mix of specific, local and general industrial interest. The reader, student or security practitioner can and should substitute and add other relatively comparable organizations, in keeping with his particular interest or field.

Clearly, participation in security-related organizations and their programs brings to the security professional an ever-increasing array of knowledge, insight and strategy that is otherwise unavailable. Failure to pursue involvement and active participation only brings stagnation and a truly narrow approach to the business of protecting one's company.

Contributions

One facet of participation is contribution. It is a rare man or woman indeed who can participate (belong to and attend) without making some form of contribution. To sit at a round-table discussion and comment does constitute contribution. One-sided participation would be selfish, denying others what the non-contributing attendee himself seeks. Participation, if open and natural in exchanges, serves others in some small measure.

But that amount of contribution, important as it is, is not sufficient for the welfare of the security industry. Where would the state of the art be today without textbooks written by security professionals and articles submitted to trade magazines? Someone must give direction to our educational institutions about appropriate curriculum for students now pursuing degrees in security management. And who is talking to the community, to service organizations, and to us about the business deemed so important in the economic health of private industry and business?

Our relationship to the security industry in general, if it is to be constructive and positive, if it is to help upgrade, if it is to continue to strive for professional recognition of our chosen careers, must have a contributory dimension. Untapped talent surrounds us in our business. A brief examination of some significant areas of contribution, such as book authorship, article authorship, public presentations and involvement in the educational process, is in order.

Book Authorship

Healy and Walsh, Gallati, Berger, Tyska and Fennelly, Broder and Barefoot, to name a few, have taken the time and energy to make a contribution to our industry. As small as their own perceptions of contribution may have seemed, they have been significant and substantial. In most instances, those in the industry who have made a literary contribution are not primarily authors. Rather, they are security professionals, willing to share their point of view, their opinions, and their experiences. In view of the past, present and projected growth of the industry and the increasing number of colleges and universities offering this discipline, security needs more people who are willing to contribute their experiences by reducing them to paper for subsequent book publication.

Magazine Article Authorship

Essentially the same thing can be said about article authorship as book authorship. At a recent meeting of security executives, one participant was overheard making relatively uncomplimentary remarks about the quality of articles in one of our important trade magazines. How much easier it is to criticize than to contribute! Trade magazines are but a vehicle through which the trade can speak. The publisher, editor and magazine staff are publishing professionals, not necessarily security professionals. The quality of trade journal content is a reflection of the quality of the trade. The security administrator who considers himself talented but fails to share that talent obviously fails to contribute to the best interests of his chosen profession

. . . and/or he fears the bright light of public scrutiny which always brings criticism.

Public Presentations

Public presentations, which include in-house talks, presentations before the industry, talks before other trades, or luncheon speaking, tend to give the security function high and positive visibility to the non-security audience and add to the professional growth of those in a security audience. Appearing before the local Rotary Club has little to do with the speaker's relationship to the security industry, except that through his presentation he may generate good will for the security cause, with some rippling effect. The same is true with in-house talks and presentations made to other disciplines, such as a Controller's Association.

The real contribution comes in making a presentation to the security industry. No matter how experienced or learned a man may be, there is something new to learn. We learn from others, through their willingness to share—if not in book or magazine article authorship, then at least in their personal presentations. For a man who is considered a leader in the industry, or an administrator with a successful track record, to refuse to make a presentation before the industry is unfortunately selfish. Security professionals have an obligation to contribute to the cause, for the good of all. They cannot in good conscience sit back and rest on their laurels.

Involvement in the Educational Process

Although not obligatory, teaching in the Security Administration field is a very marked contribution to the industry. Not everyone has teaching skills, of course, so opportunities in this area are limited. However, there is an increasing call to service in terms of participating in college curriculum advisory committees now forming in the path of the burgeoning security programs at the college and university level.

Education

The last important category of relationships with the industry is primarily self-serving, but in a positive way. The sum total of an active relationship of cooperation, participation and contribution is self-education. Keeping abreast of the industry, in terms of new technology, new case law, new legislation, innovative concepts, new trends, is as important to the security practitioner and administrator, if not in some cases more so, as are the daily operations of the organization.

For those security professionals who failed to complete their college education, now is an ideal time to return to school and earn their degree.

Security Administration programs are being established all across the country in response to a demand for formalized education in the security field.

In this business one cannot afford to sit in the backwaters and permit the rest of the industry, in all its vastness, to stream by. Time was when change came slowly in the security profession. Today we are truly in a state of "Future Shock." Changes are rapid and accelerating. Technical advances in electronics, communications, and alarm capabilities alone are almost overwhelming.

Reading is but one source of information. Discussion, explanation and demonstration are needed to supplement the written word.

The demands of the business require good communications and a participatory relationship within the industry. And this is a two-way street.

SUMMARY

In a continuing effort to improve his operation, the security administrator must look to his peers in the security industry.

Cooperation within the security industry takes the form of individual and organized efforts. Personal contacts among peers allow an exchange of ideas and strategies. Organized cooperation occurs through the activities of formal associations of security professionals.

Security professionals have the opportunity for *participation* in organizations ranging in scope from local to national. Participation usually includes some form of *contribution*. Contributions of the security professional to his field can include book and magazine article authorship, public speaking, and teaching.

Cooperation, participation and contribution form an important part of the *education* of the security professional in his effort to keep abreast of constant changes in his field.

REVIEW QUESTIONS

1.   What are the advantages to the security manager of active involvement in the security community?

2.   Find out what professional organizations are available for security managers in your area to participate in, and what their activities are.

24

Community Relations

A security department's involvement or participation in community relations activities is directly related to (1) the public's need for information, (2) the need to inform the public, and (3) security management's receptivity to such public exposure.

One might argue that there is really no difference between "the public's need for information" and "the need to inform the public." The distinction is this: the public's need is a demand and a need *they* identified, whereas "the need to inform the public" is first identified by the company.

An example of the public's need for information might well be a community's concern about the safety of a newly constructed nuclear power generating station. The utility company's Security Director could be an effective representative and speaker at local civic and business organization meetings.

In some cases local concern has taken the form of organized demonstrations, hostility and violence. When business or industry moves into a new community, they will meet with some resistance. Today there is much concern about environmental impact, which includes everything from atmospheric emissions, traffic congestion, noise pollution, architectural blight on the landscape, down to the killing of old oak trees. Reaction to such issues is often emotional. Local government is usually sensitive to the feelings of its constituency, and actions by local government such as finding fault with construction inspections, making unrealistic demands to comply with local codes, and delaying the issuance of permits and approvals can often be traced back to an ill-informed public.

Certainly senior management of the company must be visible and carry the brunt of a program aimed at establishing good community relations. The question is, does security have a role here? Indeed it does, primarily in the form of a security executive who can first establish a relationship with key local officials in public safety and law enforcement departments and then, through those officials, with community groups. Such a spokesman, if he is involved in the new business project from its early stages, can help allay fears and at the same time build good will for the company— depending, of course, upon his public speaking presence and skills.

The need to inform the public is a challenge to the retail industry, for example, with its constant problems of shoplifting, particularly juvenile shoplifting. For security representatives to go out into the community and talk about the personal consequences of theft and the impact of losses on retail prices plays an important role in educating an otherwise ignorant and apathetic public.

Security management's response (as a whole) to these needs is usually traceable to the head of the security organization. For example, if the Director of Security is gregarious, outspoken and a confident public speaker, then the department will usually enjoy a high profile in terms of community relations. Not only will the Director have public exposure, but others on the staff will be encouraged to represent the organization.

On the other hand, if the Director is uncomfortable or dislikes public exposure, he will avoid it altogether or at least minimize it, regardless of the public's or the company's needs. And it usually holds true that if the Director maintains a low profile, so does his staff. It is simple for the Security Director to avoid or minimize community relations activities; he just passes the need or the challenge to a peer in the industry, to some other Director, or to another executive in the company—someone on the legal or operations staff, perhaps, or the public relations people. It is a rare but strong Director of Security who will refer such public exposure to a subordinate, because the subordinate's high profile and recognition for his activities tends to be threatening.

Ideally, the Director will have public poise, will respond positively to the needs of the community and the company, will be supportive of his staff's participation in community events, and—by virtue of his sensitivity to his own department's role—*will actually go out and help identify needs that can be addressed through a good community relations program.*

Community relations, for the sake of this work, refers to

- Public speaking engagements
- News press appearances or interviews
- Radio interviews
- Appearances on television
- Participation in community-oriented projects
- General public contact

PUBLIC SPEAKING

The luncheon speaker, after-dinner speaker, guest speaker between the ladies' business meeting and "social hour," the classroom or auditorium speaker—each is very much part of the American scene, not only in his very presence as a vital part of the social context in which he appears, but also in the trappings and traditions that surround the speaking engagement. The process begins with the advance announcement of the program and build-up of the speaker's credentials and his topic. It continues as seating arrangements at the head table are made, as the speaker sneaks last-minute looks at his cue cards or typed text, as he is introduced by the program chairman and is greeted by applause. His opening comments are solicitous of a humorous response to "break the ice." Later comes the final, second round of applause following the presentation, expression of appreciation, and the inevitable little circle of people who surround the speaker after the meeting has been adjourned. All of this is somehow not only a natural, but an *expected* and secure process in our culture.

If the speaker does poorly—and many do—it is so noted and quickly forgotten. What was most important was that the *process itself* was right. Conversely, if the speaker did well, there tends to be a lingering sense of good will about him, his message and his organization. In short, there is little risk in public speaking in terms of ill will, but there is a great opportunity for genuine good will.

As stated earlier, the need of the public (or any segment thereof) for information, and the company's need for the public to know, represent the two *legitimate* reasons for a public speaking appearance on the part of a security executive. Something less than legitimate, then, would be an appearance where there is no need to know. That could well be a church's Ladies' Auxiliary or the local PTA, depending upon the prospective speaker. For example, what is the legitimate need for a hotel security presentation to a club of Vietnam Veterans confined to wheelchairs? Perhaps one could make a case for the presentation on the basis that such vets do travel from time to time, and security tips could be helpful.

More importantly, if an organization calls on, invites or asks for a presentation, that request in and of itself represents a need that can be filled. More often than not, filling that kind of need automatically brings about a great deal of good will.

Good will, then, is the common denominator and underlying theme, not only in public speaking appearances, but in all community relations activities, although the specific objective of any one such activity is informative in nature. Rare is the company that is not interested in good will. The Security Department, by virtue of its unique role and image, is in a position to generate good will for the organization as a whole, if it is willing to.

Some administrators called on to speak worry unduly over the topic selected by the requesting group because they feel inadequate to speak on that specific topic. Guest speakers should understand that the topics requested are usually only suggestions. The group frequently is uncertain what they want. The negotiability of topics gives the prospective speaker latitude to direct the topic and his remarks to areas in which he is more comfortable or which are even more appropriate to the occasion.

Ideally the presentation should be tailored to appeal to the audience and have some constructive application for that audience—even if the presentation is one of good will only. In the case of the veterans in wheelchairs, the hotel security administrator could not only entertain but could provide the audience security- and nonsecurity-related advice concerning hotel accommodations and services for the handicapped.

This is an important point: the security executive must recognize that he is a spokesman for his industry, be it hotel management, transportation, manufacturing, etc., as well as a security spokesman. To talk in terms of the industry, as a member of its management, adds polish and dimension to his presentation befitting his professional position. Gone are the days of the cigar-chewing security chief who did not know—or, for that matter, care—what the company's objectives were, what they were doing or where they were going.

Figure 24.1 suggests possible speech topics for a number of different security functions that might be appropriate for four different types of audiences. Needless to say, the list of security functions, the variety of audiences, and the wider variety of topics could consume pages.

NEWS PRESS APPEARANCES OR INTERVIEWS

The author's experience with the press has been that if you are wrong, the press will ensure that the public is clearly so informed, and if you are right they will serve as a powerful ally. The distortions which do creep into newsprint tend to be impartial—that is, there is as much favorable distortion as there is unfavorable.

Response to requests from the press for specific news, general news or feature material is, or should be to some measure, controlled by the public and press relations department of the company, which can aptly serve as a buffer between Security and the press if need be. A sound practice and policy is to require that all press contacts be cleared through the press relations people first. This accomplishes two things: (1) the people charged with the release of information to the press officially sanction the subsequent dialogue between Security and the press and the release of information, and (2) such sanctioning gives Security natural "protection" against criticism that can be inspired by distortions or by releases that come as a surprise to management.

Press releases can include the appointment of a new director or manager, significant criminal attacks, significant successes, or unusual achievements (such as winning in a national or local security competition).

Feature articles on a security department and its responsibilities provide interesting reading and favorable publicity for a company, particularly if slanted as an "inside look" at protection.

RADIO INTERVIEWS

So-called "talk shows" or "spot" commentaries on radio can serve in essentially the same way as public speaking engagements—i.e., informing the

	Local Business and Civic Groups (e.g., Rotarians)	School Civics Classes and PTA	Church Groups	Professional Groups (e.g., Controllers Association)
Hotel Security	• Orientation of the industry • Interesting loss statistics • Humorous anecdotes • Tips for the businessman who travels	• Career opportunities in hotel management • Humorous anecdotes • Examples of a hotel detective's day's work	• Combination of the civic and school presentation	• Case studies of internal losses • Systems modifications resulting from internal loss cases
School/Campus Security	• Need for community support for school bonds • Security costs • Examples of loss	• Vandalism problems and how they affect the quality of school life • Why the need for security	• Overview of security problems and the need for moral leadership from the church	• What's new in combating vandalism and losses, in terms of strategy and hardware
Aerospace Security	• Discussion of possible application of security technology to local businessman's problems	• A look into the future • Interesting cases and problems • Career opportunities in the industry	• As the church's goal is one of peace ... so is the industry's • Examples of attacks against that effort	• Unique problems or demands connected with present or new contracts and projects
Utilities Security	• Security measures aimed at protecting resources, the community, and the consumer	• Youth's role in conserving resources • Examples of youth's acts of vandalism and attacks	• Importance of home and church's influence in conserving resources and energy • Example of problems	• Security auditing procedures • Examples of defalcation case in payment processing center
Retail Security	• Discussion of threat and problem of internal dishonesty and ways for small businessman to detect and prevent same	• Statistics on juvenile shoplifting • Consequences of theft	• Overview of shoplifting and how the losses affect prices • Need for leadership in setting moral standards and values	• Examples of recent credit and EDP frauds and prevention efforts in those areas
Transportation Security	• Industry losses and impact on insurance and freight charges	• Transportation's role in community and economy • Attacks against the industry • Consequences of attacks	• General information, similar to that given to the schools	• Hijacking frauds and techniques to detect such frauds

Figure 24.1 Suggested speech topics for various audiences.

listening public of those things they need to know about security. One successful technique has been the recording of a retail security professional's remarks while talking with a radio reporter. One-minute sections are then extracted from the pre-recorded interview for hourly airing in support of a community's anti-shoplifting campaign during the holiday season.

Radio as well as television exposure depends a great deal on the size of the community and the sophistication of network and local broadcasting programming, coupled with the community's need for information or the considered human interest aspect of a given security department.

The important thing here is for security managers to recognize the potential of these two important community communication media, and to seize on those opportunities when they present themselves.

PARTICIPATION IN COMMUNITY-ORIENTED PROJECTS

Some community projects, whether sponsored by the Junior Chamber of Commerce, local government or the efforts of a private organization, deserve if not demand support and participation of security professionals. An example would be a community-wide campaign to reduce auto thefts by encouraging drivers to lock their cars.

Depending upon the campaign's organizing group and contact points in the community, the security executive could be the intermediary between the campaign and senior management of the company. Consequently he would be instrumental in obtaining funds for the effort. Ideally security would be in this position.

Further, those security departments which have public parking facilities, such as amusement parks, hospitals, museums, sports events facilities, shopping centers, etc., could help the cause by distributing literature or notices supporting the campaign on vehicles parked in their areas. Such notices could be in the form of 4-inch by 4-inch red cardboard octagonal "stop signs" that say "Stop Auto Thefts . . . Please Lock Your Car," or some similar message.

Such programs also provide the opportunity for radio and TV interviews with security professionals supporting that campaign. Such interviews provide excellent visibility for the company and demonstrate its concern for and support of community-wide programs that really benefit the public.

A recent community-wide project in the Los Angeles area was the preparation and distribution of a booklet, entitled "Probable Cause," on a new state anti-shoplifting law. Funding for the publication of this booklet came from four major department stores, although the real benefactors of the publication were the small or independent stores, which have little or no security. Acknowledgment of such support was printed on the back of the booklet.

Other community as well as state-wide anti-shoplifting campaigns have marshaled the support and expertise of retail security executives, with, in some instances, a profound impact on the general public—certainly a positive contribution to the community as a whole.

Again, funding, expertise, distribution, personal appearances, radio and/or television interviews are all viable ways to participate and contribute to community projects that not only serve the best interests of the community, but of the Security Department and company as well.

GENERAL PUBLIC CONTACT

Perhaps the most overlooked area of good community relations is the day-in and day-out Security Department contacts with the general public. Courtesy, good grooming, business demeanor, and the individual attitude of each member of the department can—and do—have an impact on the company's image and reputation of community good will.

SUMMARY

The Security Department's involvement in community relations activities is related to (1) the public's need for information, (2) the company's need to inform the public, and (3) security management's receptivity to public exposure. Ideally, the Security Director will respond positively to the needs of the community and will take an active part in identifying needs that can be addressed through a good community relations program.

Methods by which the Security Director can inform the public and create good will include *public speaking appearances; press appearances and interviews; radio interviews;* and *participation in community-oriented projects* such as campaigns to reduce auto thefts and shoplifting.

The Security Department's day-to-day contact with the public also contributes to the company's image and good will.

REVIEW QUESTIONS

1. List six types of activities which enable the Security Department to establish a good community relations program.

2. Suggest several possible topics for a security manager addressing a local civic group; a high school class; a women's club.

3. Give several examples of community-oriented projects in which security might participate.

V
MIS-MANAGEMENT

25

*Jackass Management Traits**

The management process of achieving organizational goals by working through other people is as much an art as a science. Those in leadership roles, irrespective of the level of responsibility, impact on the lives of every subordinate in a very dramatic and emotional way—far more than many leaders suspect. What a manager says or doesn't say, or does or doesn't do, is highly visible to subordinates and is carefully scrutinized. Flaws as well as strengths in one's management style tend to be exaggerated. By virtue of the manager-subordinate relationship the exaggerated flaw becomes dominating and overshadows or otherwise neutralizes good qualities.

Now a blunder committed in ignorance is forgivable. Theoretically, once the error is understood the manager will correct it. But there are those who understand, yet, for whatever reasons, persist in exhibiting the flaw in their daily managerial style. These flaws then become unforgivable, and hereinafter are referred to as "jackass management traits."

It only stands to reason that employees who are resentful, disgusted, disappointed, feel cheated or abused, or are angry with their bosses, are not going to do their best. But there's another dimension to this whole problem of poor managerial practices. That dimension is employee dishonesty. Social science researchers have established a relationship between theft (as well as other deviant behavior) and an employee's perception of the employer and supervisor. Clark and Hollinger, researchers with the University of Minnesota, state:

> . . . the dissatisfied employee was found to be more frequently involved in employee theft. This was especially true among the younger members of the work force. The most consistent source of dissatisfaction seemed to be the supervisor and the employer. Where the supervisory personnel were viewed as unhelpful, incompetent, and unconcerned, higher theft was detected. Where the integrity, fairness and ethical quality of the company were questioned, more theft was found.[1]

Michael Geurts, Associate Professor of Marketing with Brigham Young University, writes the following regarding employee dishonesty.

---

* Reprinted with permission of The Merritt Company. From Walsh, Timothy J., and Healy, Richard J., *Protection of Assets,* The Merritt Company: Santa Monica, CA, 1980 1981.
[1] Clark, John P. and Hollinger, Richard C., "Theft by Employees," *Security Management Magazine,* September 1980, p. 108.

Retaliation is the fourth reason for theft. The store has been offensive and retribution must be made, . . . and, . . . the employee who is insulted by a supervisor will often seek revenge by stealing.[2]

Such findings and conclusions come as no surprise to the professional security/loss prevention practitioner. It is, however, refreshing as well as encouraging to have professionals outside our industry document, in empirical terms, what we've known for some time.

The question is: are we in security management aware of, and sensitive to, the possibility of jackass traits existing within our own security organizations? Security people react to supervision and management styles (and flaws) the same as non-security people (albeit with a little more toleration). It behooves us then to eradicate jackass traits from the security pyramid by educating, training, and being examples ourselves, before we go into the greater organization and discuss causes of deviant behavior among employees. Put another way, we must practice what we preach, and put our own house in order.

The Popularity Kid

---

[2] Geurts, Michael, "Inventory Shrinkage in Retail Stores: Costs and Causes," *Retail Control,* August 1980, pp. 43–44.

1. THE MANAGER WHO SEEKS TO BE "LIKED" RATHER THAN RESPECTED

Everyone wants to be liked. Being liked gives us confidence and a sense of well-being. But the manager who strives to be "one of the gang," or wants everyone to like him or her, gets trapped into avoiding unpopular decisions and ignoring disciplinary problems. Generally, people prefer to work in a well-ordered environment. They don't really want the boss to always be a nice guy. Managers who avoid saying "no" or "don't" to individuals simply make the work load more difficult for everyone else. Employees aren't looking for a buddy in their boss. They know that too much socializing can lead to a compromised leader. What they do look for is a fair, impartial, predictable, honest administrator or leader who sets and maintains standards. Those qualities gain *respect,* which is far more important than simple likeability.

2. THE MANAGER WHO IGNORES THE OPINIONS AND ADVICE OF SUBORDINATES

One must wonder if the "know-it-all" really believes he or she knows it all, and is that smart, or if such a manager is actually insecure and is fearful

The Know-It-All

of subordinates discovering he doesn't have all the answers all the time. There's nothing wrong with saying, "I don't know."

What really turns many employees on is to be asked, by the boss, "What do you think?" And they think plenty! It's amazing how smart many people are, and it's equally amazing what they can do in terms of solving problems and coming up with creative strategies and ideas. To ask individuals such questions as, "What do you think?" "What are we doing that we shouldn't be doing?" and "What are we not doing that we should be doing?" invariably brings out startling food for thought. To deny one's self that input is to operate with one arm tied behind the back. After all, the collective wisdom of the group or department *must* exceed that of even the most brilliant managers.

The manager who can create the climate in which employees have some voice in the things that happen, in which they participate or somehow contribute to the operation as team members, will get the most out of his employees. They're on the team and want the team to succeed!

3. THE MANAGER WHO FAILS TO DELEGATE PROPERLY

The true art of delegation includes giving responsibility with commensurate authority, then holding the subordinate fully accountable for his use of that

The Judge

authority. The primary mistake made by managers is that they give a subordinate a task (responsibility), but fail to give the necessary authority to discharge that task. Put another way, the manager keeps strings attached to the assignment in terms of insisting it be done his way, not the subordinate's, and reserves for himself the final (as well as many intermediate) decisions.

Two key conditions develop with this managerial flaw: 1) the manager becomes mired down in nitpicking, relatively unimportant decisions, making everything "his" and undermining the whole point of delegation; and 2) subordinates lose "heart" because they know the boss will arbitrarily change their plans and decisions in favor of his own. They say, "What's the difference what I do? He'll change it anyhow." Not only is it demoralizing; it's a poor utilization of the managerial time and talent of all parties. It's wasteful!

4. THE MANAGER WHO IGNORES THE TRAINING AND DEVELOPMENTAL NEEDS OF SUBORDINATES

This is the manager who attends his favorite training courses, seminars and conventions, but wouldn't dream of spending the money to send subordinates. As a rule, the manager knows most of the information and data that will be presented at a seminar, so he or she is quoted as saying, "The only value of these seminars is the contacts you make and maintain, and what you pick up as news and hints during cocktails." The pity is, subordinates could learn a great deal, even if the boss can't! But when a training seminar comes to town he or she can't seem to find the funds for subordinates

The Stifler

to attend, or feels that other demands of the organization have priority. This is the same manager who resents the training department requesting or requiring that his or her people attend company-sponsored programs, because their attendance at these programs takes time away from the job.

Employees with potential and ambition thirst for education and training to help them grow. Denying them that opportunity stunts their growth, fails to maximize their latent talents, and creates resentment. After all is said and done, the greatest resource **any** organization has is its people. But this manager isn't sensitive to that.

5. THE MANAGER WHO INSISTS ON DOING EVERYTHING "THE COMPANY WAY"

Cynical humor has it that there are three ways to do a task: 1) the right way, 2) the wrong way, and 3) the company way. There really is a fourth: a *better* way.

The manager who's a stickler for compliance with the "book" (the company way), who's more concerned about the means than the end result, is the one who blocks enthusiasm, interest, creativity, and motivation. Some flexibility in standard procedures on the part of the manager can result in reduced costs and increased production. This kind of manager, who's compliance-oriented and avoids risks, typifies the person who has peaked out career-wise.

Moses

6. THE MANAGER WHO FAILS TO GIVE CREDIT WHEN CREDIT IS DUE

Nothing is more deflating, disappointing or demotivating than having the boss ignore or overlook an achievement. A sincere "job well done" or "thank you" goes a long way. A note or brief memo from the manager expressing appreciation for a task well done is treasured by the deserving employee! Even a desk-side or hallway expression of thanks means a great deal. Thoughtlessness is a mark of stinginess. Interestingly, the boss that appears to be blind to achievement more often than not is the same boss that has the eyes of a hawk when it comes to recognizing mistakes. Slow to praise, quick to criticize. Everyone can spot this jackass a mile away. People expect praise and recognition when it is earned, and expect constructive criticism when it is due. That's the way it should be.

The manager who's stingy with words is usually also stingy with salary increases. It's the nature of the beast.

The Miser

7. THE MANAGER WHO TREATS SUBORDINATES AS SUBORDINATES

Employees are people first, and employees second. Each person is the center of his or her own universe. Gather a group of employees in a room and

The Snob

pose this question, "After all is said and done, when you get right down to it, who is the most important person in this room at this very moment?" After an awkward silence someone will speak up and say, "I am," and that's right!

The manager who looks upon or treats employees as inferiors stabs their very sense of self-esteem. But he fails to kill it, and that wound never heals, but rather, at the sight or thought of the arrogant boss, festers and smolders with resentment. Wounded people may remain on the job out of necessity, and always say, "Yes, Sir" or "Yes, Ma'am," but their heart— let alone their real potential, energy, or loyalty—is not there, even though their bodies and minds are. And there are some who bide their time to return the stab in an innumerable assortment of ways. It's better to hurt a person's body than his or her pride and ego.

8. THE MANAGER WHO IGNORES EMPLOYEES' COMPLAINTS

Not listening is a luxury only jackasses and dictators can afford. How many companies today are unionized because employees' complaints went unheeded? Employees don't vote *for* unions, they vote *against* management. What kind of management do they vote against? That management that

The Deaf (and Dumb)

ignores employees' problems, real or imaginary. That's the very heartbeat of a union organizing effort. The union, in effect says, "We hear you, even if your own management won't. Vote us in. We'll represent you and then, and only then, management will listen. They'll *have* to!"

Not only should a manager listen, he or she should find ways to *encourage* employees to get things off their chests, to point out unfair practices, to complain about dirty restrooms or poor cafeteria food. Long gone are the days when the employee stoically accepted what management had to offer. The manager who ignores employees' complaints today is the kind of jackass that should have been put out to pasture at the close of the '50s.

9. THE MANAGER WHO DOESN'T KEEP HIS PEOPLE INFORMED

Whenever you hear employees say, "You never know what's going on around here," you've got a problem. Ideally, employees should not have to ask the question, "Why?" because the question should have been answered before it was asked. People spend more of their waking hours on the job than at home, or anywhere else. It's a big and important part of their lives. It's big for their families too, because the job puts food on the table, pays

The Secret Agent

the rent, buys the all-important automobile, provides the medical insurance, etc. So the job and the company (and the two are so intertwined they're hard to separate) are the source of all sustenance.

Thus everything that happens there is important, and is scrutinized with keen interest. When someone is transferred, promoted, resigns, retires, comes aboard, goes on medical or maternal leave or is laid off, in one way or another it affects someone else. The same is true with organizational realignments, benefit changes, new shifts or hours. These changes should be explained to all employees at the earliest possible time.

Frequently the official notice is prepared for distribution. The typical company distribution system is very sluggish. The line employees who type or prepare the notice know what's happening. Before the notice gets out officially, those in the know leak news and it gets distorted. On top of that, depending upon the kind of communication system in use at the company, many news items don't even get to line employees. They arrive on supervisor or manager's desks who are supposed to inform their subordinates, but don't.

To further magnify the frustration, you find the secret agent jackasses whose philosophy is, "Don't tell anyone unless there's a need to know," thus shrouding in mystery any changes and activities within their own pyramids.

This whole problem of poor communication, or no communication, breeds suspicion among the troops, and frequently more time is spent speculating over changes than is spent on the work itself.

10. THE MANAGER WHO HOLDS HIS ASSISTANT BACK

Every manager should be developing his or her assistant to take over the manager's job, as soon as possible. At the same time that manager should be preparing for a higher level of responsibility in or out of the present pyramid. Most employees want to move up the organizational ladder, and the effective manager fosters this healthy "bubbling-up" climate.

Now there are two types of managers: one has the desire and ability to move up, while the other has no desire and/or ability to move up. In the latter case, it's grossly unfair to keep a promising assistant from advancing somewhere else in the company just to have a back-up in the event of an emergency, such as a heart attack or sudden illness, in one's own office. The end result here is that the assistant, who's obviously bright enough to make the assistant level, in due time will see that he or she is being kept on ice for emergency reasons, and will simply up and leave the com-

The Jailer

pany for opportunities elsewhere. There goes a valuable and expensive investment.

11. THE MANAGER WHO VIEWS THE DISCIPLINARY PROCESS AS A PUNITIVE ACTION

Punishment isn't good discipline. In fact it's the worst type of discipline, because it's negative in nature. Regrettably, many managers equate discipline with punishment, and they're off base.

The word "discipline" is derived from the Latin *discipulus*, which means "learning." The word "disciple" comes from the same root (as, the early Christian "disciples" were "students" of Christ). The word discipline today, when understood and seen as a constructive tool, means the *training that corrects, molds or strengthens* an employee in the interests of achieving organizational goals. Punishment comes after all else fails. And punishment should be a means to an end, an end that should be organizational, not personal.

Here's a way of looking at discipline that you should never forget: the effective disciplinary process condemns the act, not the person. The approach is, "You're OK, but what you did is not OK." By attacking the

The Whipper

performance (or performance failure) rather than the person, the whole process takes on a constructive dimension and is palatable to everyone. The manager who says, "Can't you get it through your thick skull. . . ?" is condemning or attacking the person instead of the person's performance, and consequently isn't going to get satisfactory results. That manager is doing things backwards, which suggests that perhaps the *manager* has a thick skull—similar to that of a jackass.

12. THE MANAGER WHO FAILS TO BACK UP HIS PEOPLE

What a way to lose the support and respect of subordinates—hang them out to dry when something goes amiss! Employees under this manager know where they stand when trouble rears its ugly head. They stand alone, because the boss disassociates himself or herself from anything that goes wrong. After washing his hands of any guilt, he attempts to fix the blame on someone, rather than to fix the problem.

This fair-weather manager has an insatiable appetite for organizational successes—achieved, of course, by subordinates. He or she accepts full honor

The Coward

and glory for all the good things, even letting shine forth a noble hint of modesty. This manager is indeed a winner. Never makes an error and takes all the credit. This jackass actually has the traits of a pig.

13. THE MANAGER WHOSE WORD CANNOT BE TRUSTED

The Pretender is a slippery character with an almost uncanny ability to cloud up issues and renege on earlier promises or statements. Subordinates walk out of the office confused and baffled after a session with this kind of manager. A subordinate may walk into that office to inquire about a promised early performance review (with a possible increase), but the manager pretends he or she is confused about any earlier promise and then suggests the subordinate must be confused. To cap off this tragicomedy, this kind of boss righteously points to the very source of his wisdom and power, the sign on the wall that reads: "I know you believe you understand what you think I said, but I am not sure you realize that what you heard is not what I meant."

Talk about tragedy. This kind of manager loves the pretender style, believes it's inspired in heaven, and believes the style contributes to the

The Pretender

overall success of the organization. The truth is, this manager is viewed with suspicion and disdain, not only as a manager of people, but as a human being. What a tragic work climate this manager creates.

14. THE MANAGER WHO AVOIDS MAKING DECISIONS

Nothing can be quite as exasperating as waiting for the boss to make a decision. Until the decision is made the project related to the decision remains motionless. Nothing happens.

Some flaws in management styles never get outside a given sub-pyramid, but this particular flaw has a way of becoming widely known and snickered over. This is true because sooner or later "Ol' Undecided" will be faced with a decision that will affect the entire company and not just his own department. How many times has the following occurred? Employee A asks employee B, "What's the status on the new proposal for interstore transfers?" Employee B answers, "It's sitting on Harry's (The Undecided) desk." Employee A just rolls his or her eyes back.

The unwillingness to make decisions clearly reflects a lack of self-confidence, or fear of making the wrong decision (an error!). A key leadership responsibility is to give direction. Decisions give direction. Failure to act, let alone act in a timely fashion, is a serious deficiency that breeds frustration and a "don't-give-a-damn" attitude among subordinates.

The Undecided

15. THE MANAGER WHO "PLAYS FAVORITES"

Showing partiality to one or more employees at the expense of others quickly generates hostility toward the "favored" and resentment against the manager. The manager has no choice but to discharge his office in an objective, impartial manner. Anything less than that is blatantly unfair. It causes problems in such institutions as the schools, government, and the home. It invariably leads to organizational disharmony.

A manager may well harbor personal likes and dislikes for various employees, but if he or she has any class, or sense of professionalism, no one will ever know. Of course, jackasses lack class.

The Bestower

16. THE MANAGER WHO FAILS TO STAY CURRENT IN HIS FIELD

Keeping up with the "state of the art" in terms of new technology, new concepts, new studies, changing laws, changing attitudes, trends and needs is a very personal as well as professional requirement, especially for those in leadership roles. To discover the manager is "behind the times" is a source of wonderment to subordinates, one which ultimately leads to a credibility gap. And there's no way to bridge that gap once it has developed, except of course, to become current. Catching up is an awesome task when

Rip Van Winkle

one considers that the reason behind the need to catch up is only that the manager is too lazy to stay current. That very laziness is like a disease that accelerates in its crippling growth. Reversal is rare.

A manager can't just reach the top of any given plateau and rest on the laurels of that accomplishment. If you don't grow vertically then at least grow horizontally, i.e., stay abreast of your business, keep learning, keep improving.

Absolutely nothing remains constant or static, except the intellect of a jackass.

17. THE MANAGER WHO ENJOYS "POURING ON" MORE WORK THAN A SUBORDINATE CAN HANDLE

No useful purpose is served by inundating employees with more work than they can handle. Invariably quality is sacrificed for quantity, and desperation over too much to do in too little time leads to compromises which can include deception and destruction of assignments. Most people enjoy their work and find satisfaction in a job well done, in terms of achievement. To purposely overload subordinates "just to be sure they're kept busy," directly contributes to high turnover, mental fatigue, some physical disabili-

The Slave Driver

ties with resultant lost time, and general resentment and frustration. This jackass categorizes those who stay home ill as malingerers, and those who object to the way work is assigned as "lazy." The manager is so dedicated to getting the maximum work out of every employee, that coffee breaks, lunch breaks, holidays (particularly birthday holidays), and vacation breaks are resented. This jackass is happiest when people come in early, work late, and come in on their day off when such extra time is off-the-record and without compensation.

Only a jackass is blind to the fact that maximum production and organizational efficiency come from employees who enjoy their work and produce willingly.

18. THE MANAGER WHO ACTS OR OVERREACTS TOO QUICKLY

This manager would be dangerous if armed—leaping before looking, acting before thinking, and shooting without aiming (always from the hip). Making on the spot decisions without the facts is another characteristic of this kind of manager. This jackass also changes subordinate's plans without the benefit of discussion. Those who are in charge of executing the manager's plans

Hair-trigger Harry

are never given any notice if the plans are changed. This managerial type reacts to normal problems as though they were crises. When the smoke clears, others are blamed for the mess this jackass caused.

People resent taking the blame or being criticized for conditions created by the boss. That leads to secrecy. The boss can't react to something unknown. Employees say, "We'll handle it ourselves and the boss will never know the difference." What a breakdown in communications! Then this jackass becomes suspicious. So, the boss goes on the prowl and reacts that much more irrationally. It becomes a vicious circle that causes an unhealthy work environment.

19. THE NEWLY PROMOTED MANAGERS WHO BELIEVE THEIR MANURE IS ODORLESS

Now that this jackass received a promotion and is taking over the department, everything will be OK. All the problems are in the past. All the earlier failures will be corrected. Everything will be changed for the better. How horrible everything was before. The new manager arrives like a knight in

The Lifeguard

shining armor who is going to "clean house" and get this organization on its feet and moving forward again.

Talk about a dumb jackass. Doesn't the new boss realize a lot of people were quite happy under their old boss (who they were sorry to see go, but pleased about the promotion), and honestly believed the department had been doing an effective job before the change? Even if an effective job was *not* being done, only a jackass would come in and make a lot of noise about how bad things have been. It only alienates the staff.

Newly appointed managers should heed the warning given to little children when taught how to cross a railroad track: Stop, Look, and Listen.

And who's to blame for this kind of jackass? The jackass's boss! That boss failed to prepare the new manager for this new venture; this new level of responsibility. The new boss was told: "You're the best candidate, you have all the qualifications, I have great confidence in you, now go in there and do one helluva job!" This kind of pep talk creates giant egos, leaving anyone giddy from the rapid elevation. The new manager must be the best and the only one to save the sinking ship. If anyone is in deep—and hot—water, it will be the newly promoted manager. However, with such a swelled head, the new boss probably won't go under.

20. THE MANAGER WHO'S MOODY

Everyone who works for this jackass speculates, on a daily basis, what kind of mood the boss will be in today. And those who indulge in moodiness tend to have a fascinating array of personalities: cheerful, mean, silly, argumentative, sullen, aggressive, charitable, condescending, and magnanimous, to name a few. Sometimes the same mood will last for *two* consecutive days, which of course prompts a great deal of discussion among the ranks. The key to all activity in a given day is this jackass's secretary who everyone counts on for relating the "mood of the day." "Barbara," they'll say on the phone, "is it safe to come up to discuss a budget revision?" "Oh no, not today," she may answer, particularly if she likes you. And God help you if Barbara doesn't like you because she could send you into the lion's den, a hapless victim.

This managerial style doesn't breed respect, it breeds cynical disdain for those who indulge in the usurpation of authority. Managers must be predictable and consistent. They should be available to advise, counsel, assist, and work with all employees when the need surfaces. The whole idea of being required to throw your hat into the office to see if it'll be stomped flat and thrown back out, or if you're welcome to enter, is juvenile. Perhaps this is an immature jackass.

Ol' Unpredictable

21. MANAGERS WHO FAIL TO PLAN AND PUT PRIORITIES ON THEIR WORK

The difference between a fire chief and a fire fighter is that the former directs the efforts of the fire fighters who make up the company or battalion and the fire fighter extinguishes the flames. When you hear a manager say "All I did today is put out fires," that's telling you the manager abrogated his authority as a leader and inserted himself into the line activity of the organization. Now there are occasions when absolutely everyone must pitch in to get a job done, but jackass fire fighters are consistently in the smoke. There are several explanations for this. First, they failed to plan their day's activities and/or failed to stick to the plan. Second, they either failed to put priorities on their work (first things first, etc), or didn't know how to identify their tasks in descending order of importance and then attack those tasks. Third, they find problems surfacing that they choose not to delegate to subordinates (and delegation is the key to good management) and get in there to resolve the problem themselves. And fourth, they are comfortable with and love fires and putting them out.

There are four problems here: (1) these managers are not properly managing, i.e., they are not getting the job done through others; (2) they are not discharging their responsibility to plan, organize, budget, control,

The Fire Fighter

direct, staff, and delegate; (3) subordinates are denied the opportunity to perform; and (4) they are not *available* as leaders because they are up to their shins in cinders.

The need for managers of people to be *available* to subordinates cannot be over stressed. Employees look for, expect, and need leadership. If a subordinate needs assistance or advice, or has a work or personal problem, and the boss is not in, where do they go? They go into a state of frustration, that's where they go! And where does frustration lead?

22. THE MANAGER WHO LACKS EMOTION AND EMPATHY

I want you to reflect back over the years and recall the person who you would designate as "The Best Boss I Ever Worked For." Everyone has one! Now recall the "Worst Boss I Ever Worked For." Everyone has one of those too. The difference between the two? One was warm and sensitive, and truly cared about you as a person. The other was cold, indifferent, and cared less about you. For which of these two bosses did you give your all? With respect to the poor manager, is it not true you harbored some resentment against management generally, for supporting such a manager?

The interrelationship between people is a very dynamic and emotional

The Iceman Cometh

process. The jackass that functions like an inanimate robot turns people off emotionally. An organization is not a chart with blocks, lines, department names and ranks. It's comprised of people—people with human needs and feelings. On the job a primary feeling is one of self worth. And this need for self worth spans the entire organization from the chief executive office to the lowest paid, entry level position. The manager who is sensitive to that value of worth, who genuinely is concerned about each employee, evokes a reciprocal feeling—as does the unemotional, cold, oblivious manager.

Regrettably, too many managers are simply sharp technicians. They understand and excel in the workers' tasks and tools. Good managers understand and excel (or at least try) in dealing with people who perform the tasks, use the tools, and bring profitability to the enterprise.

23. THE MANAGER WHO HIRES RELATIVES INTO THE ORGANIZATION

To bring members of one's family into the organization is a no-win situation for everyone. Such family members are not fully accepted by the work force.

The Nepotist

Employees feel, right or wrong, that relatives have an unfair advantage, and the boss's decisions on every aspect of internal affairs that affects relatives is viewed with suspicion and criticism. That's why many enlightened organizations prohibit this practice.

Why are family members not accepted by the staff? There are three reasons: (1) as a rule employees resent others getting a job through "connections"; (2) most employees refuse to believe that relatives who are promoted earned that promotion; and (3) most employees suspect relatives are a "pipeline," and funnel information to the boss. The end result is employees are resentful and guarded.

Only a jackass would opt for the problems incurred when hiring relatives.

24. THE MANAGER WHO VIEWS FEMALES AS BEING LIMITED TO PLEASURE, BREEDING, AND MENIAL FUNCTIONS, SUCH AS CLERICAL AND ASSEMBLY DUTIES

This jackass is from a herd that's slowly dwindling, but is not yet extinct! It's virtually archaic to believe that all women should be subdued, lovely, barefoot, pregnant, and in the kitchen. Gender has nothing to do with one's

The Sheik

intellectual capacity, leadership potential, or administrative and executive skills. The whole issue of sexual discrimination is no more or less than a hangover from a society and culture now in the distant past. Today we're in a fast moving, highly technical, computer-oriented, sophisticated business and industrial era, where pure talent should be the only criteria for advancement into positions of greater responsibility. More women than ever before are in the work force. In many industries the percentage of females to males is significant. What a marvelous pool of talent! Only a jackass would purposefully kindle discontentment and resentment in the work place by engaging in sexual discrimination! The mainstream of commerce today is maximizing those human resources represented in the female work force. This jackass isn't in the mainstream, but still watering in a stagnant billabong.

25. THE MANAGER WHO FAITHFULLY PRACTICES THE ART OF PESSIMISM

This manager sleeps under a wet blanket and throws cold water on every innovative, creative, new or different idea, or strategy. Consistently pat an-

Ol' Negative

swers include: "We can't," "It won't work," "We tried that before and it didn't work," "No way!", "We can't afford it," "I'd look stupid trying to sell that," "Management won't buy it," "It's not in the budget," "Too risky," "We're not ready for it," "Where the hell did you come up with that idea?", "Let's not make any waves," "Don't rock the boat," and, of course, "No."

This manager is flawless in terms of predictability, and is unequivocally insurmountable. Enthusiasm within the department is effectively blocked, causing creative employees to grind their teeth in resentful frustration. Subordinates just marvel at how this "Loser" holds the seat of power.

Ol' Negative is also pessimistic about future plans, the future of the company, the skills of subordinates, the future of the country, and probably believes Apocalypse is just around the corner. Worse yet, this pessimism is contagious. Just ten minutes around Ol' Negative and you're depressed too. That's why this manager is avoided like a jackass afflicted with the plague.

26. THE MANAGER WHO STEALS SUBORDINATES' IDEAS

The following is a four-act play. As the curtain opens on Act I, Mary Clark, the subordinate, is seated in front of her boss's desk. She's talking with her boss, Harry the Pirate. "Harry," she says, "I have what I think could be a dynamite suggestion for our marketing campaign on the XL4300." Harry's interested and asks Mary to spell out her suggestion. When she's done, Harry says, "Well, let me think about it, Mary. I'll get back to you later. Thanks."

Act II. The curtain opens and we see Harry the Pirate sitting in his boss's office talking to Walt Big. "Walt, I've been giving a lot of thought to our marketing strategy on the XL4300. Let me bounce this idea off you, for your reaction." Harry then reiterates Mary's suggestion. When he's done, Walt jumps up and says, "Harry, you've done it again! By God, that's one helluva idea. How long would it take you to flesh-it-out and formalize it on paper, I want to take it upstairs." Our Harry, who's now beaming with modesty replies, "You know I'm up to my ears on the Big B project. Tell you what I can do. I'll get Mary Clark to pull it together. We've talked about it already. I'll have her get it up to you before the day's out. She does good work." "Great," says Walt, unsuspecting of Harry's slight-of-hand act of theft.

Act III. Mary has been called back into Harry the Pirate's office and Harry is talking to her. "Mary, the more I think about the XL4300 suggestion the more I'm convinced you should go ahead and formalize it. Drop everything else, pull it together, and take it up to Walt's secretary." "Oh, that's exciting," says Mary, "I'll do it right away," and out she goes, unaware she's been victimized.

The Pirate

Act IV takes place the following day in the employee cafeteria, where Mary is having lunch with co-workers Tom and Dick. Tom says, "I overheard Walt Big's secretary telling some of the girls how Chairman Grand came down to Walt's office, all excited about a new marketing strategy that came from Harry." "Why, that wasn't Harry's idea. That was mine!" exclaims Mary, almost in tears. "The use of the word *was,* past tense, is correct, my dear," says Dick. "It is now Harry's. You do the work and he takes the credit. It's his style, you know!" "That's dishonest," says Mary. All nod in agreement as the lights dim and curtain closes.

27. THE MANAGER WHOSE STYLE AND AUTHORITY IS BASED ON ABSOLUTE POWER

There's no joke about the fact that despots still exist in management circles today. They're formal officious little dictators. Interestingly enough, most are of small stature. They know best and the subordinate's role is to do as told without questioning why.

One can't help but think this jackass is indeed playing a role on stage because it's so much in contrast to modern practices. But they're still around. They tend to intimidate everyone around them, love to have people speak in hushed tones in their presence, as well as step aside as they move straight

The Despot

ahead. To them the organization is like a supreme "state," and it's their sacred duty to rule with an iron hand. A strategy they share in common with one another is to call subordinates to their office to make them sit outside, agonizing over why they were called.

Earlier in this century, they constituted the majority of managerial/ supervisorial styles and were accepted as a way of organizational life. Today they are despised with a passion. No one will ever know how much theft, arson, sabotage, and successful union organizing efforts can be directly attributed to this strutting jackass.

28. THE MANAGER WHO SEEMS OBLIVIOUS TO WHAT'S HAPPENING

Managers of people don't have the freedom to pick and choose what they want and don't want to see. But there are those who seem to have blind spots when it comes to certain acts or people within their own pyramid. The visual impairment runs a range from "spots" to "tunnel vision" to "total." If effective and professional managers came on the scene, they would be horrified to find the chaos that occurs when a supervisor chooses not to see unchecked behavior that's not acceptable in the organization. The truth

The Visually Handicapped

is, if one member of the staff starts "getting away with murder," it becomes common knowledge among the troops and others will follow suit. Many times blindness comes from fear of taking corrective action—not wanting to be disliked or considered "mean."

When employees "goof off" it's not because they prefer that conduct over productive work. It's because productive work is not necessarily rewarding in a poorly disciplined environment. Most of us tend to gravitate to where the rewards are. If rewards don't come from the boss, but come from peers instead, then such rewards are sought. Lone workers who keep their nose to the grindstone in this kind of work place will probably be ridiculed. Better to be rewarded then ridiculed, right? And if you can get away with making long distance personal phone calls and taking company postage stamps, what else can you get away with?

29. THE MANAGER WHO LOVES TO "SACK" EMPLOYEES

There are those jackasses that take absolute delight in firing employees. They'll diligently monitor a likely prospect, allowing correctable failures to mount and accumulate, so that the killing blow will not be deflected by some do-gooder personnel representative or otherwise rational executive.

The Headhunter

And when *that* prospect receives walking papers, the headhunter goes about, unproductively, selecting a new victim. One suspects these manager's notch the edge of the desk with each "kill" (little notches if on probation, big notches if past probation).

The truth is, it's relatively easy to terminate someone, compared to working with a marginal employee and salvaging the initial investment that goes into the recruiting, selection, processing, orientation, and training. Most employees are salvageable and want constructive criticism and guidance to achieve acceptable company standards. Headhunters are easy to spot because they tend to sneak about, noting observations in little books from behind pillars. Although they're loathed, they wear the mantle proudly because they perceive their mission as one of purging the impure from the organization.

The tragedy here is some fall victim to this jackass and their termination is unfair. When managers and organizations are perceived as "unfair," the variety and magnitude of subsequent consequences can be costly.

30. THE MANAGER WHO EMBARRASSES SUBORDINATES IN THE PRESENCE OF OTHERS

Discipline, corrective action, constructive criticism, or reprimands constitute a necessary and on-going activity in every organization. Good managers

WHAT A STUPID MISTAKE!

The Humiliator

know when and where to conduct such activity. Jackasses don't! Every employee understands and should expect correction, if warranted. But they have natural expectations as to how, when, and where that correction will take place. If handled in the privacy of an office, and it is a discussion about performance (or nonperformance) rather than a personal attack, more often than not, the employee will listen to what's said and correct the questionable performance.

But employees who are tongue-lashed, shouted at, or are "chewed out" in the presence or earshot of others, are embarrassed and humiliated. They focus and dwell on the humiliating experience. They profit or learn nothing constructive or positive from the correction, but rather shift guilt, as it were, from their performance to the equally wrongful performance of the Humiliator. Not only does the victim harbor resentment, but peers who witnessed the public display identify with the victim, and they too harbor rejection and resentment against the boss.

All this to what good end? No good. Only jackass bad!

31. THE MANAGER WHO FOLLOWS "DOUBLE STANDARDS" IN THE ORGANIZATION

A key responsibility of every manager is to set a proper example. If the work day begins at 9:00 A.M., the manager should be there at 9:00 A.M.

Rules that apply to the staff should apply to the boss. If employees are entitled to purchase company goods, products, or services at a discount, the discount percentage for the boss should be the same, not higher. If the company allows employees to travel on business via aircoach and the boss travels with subordinates, he too should ride coach and not first cabin. Certainly R.H.I.P. Everyone recognizes that. But it shouldn't be flaunted, and subordinates shouldn't have their noses rubbed in it. Privileges in rank are manifested in salary differences, as an example. Yet, aren't executive salaries usually treated as confidential? If confidential, why? Because obviously the disparity would only cause problems. Wisdom and common sense dictate that conspicuous disparities be avoided.

The jackass managers who flaunt their privileges by parking in restricted areas, coming in late, enjoying long breaks and lunches, going home early, having their secretary do personal business for them, staying in fancy hotels next to the hotel where their staff stays, bragging about their higher travel per diem, and generally relishing their advantages in open view of subordinates who work shoulder to shoulder with them are inviting problems.

Mr. R.H.I.P. (Rank Has Its Privileges)

32. THE MANAGER WHO'S A RELIGIOUS OR RACIAL BIGOT

This is a close cousin to the Sheik or sexist who we've already identified as a managerial jackass. The difference between the two is the sexist simply feels females have limited value, whereas the Night Rider is fundamentally opposed to either Jews, Protestants, Catholics, Mexicans, Blacks, Orientals, or in some cases, all of them. It's simply ridiculous to categorically state that given classes, groups, or races of people have no executive or managerial potential. Now a simple jackass can take that position. But an effective and intelligent leader knows otherwise. Identifying and then maximizing individual talent to achieve organizational goals is a requisite and responsibility of sound management. I personally care less if an individual has a different religious conviction (although I'm certain I'd be pleased if he has *a* conviction) or a skin pigmentation different from mine. My concern is: can this person do the job, and do it well.

For just a moment, forget managers denying themselves and the organization the full spectrum of talent present in the greatest resource any firm has—the human resources of its employees. Prejudice, be it racial or religious, consistently has bred discontentment and confrontation. What else can it breed in organizational life?

The Night Rider

SUMMARY

Now we have a grand total of thirty-two supervisory and managerial flaws found in organizational life. We've chosen to call them jackass management traits. Though it's good to poke fun at some of these otherwise tragic characters, it's sad to consider so many negative traits still existing, and in some cases, prevailing. But there's good news, too. These failings which exist in the very source of our strength, our economic base, are rapidly being replaced with a new breed of leadership that understands and appreciates the values of human dignity and worth. And this is not coming from the bottom up, but from the top down; i.e., senior management's growing recognition that good leadership inspires self motivation among the troops, rather than harsh or otherwise insensitive managers prodding employees down the jackass trail.

Appendix A

EMPLOYEE PERFORMANCE EVALUATION

HOURLY AND WEEKLY RATED
NON-SUPERVISORY PERSONNEL

NAME _____   DATE OF RATING _____

JOB TITLE_____   ON PRESENT JOB SINCE _____

EMPLOYEE NUMBER _____   SERVICE DATE _____

INSTRUCTIONS: Read the definitions under each factor listed below and check (✓) the box that best describes this employee's overall performance for the past year. To the right of the definitions are various elements for each factor, again check as appropriate. Any BAS rating must be explained in the comments sections.

RATING CODE DEFINITIONS

(O)   OUTSTANDING: Performance of extraordinary or rare nature. Consistently exceeds normal job requirements. Makes substantial contributions to the success of the department.

(AAS)   ABOVE ACCEPTABLE STANDARDS: Performance that frequently exceeds normal job requirements. Makes definite contributions to the success of the department.

(MAS)   MEETS ACCEPTABLE STANDARDS: Performance that meets normal job requirements. There is no evidence of any major deficiency.

(BAS)   BELOW ACCEPTABLE STANDARDS: Performance that is frequently below normal job requirements. Evidence of major deficiencies. Improvement is required to meet job requirements.

PART I

1. KNOWLEDGE OF JOB

The understanding of basic fundamentals, methods and procedures of the job.

A. KNOWS PROCEDURES
B. LEARNS WORK QUICKLY
C. KNOWS EQUIPMENT AND FORMS
D. KNOWS WHY THINGS ARE DONE

O A M B

O   AAS   MAS   BAS

COMMENTS: _____

_____

2. QUALITY OF WORK

Grade of acceptable work compared to what might reasonably be expected.

A. ACCURACY OF WORK
B. THOROUGHNESS OF WORK
C. NEATNESS OF WORK

O A M B

O   AAS   MAS   BAS

COMMENTS: _____

_____

3. QUANTITY OF WORK

Volume of acceptable work compared to what might reasonably be expected.

A. OVERALL VOLUME OF WORK
B. CONSISTENCY OF OUTPUT
C. EFFORTS TO IMPROVE OUTPUT
D. UTILIZATION OF TIME

O A M B

O   AAS   MAS   BAS

COMMENTS: _____

_____

4. ADAPTABILITY

Quickness to learn new duties and to adjust to new situations encountered on the job.

A. ADJUSTS TO NEW SITUATIONS
B. QUICK TO LEARN NEW DUTIES
C. FOLLOWS COMPANY POLICY

O A M B

O   AAS   MAS   BAS

COMMENTS: _____

_____

5. ATTITUDE

O A M B

The interest, enthusiasm
and cooperation shown in
the work, in the company,
and with associates.

A. INTEREST IN WORK
B. COOPERATION
C. RESPONDS TO CONSTRUCTIVE
   CRITICISM
D. RESPONDS TO TRAINING
E. ALWAYS DOES HIS BEST
F. HELPS FELLOW EMPLOYEES
G. KEEPS SUPERVISORS WELL
   INFORMED
H. RESPONDS TO CHANGES

O   AAS   MAS   BAS

COMMENTS: _____

6. DEPENDABILITY

O A M B

The ability to work without
close supervision. Accuracy
and follow through on
assignments without
constant checking.

A. FOLLOWS THROUGH ON
   ASSIGNMENTS
B. EFFECTIVE UNDER PRESSURE
C. FOLLOWS INSTRUCTIONS
D. ACCURACY IN HANDLING
   PROCEDURES WITHOUT
   CONSTANT CHECKING

O   AAS   MAS   BAS

COMMENTS: _____

7. JUDGMENT

O A M B

Ability to decide course of
action when some choice
can be made.

A. PROPER ATTENTION TO DETAILS
B. REASONING IS SOUND AND
   CONSISTENT
C. TAKES PROPER AMOUNT OF
   TIME TO CONSIDER FACTS AND
   THEIR APPLICATION

O   AAS   MAS   BAS

COMMENTS: _____

8. INITIATIVE

O A M B

The ability to perform
assigned jobs in a self-
confident, eager manner
without detailed instruc-
tions.

A. EAGER TO IMPROVE OWN
   PERFORMANCE
B. TACKLES DIFFICULT JOBS
C. SEES THINGS TO BE DONE
D. INQUISITIVE

O   AAS   MAS   BAS

COMMENTS: _____

_____

9. CUSTOMER SERVICE (As Applicable)

Alertness to, acknowledg-
ment of and interest in the
customer.

A. IMMEDIATE APPROACH AND
ACKNOWLEDGMENT OF
CUSTOMER
B. RECOGNITION OF WAITING
CUSTOMER, IF BUSY
C. GRACIOUS, COURTEOUS AND
ATTENTIVE

O	AAS	MAS	BAS

D. GIVES ALERT AND
INTELLIGENT SERVICE

O	A	M	B

COMMENTS: _____

_____

10. MERCHANDISE KNOWLEDGE (As Applicable)

Well informed on entire
stock in department.

A. VOLUNTEERS MERCHANDISE
INFORMATION
B. GIVES ACCURATE INFORMATION
C. USES FASHION AND AD-
VERTISING INFORMATION
D. DEMONSTRATES USE AND CARE
OF MERCHANDISE

O	AAS	MAS	BAS

E. INQUISITIVE

O	A	M	B

COMMENTS: _____

_____

11. SALES PERFORMANCE (As Applicable)

Overall selling performance.

A. VOLUME
B. ATTITUDE
C. SUGGESTIVE SELLING
D. CLOSING THE SALE

O	AAS	MAS	BAS

O	A	M	B

COMMENTS: _____

_____

12. APPEARANCE

The overall impression
given to the customer. Neat
and businesslike or some-
times careless and untidy.

A. APPROPRIATE FOR THE JOB
B. IN GOOD TASTE
C. WELL GROOMED

O	A	M	B

O	AAS	MAS	BAS

COMMENTS: _____

13. ATTENDANCE
 A. NUMBER OF DAYS ABSENT_____SINCE_____
 B. NUMBER OF OCCASIONS ABSENT_____SINCE_____
 C. OVERALL DEPENDABILITY AS RELATES TO ATTENDANCE
   AND TARDINESS

O A M B

COMMENTS:_____

PART II NAME_____

SUMMARY RATING

Overall job performance and contribution to   COMMENTS:
the success of the department.

OUTSTANDING

ABOVE ACCEPTABLE STANDARDS

MEETS ACCEPTABLE STANDARDS

BELOW ACCEPTABLE STANDARDS

PART III

1. DISPOSITION

_____IMMEDIATELY PROMOTIONAL TO:_____

_____PROMOTIONAL IN _____ MONTHS TO:_____

_____RECOMMEND TRANSFER TO: _____

_____LEAVE ON PRESENT ASSIGNMENT _____

_____PLACE ON JOB PERFORMANCE CAUTION

1   2   FINAL

OR WARNING   _____TOO NEW TO SPECIFY

2. RECOMMENDATIONS FOR TRAINING OR OTHER ACTION: _____

_____

_____

3. REMARKS: _____

_____

_____

_____

| RATER | DATE | SENIOR RATER | DATE | PERSONNEL MANAGER | DATE |

PART IV

NOTE: Do not conduct interview until Senior Rater and Personnel Manager have signed this form.

1. REPORT OF INTERVIEW _____

_____

_____

_____

_____

_____

| DATE OF INTERVIEW | SIGNATURE OF INTERVIEWER |

Appendix B

SECURITY VULNERABILITY SURVEY

Facility _____ Survey Date _____

Address _____ Facility Manager _____
                                           Telephone No. _____

I. GENERAL FUNCTION

Leased
Owned
_____

No. Employees Assnd. _____

Operating Hours:	Weekdays	Saturday	Sunday
	Opens _____	Opens _____	Opens _____
	Closes _____	Closes _____	Closes _____

Address & Phone of Police Jurisdiction: _____

Area Evaluation: _____

II. BUILDING & PERIMETER

_____ 1. Type of construction?

_____ 2. Door construction (hinges, hinge pins, solid core, etc.)?

_____ 3. Total number of perimeter entrances?

_____ 4. Are all exits & entrances supervised?
If not, how controlled?

_____ 5. Are there perimeter fences?
Type?
Height?
Distance from bldg.?
Cleared areas?
Barbed wire top?
Roof or wall areas close to fence?

_____ 6. Are there any overpasses or subterranean passageways?

_____ 7. Height of windows from ground?
Adequately protected?

_____ 8. Any roof openings or entries?

_____ 9. Any floor grates, ventilation openings?

_____10. Any materials stored outside bldg.?
How controlled?

_____11. Adjacent occupancy?

Comments:

III. VEHICULAR MOVEMENT

_____ 1. Is employee parking within perimeter fence?

_____ 2. Are cars parked abutting interior fences?

_____ 3. Are cars parked adjacent to loading docks, bldg. entrances, etc.?

_____ 4. Do employees have access to cars during work hours?

_____ 5. Vehicle passes or decals?

_____ 6. Are guards involved in traffic control?

Comments.

IV. LIGHTING

_____ 1. Is perimeter lighting provided?
Adequate?

_____ 2. Is there an emergency lighting system?

_____ 3. Are all doorways sufficiently lighted?

_____ 4. Is lighting in use during all night hours?

_____ 5. Is lighting directed toward perimeter?

_____ 6. Is lighting adequate for parking area?

_____ 7. How is lighting checked?

_____ 8. Is interior night lighting adequate for surveillance by night guards (or by municipal law enforcement agents)?

_____ 9. Are guard posts properly illuminated?

Comments:

V. LOCKING CONTROLS

_____ 1. Does the facility have adequate control and records for all keys?

_____ 2. Is a master key system in use?

_____ 3. How many master keys are issued?

_____ 4. Are all extra keys secured in a locked container?

_____ 5. Total number of safes?

_____ 6. Last time combination(s) changed?

_____ 7. If combination is recorded, where is it stored?

_____ 8. Total number of employees possessing combination?

_____ 9. Review procedures for securing sensitive items, i.e. monies, precious metals, high dollar value items, narcotics, etc.?

_____10. Who performs locksmithing function for the facility?

_____11. Is a key inventory periodically taken?

_____12. Are locks changed when keys are lost?

Comments:

VI. ALARMS

_____ 1. Does this facility utilize any alarm devices?
           Total number of alarms?

Type	Location	Manufacturer	Remarks

_____ 2. Are alarms of central station type connected to police department or outside guard service?

_____ 3. Is authorization list of personnel authorized to "open & close" alarmed premises up to date?

_____ 4. Are local alarms used on exit doors?

_____ 5. Review procedure established on receipt of alarm?

_____ 6. Is closed circuit TV utilized?

Comments:

VII. GUARDS/SECURITY CONTROLS

_____ 1. Is a guard service employed to protect this facility?

If yes. Name:_____ No. of guards_____ No. of posts_____

_____ 2. Are after hours security checks conducted to assure proper storage of classified reports, key controls, monies, checks, etc.?

_____ 3. Is a property pass system utilized?

_____ 4. Are items of company property clearly identified with a distinguishing mark that cannot be removed?

_____ 5. Review guard patrols & frequency?

_____ 6. Are yard areas and perimeter areas included in guard coverage?

_____ 7. Are all guard tours recorded?

_____ 8. Are package controls exercised re packages brought on or off premises?

_____ 9. Does facility have written instructions for guards?

_____10. What type of training do guards receive?

_____11. Are personnel last leaving building charged with checking doors, windows, cabinets, etc.?
        Record of identity?

_____12. Are adequate security procedures followed during lunch hours?

Comments:

VIII. EMPLOYEE AND VISITOR CONTROLS

_____ 1. Is a daily visitors register maintained?

_____ 2. Is there a control to prevent visitors from wandering in the plant?

_____ 3. Do employees use identification badge?

_____ 4. Are visitors issued identification passes?

_____ 5. What type of visitors are on premises during down hours and weekends?

_____ 6. Does any company's employees other than _____ have access to facility?
        List Company Names   Type Service Performed

_____ 7. Are controls over temporary help adequate?

Comments:

IX. PRODUCT CONTROLS (Shipping and Receiving)

_____ 1. Are all thefts or shortages or other possible problems, i.e., anonymous letters, crank calls, etc. reported immediately?

_____ 2. Inspect and review controls for shipping area.

_____ 3. Inspect and review controls for receiving area.

_____ 4. Supervision in attendance at all times?

_____ 5. Are truck drivers allowed to wander about the area?
Is there a waiting area segregated from product area?
Are there toilet facilities nearby?
Water cooler?
Pay telephone?

_____ 6. Are shipping or receiving doors used by employees to enter or leave facility?

_____ 7. What protection is afforded loaded trucks awaiting shipment?

_____ 8. Are all trailers secured by seals?

_____ 9. Are seal numbers checked for correctness against shipping papers?
"In" and "Out"

_____10. Are kingpin locks utilized on trailers?

_____11. Is a separate storage location utilized for overages, shortages, damages?

_____12. Is parking (employees and visitor vehicles) prohibited from areas adjacent to loading docks or emergency exit doors?

_____13. Is any material stored in exterior of building?
If so how protected?

_____14. Are trailers or shipments received after closing hours?
If so how protected?

_____15. Are all loaded trucks or trailers parked within fenced area?

_____16. Review facility's product inventory control.

	Loss	Breakage	Returns
Average Monthly			

_____17. Review controls over breakage.

Comments:

X. MONEY CONTROLS

_____ 1. How much cash is maintained on the premises?

_____ 2. What is the location and type of repository?

_____ 3. Review cashier function.

_____ 4. What protective measures are taken for money deliveries to facility? To bank?

_____ 5. If armored car service utilized, list name and address.

_____

_____ 6. Does facility have procedure to control cashing of personal checks?

_____ 7. Are checks immediately stamped with restricted endorsement?

_____ 8. Are employee payroll checks properly accounted for and stored in a locked container (including lunch hours) until distributed to the employee or his supervisor?

Comments:

XI. PROPRIETARY INFORMATION

_____ 1. What type of proprietary information is possessed at this facility?

_____ 2. How is it protected?

_____ 3. Is "_____ Restricted" marking used?

_____ 4. Are safeguards followed for paper waste, its collection and destruction?

_____ 5. Are desk and cabinet tops cleared at end of day?

_____ 6. Is management aware of need for protecting proprietary information?

Comments:

XII. OTHER VULNERABILITIES

_____ 1. Trash pick ups. (Hours of pick ups, control of contractor, physical controls).

_____ 2. Scrap operations. (Physical controls of material and area, control over scrap pick ups, etc.).

_____ 3. Other.

Comments:

XIII. PERSONNEL SECURITY

_____ 1. Are background investigations conducted on employees handling products?
Handling cash?
Engaged in other sensitive duties?
Supervisory position?
All employees?

_____ 2. If so, who conducts background investigation?

_____ 3. Are new employees given any security or other type of orientation?

_____ 4. Do newly hired employees execute a corporate briefing form for inclusion in their personnel file?

_____ 5. Are exit interviews conducted of terminating employees?

_____ 6. Is a program followed to insure return of keys, credit cards, I.D. cards, manuals, and other company property?

GENERAL COMMENTS

Appendix C

SECURITY DEPARTMENT
LOSS PREVENTION CHECK LIST

STORE NO._____

Legend:
A—Satisfactory
B—Corrected During
   Inspection
C—Requires Corrective
   Action

INSTRUCTIONS

All areas applicable to this store are to be inspected during course of month. Indicate condition by marking "X" in appropriate box. Areas requiring corrective action should be reviewed with store management prior to turning in check list. Use Part II for explanatory details.

A	B	C	PART I	Date Inspected
			Securement of Theft Prone Merchandise	
			1. Calculators properly secured to display fixture, (Dept. 13)	
			2. Display typewriters are secured (Dept. 15)	
			3. Lockbars in Suit Dept. are in place & kept locked.	
			4. Men's Leathers are chained or are under lockbar.	
			5. Stoplifters are used on higher priced RTW fixtures adjacent to street exits.	
			6. Stoplifters are utilized on floor fixtures in Dept. 9-48-61.	
			7. Men's Accessories showcase are kept locked (Dept. 105)	
			8. Ciani counter fixtures are secured to counter (Dept. 20)	
			9. All portable TV's are secured with cord locks. (Dept. 72)	

A	B	C		Date Inspected
			Physical Security	
			10. Firelocks on stairwells & emergency exits have been tested.	
			11. Locks & electric latch on vault man-trap are functional.	
			a. Access list to Cashier area and vault are current & posted.	
			12. All Ultrasonic Alarms (Fine Jewelry, Furs, Escalators) walk tested.	
			13. Restricted area signs posted at inner hallways to dock & back areas.	
			14. Rear exit door from restaurant kept locked at all times & key under control of restaurant manager.	
			15. Alteration Room secured whenever unoccupied or closed.	
			16. Watchman is assigned to employee door after employee system is turned off.	
			Merchandise Counts	
			17. TV counts taken prior to store opening.	
			18. Daily suit counts accurately taken on timely basis.	
			19. Fur counts are taken at store opening & closing & include all furs in stockroom (include holds & customer repairs).	
			Stockrooms	
			20. All stockroom doors located in fitting room banks are equipped with self locking hardware.	
			21. Lockable stockrooms are kept locked.	
			22. Stockrooms utilize only one entrance (alternate entrances are closed off).	
			23. TV stockroom is completely enclosed, adequate in size & kept locked at all times.	
			24. Keys to TV stockroom controlled only by Dept. Manager & store management.	
			25. Stockroom Doors are not propped or tied open unless employee continuously present.	
			Dock, Wheeler, Basement, Penthouse	
			26. Access to customers is secured during night hours & Sundays.	
			27. High theft type merchandise not stocked in open Wheeler areas.	
			28. Transfer trailer seals are stored in secure location.	
			29. Customer pickup log is properly maintained (include vehicle license number).	
			30. Dock doors kept closed when loading operation not in progress.	
			31. Employee always present when dock doors open.	
			32. Marking room kept locked when unattended.	
			33. Trailers are secured during lunch breaks & end of day.	
			Fitting Rooms	
			34. Each fitting room & fitting room hallway is properly signed with signs in good condition (1-2-3, policy statement & shoplift picture).	

A	B	C		Date Inspected
			35. Garment limit sign clearly visible in each entrance foyer area.	
			36. Fitting room doors properly cut (top & bottom) to permit surveillance, or vented in proper direction.	
			37. Fitting room has only one entrance/exit.	
			38. Store is equipped with adequate supply of fitting room discs and disc holders.	
			39. Fitting rooms are not used as stock storage areas unless modified to provide secure storage.	
			40. Fitting room wall abutting stockroom has floor to ceiling wall.	
			41. Fitting room walls of one department abutting departments fitting room bank to have floor to ceiling wall.	
			42. Merchandise is cleared out of all fitting rooms on timely basis.	
			High Shrinkage Departments 43. Costume Jewelry	
			a. Counter fixtures with higher priced merchandise located closer to register stand & in unobstructed view.	
			b. All display cases & drawers are equipped with locks & all locks are functional.	
			c. All display cases & drawers are locked each night (verify).	
			d. Countertop fixtures are covered with dust covers at store closing.	
			44. Wallets (Dept 86) displayed only one deep & in manufacturer's box when reserve stock can be kept in dept. area.	
			45. Furs	
			a. No fur piece in excess of $995 is displayed on selling floor, except on mannequin with arms.	
			b. Furs not displayed on more than 4 floor fixtures & each display is balanced.	
			c. Keys to fur vault during day are retained in register or on salesclerks' person. (Not in unlocked desk)	
			d. Furs are removed from floor display and secured when employee with 60 number is away from Dept. (including breaks, lunch, etc.)	
			e. Fur dept. & PBX employees are familiar with procedure to be followed re: Fur Dept. buzzer & buzzer is functional.	
			46. Cosmetic testers are properly marked.	
			47. Dept 106 Jewelry is displayed in area clearly visible from register stand.	
			48. Dept 102 Jewelry is displayed in area clearly visible from register stand.	
			49. All TV's not displayed on selling floor are stored in TV stockroom and placed in stockroom immediately upon receipt.	

A	B	C		Date Inspected
			Administration	
			50. Security Officer is regular attendee at store's Group Manager meetings.	
			51. Store management is kept informed of attempted theft activity (burns).	
			52. Store management/Security periodically monitors employee door during early shift breaks, i.e. House-keeping crews, Stock, Display.	
			53. Store management representative periodically reviews loan books to insure accuracy.	
			a. Audit loan book for 2 depts. and note findings in Part II.	
			54. Over & short records are kept posted on a current basis.	
			a. How far behind are postings?	
			b. Name of store representative specifically designated to be responsible to monitor Over & Shorts:	
			55. Periodic store walk-throughs are conducted by either Senior or Security Officer with a member of store management.	
			a. Date of last joint walk-through	
			b. Note in Part II conditions noted in walk-through not yet corrected.	
			56. Are checker schedules filled as planned?	
			a. Store includes Checkers in break relief schedule.	
			57. Are Checkers hired on non-sell number where possible instead of using contingent sales personnel?	
			58. Are proper employee lockering techniques followed?	
			a. Spot check 3 employee sealed lockered packages.	
			59. Are employees wearing their store badges?	
			a. Take count of all employees visible on one tour of the store. Employee's badged_____Not badged_____.	
			60. Is store initiating loss reports for suspected losses?	
			a. Turn in quantity of Kimball Tickets recovered from fitting rooms.	
			Qty. turned in_____Loss Reports prepared_____ (explain in Part II)	

PART II

Use this section to elaborate on any answer in Part I or to make additional comments in other areas. Continue comments on reverse side. Attach additional sheets if needed.

PART III

List by item number the inspection items reviewed with store management.

Member of Store Management with Whom Reviewed: _____

_____   _____   _____
Name of Security Employee   Signature   Date of Report
Conducting Inspection

INDEX

Accountability, authority with, 17–18
Achievement, as motivator, 120, 122–123
Advancement, as motivator, 120
Advertising
  of job openings, 77–78
  by Security Department, 245
Alarm systems, 37–38, 187
American Management Association, 205
American Society for Industrial Security, 262, 263
Assets, and risk identification, 200–201
Assignments, 109–110
Attitude, 72
Audio-visual materials, 243–244
Authority
  functional, 20
  line and staff, 14
  and responsibility, 17–18
  supervisory, 57–58
Authorship, 264
Auto thefts, 272
Autocratic theory, of organizational behavior, 119

Background investigation, 228–229, 230
  and criminal histories, 250–251
  for security employees, 75, 83–84, 224
  and Stores Protective Association, 261
Bodyguard/escort service, 38
Book authorship, 264
Budget, 161–177
  and career and non-career employees, 151, 152, 154
  justification of, 174–176
  and organizational structure, 30
  salary expense, 166–171
  sundry expense, 172–174
  top-down and bottom-up, 164–165

Bulletins. *See* Newsletters
Business
  attitude toward security, 208–209
  crime loss to, 205–207

Campus recruiting, 47
Capital expenses, 161
Career path, 149
Chain of command, 31, 60–61
Chamber of Commerce, U.S., 206
Chief Special Agents Association of Southern California, 262–263
Clark, J. P., 277
Cleanliness, 70
Clerical duties, 219
Closed circuit television, 187, 189
Command
  chain of, 31, 60–61
  unity of, 16–17, 59–61
Communications, 139–147
  horizontal, 140, 142–143, 145
  interdepartmental, 48
  stovepipe, 139–140
  verbal, 139–140, 145
  written, 140–144, 261
    handbook, 104, 231–235
    newsletter, 142–144, 261
Community, role in crime prevention, 272–273
Community relations, 267–273
  press interviews, 270
  public speaking, 268–272
  radio-television interviews, 265
Company growth, 29–30
Company rules, 110–111
Company security, 21–25
Compliance inspections, 189–190
Conduct, 65–72
Consistency, and discipline, 111
Constructive discipline, 107–108
Consultant, security, 154

Control
    span of, 16, 58–59
    supervisory, 3–4, 107, 58–59
Control card ledger, 222
Cooperation, 68–69
Coordination, 3, 18–19
Courtesy, 66–67
Crime
    cost to business, 205–206
    white collar, 206
Crime prevention, 19–20, 41, 272
    and criminal histories, 251
    and security survey, 210
Crime statistics, 255–256
Criminal histories, 84, 250–253
Custodial theory, of organizational behavior, 119

Delegation of work, 17–18, 280–281
Demotivators, 124–127
Directing function, of management, 3
Discipline, 107–115
    constructive, 107–108
    and mismanagement, 288
    rules of, 110–113
    self-discipline, 113–115
    supervisor's role in, 57, 58, 108–110, 113–115
Discrimination, in hiring practices, 79
Documentation, in disciplinary process, 112–113
Due process, 67–68

Education. *See* Training
80/20 rule, 6
Electronic countermeasures, 187
Emergency planning, 39, 60, 164
Employees
    career, 149–152, 156
    conduct of, 65–72
    and due process, 67–68
    evaluation of, 57–58, 315–320
    file of infractions by, 112
    hiring of, 75–85
        interviewing, 78–82
        recruiting, 77–78
    induction programs for, 40–41
    integrity of, 69–72

    non-career, 152–156
        contractual, 154–156
        part-time, 152–154
    promotions, 129–137
    salary expense budget for, 166–171
    self-protection programs for, 41
    selling security to, 242–243
    theft by, 206–207, 277–278
Employee Performance Evaluation chart, 315–320
Employee Screening. *See* Investigations, background
Entry level recruiting, 77
Escort service, 38
Executives
    orientation in security for, 244–245
    protection of, 37, 198
    special services by security for, 37–39
        bodyguard/escort service, 38
        emergency service, 39
        home security services, 37–38
    security director as, 46–47

Fair Credit Reporting Act, 84
Feinberg, Mortimer R., 124, 125
Felony convictions, 75–76
Fidelity, 70–71
Filing system, 220–223
Fire risk analysis, 198
Functional supervision, 61

General Security Program, 40
Geurts, M., 278
Goal-setting, 51
Good will, 269
Growth, as motivator, 120, 123
Guidelines, vs. policies and procedures, 231

Handbooks. *See* Manuals
Hardware countermeasure, 186–187
Herzberg, Frederick, 120, 124
Hiring practices, 75–85, 230, 251
Holidays, 168
Hollinger, R. C., 277
Home security surveys, 37–38
Honesty, 69
Human behavior, theories of, 117–118, 120, 124

Humiliation, and discipline, 111–112
Humility, and self-discipline, 114–115
Hygiene, 120–121

Information, in POP formula, 100
Inspections
    checklists for, 182, 329
    in program management, 179–184, 189–190
    and supervision, 55–56, 182–184
Integrity, 69
Intelligence gathering, 250–255
International Association of Chiefs of Police, 19–20
International Association of Professional Security Consultants, Inc., 262–263
Interviews
    bias in, 82
    of employee applicants, 78–82
    for promotions, 132–133
Inventory shrinkage, 242
Investigations
    background, 228–229, 230
        and criminal histories, 250–251
        for security employees, 75, 83–84, 224
        and Stores Protective Association, 261
    coordination with law enforcement in, 250–255
    of labor disputes, 255
    policies and procedures for, 232–233

Job descriptions, 87–95
Job performance, 130–131
Job satisfaction, 71
Job security, 151
Job surroundings, 120–121

Kidnapping risk analysis, 198
Kidnapping prevention, 41

Labor disputes, 255
Law enforcement
    records of, 250–251
    relationship with private security, 249–258
Leadership, 5, 32–33, 45–46
Liability risk, 195

Line authority, 14
Litigation, 152
Lobby Desk Office training, 101
Loss prevention, 199, 200
    checklist, 329–333
    manual, 234–235
Loyalty, 70–71

McCauley, Paul R., 176
McGregor, Douglas, 117, 120, 124
Mail processing, 223
Management
    and budgeting, 176
    functions of, 2–4
    and program management inspections, 180–181
    and risk analysis, 196–198
    selling security to, 211–212
    and training, 99
Managers
    flaws in, 277–311
    self-discipline of, 113–115
    successful, 1–2, 4–5, 139
    See also Security Manager
Manuals. *See* Security manual
Manufacturing firm, organizational chart of, 22
Master index cards, 222–223
Misdemeanors, 75, 76
Mismanagement, 277–311
    and employee theft, 277–278
    and training, 281–282
Momboisse, R. M., 205
Morale, 117–127
Morality, 71
Moral turpitude, 75, 76
Motivation, 117–127
    and achievement, 120, 122–123
    autocratic theory of, 119
    custodial theory of, 119
    demotivators, 124–127
    and promotions, 133
    and responsibility, 120, 121–122
    supportive theory of, 119–120, 124
    Theory X and Y of, 117–118, 120, 124
    work motivation theory, 120–124

National Retail Merchants Association, 262, 263

Neighborhood checks, 90–91
Nepotism, 300–301
Newsletters
    departmental, 142–144
    Stores Protective Association, 261

Objectivity, 111, 114
Office administration, 215–225
Office equipment and furniture, 66
Organizational structure, 27–33
    charts of, 14–16, 30–31
    company and corporate, 21–25
    departmental, 27–31
    formal and informal, 27–31
    functional, 13
    horizontal and vertical planes of, 27
    multiple layers of, 134–135
    principles of, 11–19
    pyramidal, 14–16
    security's place in, 19–25, 35–43, 104
    sub-unit, 31–33
    theories of, 119–120
Organizing function of management,
    2–3
Orientation, vs. training, 97–98

Parking environments, 35–36
Performance evaluations, 55–56
    chart of, 315–320
    and job description, 90–91
    policies and procedures for, 230
    and supervision, 55
Personal risk, 195
Personnel Department, 30–31, 187–188
    in hiring security employees, 79
"Peter Principle," 135
Petty cash box, 185
Planning, 2, 161–177
Police. *See* Law enforcement
Policies and procedures, 227–237
    benefits of, 229–230
    compliance with, 230–231
    free-standing, 233
    format and mechanics of, 235–237
    and security manual, 234–235
Political activists, 254–255
Polygraph, 83, 84
POP training formula, 99–102
Press interviews, 270

Press releases, 270
Privacy rights, 111, 250–251
Problem-solving, 121, 122
Procedural controls, 99, 100–102, 186, 189–
    190
Profits, 20, 206, 207–208
Program management, 179–194
    countermeasure assessment, 188–189
    countermeasure selection, 185–188
    inspections, 179–184, 189–190
    risk assessment, 184–185
    statistics in, 190–193
Promotions, 129–137
    identification and selection of candi-
        dates for, 129–132
    as motivator, 123
    outside department, 134
    Promotion Board, 131, 132–133
    retreating, 135–136
    temporary, 135
    from within, 133–134
Property risk, 195
Protection, 35–36
Psychological testing, 228
Public relations, 241–248
Public speaking, 264–265, 268–272
Punishment, and discipline, 107
Pyramidal organization, 14–16

Radical activists, 254–255
Radio-television interviews, 270–272
Rape prevention, 41, 244
Receptionists, 218
Recognition, as motivator, 120, 123
Records, 219–220
    control of, 223
    filing system for, 220–223
Recruiting, 77–78
Respect, 66–68
Responsibility, 67
    and authority, 17–18
    delegation of, 17–18
    as motivator, 120, 121–122
Retail security
    inventory shrinkage, 242
    organization of, 23, 134
    "red coat" approach to, 48–49
Risk, definition of, 195
Risk analysis, 195–203

Risk assessment analysis, 184–185, 196
Risk exposure assessment, 198–199, 200
Risk identification, 199–203
Rules
    company, 110–111
    of disciplinary process, 110–113

Salary expense budget, 166–171
Secretaries, 216–218
Security checklists, 203, 329–333
Security countermeasures, 185–189
Security Department
    budget, 167, 173–176
    communications, 48
    community services, 255–257
    corporate and company, 21–25
    and crime prevention, 19–20
    division of work within, 12–14
    involvement programs, 247–248
    loss prevention checklist, 203, 329–333
    meetings, 246–247
    motivation in, 121–122
    newsletter, 245
    place in organization, 19–25, 35–43
    and profits, 20
    relationship with law enforcement, 249–258
    relationship to security industry, 259–266
    selling to management, 211–212, 241–248
Security Director
    and community relations, 268
    corporate, 21–25
    place in organization, 20–21
    role of, 45–53, 246–247
    vs. Security Manager, 45
Security industry, 259–266
    attitude of business toward, 208–209
    changing role of, 19–20
Security management, 13–14, 42
Security Manager, 260
    flaws in, 277–311
    inspections by, 182–184
    role of, 246–247
    vs. Security Director, 45
Security manual, 104, 141–142, 234–235
Security newsletter, 142–144, 261
Security of Objectives theory, 176

Security office administration, 215–225
Security presence, 36
Security seminars, 41–42, 102–104
Security survey, 205–213, 321–327
Security Training Officer, 102
Self-discipline, 113–115
Self-respect, 69–70
Sennewald, Charles, 210
Sex discrimination, 301–302
Shift rotation, 13
Shoplifting, 100, 244, 272
Skill development, 100, 101
Special Agents Association of Southern
    California, 262
Speech topics, 270, 271
Stability, 70
Staff authority, 14
Staff supervision, 61
Stanford Research Institute, 206
Statistics
    crime, 190–193
    and program management, 190–193
Stores Protective Association (SPA), 84,
    261, 262
Sundry expense budget, 172–174
Supervision, 55–63
    and assignment failures, 109
    and authority, 57–58
    and discipline, 108–109
    and employee differences, 56–57
    functional, 61
    and inspections, 55–56
    in office administration, 216
    and promotions, 132
    and self-discipline, 113–115
    span of control, 16, 58–59
    and training, 40–41, 47, 61–62
    and unity of command, 59–61
Supplies budget, 175

Teaching, 265
Temper, 114
Thefts
    auto, 272
    cost to business, 205–206
    and disciplinary action, 113
    employee, 272
Threats, and risk analysis, 197–198
Time management, 6–7, 13

Traffic control, 252
Training, 39–42, 97–105, 265–266
  career employee, 150
  definition of, 99
  and discipline, 107, 111–112
  and job description, 90
  and mismanagement, 281–282
  on-the-job, 98
  vs. orientation, 97–98
  POP formula for, 99–102
  Security Degree options, 250
  Security Director's role in, 49–50
  shortcomings of, 97–99
  supervisory, 61–62
  Training Officer, 102

Travel expense account, 172
TRW, 84

Uniform Crime Reports
Uniforms, 66

Vanity, 113–114
Velde, Richard W., 19–20
Vertical organizational structure, 27
Vulnerability, 198, 321–327

Warehouse inspection, 183
Work, division of, 12–14
Work habits, 114
Work motivation theory, 120–124